MEMOIRS OF A
DISSIDENT PUBLISHER

HENRY REGNERY

MEMOIRS
OF A DISSIDENT
PUBLISHER

HBJ

New York and London

HARCOURT BRACE JOVANOVICH

BR 341 m

Library of Congress Cataloging in Publication Data
Regnery, Henry, 1912-
Memoirs of a dissident publisher.

Includes index.
1. Regnery, Henry, 1912-
2. Publishers and publishing—United States—Biography.
3. Conservatism—United States.
I. Title.
Z473.R43A35   070.5′092′4 [B]   78-22269
ISBN 0-15-173752-5

First edition

B C D E

For E. S. R.

with gratitude and affection

CONTENTS

Contents

Contents

12

OTHER BOOKS: GOOD AND BAD

INDEX

Acknowledgments

I wish to thank the publishers of *Modern Age, National Review,* and *The American Spectator* for permission to use the parts of the book that appeared in their magazines.

Eliseo Vivas read the manuscript while it was being written, made many helpful suggestions, and offered much encouragement, which, coming from a man of his knowledge and experience, was all the more appreciated. David Collier was equally helpful, and by using several chapters in *Modern Age,* of which he is editor, made me feel that what I was writing might be of interest to others besides myself.

Finally, I want to acknowledge my debt to that stern, sharp-eyed editor Dan Wickenden, who trimmed the manuscript down to size and smoothed out many rough spots, and in so doing made it far more effective than it otherwise would have been. For its substance, of course, I alone am responsible.

PREFACE

Every book requires justification, but none more than a book by a publisher, who, if anyone, should be aware that there are far too many books.

The first books to carry the imprint of the firm I founded appeared in 1947, just two years after the shooting had finally stopped in World War II, and were strongly in opposition not only to the official policy of the time, but also to the position of those who formed public opinion. When I set out to challenge the governmental and intellectual establishment, it was with an apparatus that fitted very comfortably into a small office above a drugstore in Hinsdale, a Chicago suburb; I had no conception either of the power and influence of the group I set out to do battle with or of my own inadequacy, but I was not entirely alone, as I soon discovered, and my innocence was a form of protection.

The firm I founded was born in opposition, and, for the most part, remained in opposition for the twenty-five years or so it remained under my direction; it was this ·fact that gave it whatever distinction it attained and provides the justification for describing some of the more significant books we published and their impact on public opinion. We published books on foreign policy, politics, economic policy, education, philosophy, and religion; we launched two authors who have since become well known, Russell Kirk and William F. Buckley, Jr.; and we contributed substantially to the development of the modern conservative movement. The fact that the general trend of our books was consciously in accord with the traditional values of Western civilization was sufficient, in the climate of opinion that prevailed in the period following World War II, to cause us to be regarded, especially by the intellectual establishment, as controversial publishers.

Although I did not necessarily agree with every book I published, and published a number of books of little or no value, my firm, for better or for worse, reflected my personality, background, experience, and limitations. For this reason, I hope that I shall be forgiven if I begin this account with a description of my own background and of the experiences that formed my attitudes and opinions; for the rest, I shall let our books speak for themselves.

MEMOIRS OF A
DISSIDENT PUBLISHER

1

BACKGROUND AND EDUCATION

F_{ATE}," according to Oswald Spengler, "is who one is, where one is born, in which year, in which nation, in which class, with which body and soul, with which character traits." It was my fate, by this definition, to be born in Hinsdale, a suburb of Chicago, in 1912, the year in which Woodrow Wilson was elected President, an event that had a profound effect on American society, and in the end contributed to the partial destruction of Europe. The world I was born into, however, seemed secure and safe, and looked to the future with confidence. My father, who was a successful manufacturer of textiles, had been born on a farm in Wisconsin of German Catholic forebears. His father came from a wine-growing family from the Mosel valley near the old Roman city of Trier, and his mother's family—she was born in Wisconsin—from the Saar valley, a few miles south of Trier. Her father had emigrated because of having participated in the uprisings of 1848, which in the Rhineland had strong anti-Prussian overtones.

While he was still a small child, my father was taken by his parents to a farm in the northeastern part of Iowa, near a place called St. Lucas, where they lived until he was about fourteen. This must have been a happy time for him. I loved to hear his stories of his boyhood on the farm, and he enjoyed telling them— about making their own soap and yeast, growing vegetables and gathering seed, shearing sheep and spinning wool, and of the long walks to school in the cold winters, with snow drifting across the prairie.

My mother, whose maiden name was Thrasher, was of English and Welsh descent. Her father came from a small place near Harpers Ferry and her mother from Hancock, Maryland; one of her grandfathers was a country doctor, and the other had a farm and gristmill in the Potomac valley. Her father had served in the Union army from the beginning of the Civil War to the end, attaining the rank of captain, and had taken his family west when it was all over. They lived in several places, and finally settled in Kansas City, where my mother met my father and where they were married. By then my father was living in Chicago, but after their first child was born he and my mother moved from Chicago to Hinsdale, and they lived there the rest of their lives. They had four more children, of whom I was next to the youngest. By the time they celebrated their fiftieth wedding anniversary they had twenty-one grandchildren.

When I started school in 1917, Hinsdale still had many of the characteristics of a small town. There were woods, open fields, and farms just outside of the town; and there were two blacksmiths, a harness maker, and a woodworking shop. The stores were small and locally owned, and deliveries were generally by horse-drawn wagons. Most people had vegetable gardens, many kept chickens, and a few still had horses. I came long after the McGuffey readers and had the good fortune to miss "Dick and Jane." The stories we read in school, which came largely from Greek and Germanic mythology, stimulated the interest and imagination of a child. A teacher, who went from one school to another on foot, arrived several times a week to teach us the notes of the scale and the rudiments of music. All our teachers for the first eight years were unmarried women who rented rooms from widows who made a practice of "taking in teachers." They were probably not as well versed in educational psychology as their present-day counterparts, but they had standards, kept order, and took their profession seriously. I remember many of them with gratitude.

The twelve years I attended public school almost exactly covered the period between the end of World War I and the beginning of the Great Depression. During those years Hinsdale changed from a rather simple, unassuming small town to an aggressive, self-assertive suburb—a process that typifies what was happening in

4

the country as a whole. It was the time during which the transition from the nineteenth to the twentieth century was completed.

We lived in an ample, comfortable house surrounded by a fairly large property. There was room for baseball, and there was a big, old barn that became a gathering place for all the children in the neighborhood. We had a vegetable garden and fruit trees, and when I was small we kept chickens. The chicken yard was later converted into a tennis court, which was probably symbolic of the change from small town to suburb. One of my older brothers, although rather small of stature, as most of us in my family were, excelled in sports and was very popular with other boys. Both of these facts probably made me more conscious than I might otherwise have been of my own deficiencies in such matters. I spent many days with a friend or a younger brother in a nearby woods, where we built a shack, cooked our lunch, and imagined ourselves to be Indians, or at least trappers or woodsmen. As I grew older I read a good deal. My father, who was self-educated, had read widely as a young man and had an excellent collection of books. I went through much of Dickens, Stevenson, and Mark Twain, and, while in high school, of Thomas Hardy. At one point I developed an enthusiasm for Thomas Paine, whom my father did not greatly admire, but he made no objection when I bought, with money I had earned selling the *Saturday Evening Post*, a complete set from a foundation that was pushing Paine. My enthusiasm waned, not surprisingly, before I had read more than a volume or two.

My mother had a strong personality and very definite opinions on most subjects, particularly those involving behavior, but our household pretty much revolved around my father. He was an unusual man, highly successful in business, but, unlike many successful businessmen, modest, unassuming, and generous. Although his substantial business interests were demanding, he always had time for others and his family. Many people came to him with their problems, particularly during the Depression, and he was always helpful. He had few illusions, and certainly none about his fellow man, but he was always glad to help when he could, without expecting anything in return. When any of his numerous acts of generosity turned out well, as on the occasion of his teaching a local painting contractor how to keep books, he was gratified; but he was too wise to be upset about those that did not. He had an excellent sense of humor, and the rare ability to keep things in proper proportion. He was successful and enjoyed what his success

5

had brought him, made money but knew when to stop, and above all did not regard money as an end in itself. He once remarked to me that making money was a knack and had nothing to do with intelligence, but he also possessed remarkable intelligence.

World War I was a difficult time for my father. He felt himself to be completely American and had never been involved in German-American affairs of any kind, but he was conscious of his Rhenish-German heritage and saw no reason to be ashamed of it. The propaganda stories of World War I infuriated him, as did the stupid anti-German hatred they aroused. The Versailles Treaty, which he regarded as an abomination, confirmed his poor opinion of Wilson. A welcome change from all this occurred some months after the war had ended, but while the Allied food blockade of Germany and Austria was still in effect. I remember very clearly his arriving home one evening and telling us that some people had come to see him that day who were raising money, not to buy bombs or guns, but for food to send to starving children. They were from the American Friends Service Committee. As things turned out, I married the daughter of the Philadelphia Friend who supervised the child-feeding program in Germany, Alfred G. Scattergood. It was known as the *Quäker-Speisung*, and for a time supplied supplemental food to more than a million children a day. That there were people willing to undertake such a mission from purely Christian motives after the hatred and bitterness aroused by the war made a deep impression on my father, and through him on me also.

Hinsdale High School, when I attended it, was rather small, and the general atmosphere relaxed and informal. There were some good teachers, but academically it was not distinguished. For most of the students the four years were largely wasted, and those who did get something should have been offered more. The director of school music was a good musician and teacher, and I thank him for introducing me to what became an important part of my life. There was also an English teacher, during my last year, who greatly stimulated my interest in literature and opened my eyes to a world I had been only dimly aware of. I finished high school in the spring of 1929, at the peak of the postwar boom, determined to become an engineer. My two older brothers had gone to Amherst, which my oldest brother, whose opinions I greatly respected even then, urged me to do also; but I wanted to go my own way, and in the fall of 1929 entered Armour Institute of Technology, now the

6

Illinois Institute of Technology, to study mechanical engineering.

I worked hard at Armour Tech—it was that kind of place—and did well, but by the end of the second year had come to the conclusion that engineering was not for me. I had no problems with my work, but began to question the whole world of technology and whether I wanted to be a part of it. I had done particularly well in mathematics, and for the lack of any better ideas transferred to M.I.T., intending to major in that discipline. But I was able to pursue other subjects as well, and took all the courses that were offered in French, German, English, and philosophy. Some were of the highest quality. I particularly remember a professor of English we called "Tubby" Rogers, who was an excellent and stimulating teacher, and a course in philosophy, with no more than ten students taking it, given by Norbert Wiener. I took cello lessons at the New England Conservatory, heard the Boston Symphony every week, played in the M.I.T. orchestra, which in those days we had to maintain with our own funds, and read widely. The three books that made the greatest impression on me were Krutch's *Modern Temper*, Goethe's *Wilhelm Meister*, and Mann's *Magic Mountain*. Mathematics remained my major, although I had soon discovered that my talent for it was limited; but my three years at M.I.T. were not entirely lost, and I discovered where my interests and abilities did not lie.

While at M.I.T. I made one friendship that had a lasting and decisive influence on the course of my life. A German exchange student who lived in the same rather dreary dormitory I did and who was an accomplished pianist, invited me toward the end of my first year at M.I.T. to have supper with him and another German exchange student, an art historian at the Fogg Museum. Afterward we went to my room and played several records on my wind-up Victor machine. One was a recording of the Schumann *Carnaval*, by Rachmaninoff, which our new friend particularly enjoyed; I later discovered that he could play it almost as well. We liked each other immediately, met several times before the end of the term, and agreed to meet again the following fall.

After returning to Cambridge at the end of the summer I went to the Fogg Museum to find my new friend, and was told, incorrectly, that he had gone back to Germany. The news was a great disappointment to me, so I was all the more pleased to meet him by chance at a concert of the Boston Symphony some months later. We saw each other frequently from then on, became close friends, and remained so until his death more than forty years later. He came from a beautiful old town on the German-Belgian border some thirty miles south of Aachen (Aix-la-Chapelle); he had studied in Berlin and Munich and finished his doctorate at Bonn and was fluent in French and Italian as well as in English. He quickly decided that my education had been sadly deficient; he was appalled to discover that I did not know the meaning of the word *baroque* (I may say in my own defense that it was not so frequently used in those days as now) or the dates of Peter Paul Rubens, and, born teacher that he was, he took me in hand. We went through the Boston museums together, the Fine Arts, the Fogg, and the Gardner Collection, and attended concerts and recitals. He played the piano for me, particularly *Tristan*, which was his current passion, and he gave me books to read, among them Thomas Mann's *Tonio Kröger*, which he insisted that I read in German, a slow process in that stage of my development. And we talked. Such a spring, following a dull winter of mathematics and physics, was an intoxicating experience for me. He urged me to come to Bonn for a year or two after I finished M.I.T., and that is what I did.

I arrived in Germany in August, 1934. The Roehm purge, when Hitler had a number of his close associates murdered for allegedly conspiring against him, had taken place the previous June. I had no idea what to expect, but was fully prepared to find a country in a state of turmoil. I went directly to Koblenz, an old city at the confluence of the Mosel and the Rhine, which had once been a fortified Roman town, because that is where my friend Hermann was working. He had suggested that I spend the month or two with him before the university opened, which would give me a chance to begin the arduous task of learning German and to see something of the country.

He was working for a department of the provincial government that was concerned with the preservation of historic monuments; his specific assignment was to make an inventory of anything of artistic or historic value in the area in and around Koblenz. He had rented a room in a large, comfortable Victorian house on a quiet street not far from the Rhine, and I was able to get a room in the same place. It was a pleasant, intensely interesting time for me, and a perfect if somewhat one-sided introduction to Germany. We spent our days measuring churches and taking pictures of sculpture, old houses, castles, and so on. The late summer and early fall were sunny and warm, the countryside lovely, and the grapes in the vineyards beginning to ripen; to me, fresh from the prairies of the Middle West, it all seemed incredibly beautiful and romantic.

One evening, shortly after I arrived, we took a little train to a village on the Mosel for supper. The local inn, said Hermann, who was very knowledgeable in such matters, had an excellent kitchen. We ordered our dinner and then walked through the vineyards to the top of a hill, behind the village, to see a perfectly preserved Romanesque chapel a crusader had built to express his thanks for his safe return from the Holy Land. It was getting dark as we walked back, the Mosel valley lay stretched out before us, the silhouette of a ruined castle on the other side, and an unforgettable meal waiting for us: Mosel *Hecht*, or pike, from a river clean enough then to produce good fish, with a delicious sauce that was a specialty of the house, fresh salad, and, of course, the local wine. We made many such trips, on one occasion to Trier, where we spent several days visiting the Roman ruins; the cathedral, which is one of the most impressive in Europe and includes every style of architecture from Roman to baroque; the beautiful Gothic *Liebfrauenkirche*; and the elaborate, late baroque St. Paul's, for which I was completely unprepared and which rather shocked me. We walked for several days through the terraced vineyards on the Mosel, helping ourselves to the grapes as we went, in spite of a warning in the form of a medieval representation of two boys who had been turned to stone for having done just what we were doing.

One especially beautiful day we walked to Bad Ems, which lies on the Lahn a few miles east of Koblenz. We crossed the Rhine on the pontoon bridge, went up the road past the fortress of Ehrenbreitstein, which for centuries was one of the most strategic and most heavily fortified points in Europe and affords a fine view of the Rhine valley and of Koblenz, and then on quiet back roads to Ems. The countryside was well cultivated and orderly, there were fruit trees along the roads, and the farmers were bringing in their crops—in wagons drawn by horses, oxen, or cows. It all reminded me of the description of a similar countryside in Goethe's *Sorrows of Werther*. Hermann's associate went with us. He was a member of the Nazi Party, and a storm trooper besides. Actually he was a mild, scholarly, completely idealistic young man, who later gave up the whole thing in disgust, but at that point he saw it all as the great hope for his country. Hermann, on the other hand, took a

9

dim view of Hitler and all his works. They argued about it a good deal, but were firm friends and never became angry. At lunch, Hermann's associate ordered milk instead of beer, at which point Hermann, turning to me in perfect disgust, said, "You can see what these people are doing to this country." Later, as we sat on a grassy hilltop admiring the rolling countryside stretched out before us, the storm trooper turned to me and said, "But if it weren't for Hitler you wouldn't have been able to come to Germany at all, because we would have been in the midst of a civil war," to which Hermann replied, "Yes, of course, because *he* would have started it."

A most memorable occasion was a performance of *Figaro* in Cologne, which made an enormous impression on me. I had heard opera before, even a Mozart opera, but until then it had never meant much to me. Circumstances must have been exactly right; at that performance of *Figaro* I became aware of the ineffable magic of the music of Mozart and of the mystery of creativity.

In October I registered at the university and found a room in a large, airy house in a pleasant part of Bonn, which was still a quiet university town. My landlady, I soon discovered, was a direct descendant of the prominent, cultivated Bonn family who had befriended Beethoven as a young man and had played an important part in his life—a fact of which she was inordinately proud. She had a well-trained voice and as a younger woman had made a specialty of singing Beethoven songs, wearing the dress of Beethoven's friend, and her ancestor, Eleanore von Breuning. On one occasion, she told me, she had done this in the Redoute, the elegant eighteenth-century building in nearby Bad Godesberg where the young Beethoven had played for Haydn.

I registered in the faculty of economics, but for the first semester devoted most of my attention to learning German. There were a number of foreigners in Bonn, including several from Scotland, Wales, and Ireland who had come to Bonn to study Gaelic, since the leading authority on Celtic languages was a Bonn professor. The university offered an excellent course in German for foreigners, which we all took and which brought us frequently together. A number of us, mostly British and American, formed a little club. We bowled, in the relaxed German fashion that seemed to consist largely of drinking beer to congratulate each other for a particularly lucky shot; we made bicycle trips, and in the spring several of us took the train to Trier, rented boats, and for several days paddled down the Mosel. We also did some work, several of us got degrees, and I learned to speak and write quite presentable German.

The two Christmas holidays during my stay in Germany were spent on a large farm in Silesia. The oldest of the three sons of the family was an art historian and a friend of my friend Hermann, who arranged the invitation for me. This son had joined the Nazi Party some time before Hitler came to power, which would have given him a privileged position, but he resigned when it became evident what National Socialism meant in practice. Their father had been killed in World War I, and their mother, who was a remarkable woman, had managed the farm ever since. It was a highly productive, well-cultivated property, and for an American an interesting place to visit. We were met at the station by an open carriage drawn by two handsome horses, with a coachman on the box—no self-respecting Silesian landowner at that time, I was told, would have had a car. Not long after I arrived I was taken to the barn to see the stock, among which was an old mule with the letters *USA* branded on one side—a prisoner of war, apparently, who was spending his declining years on a Silesian farm. The Christmas holidays were observed with much festivity. There were a Christmas tree and other decorations, of course. On Christmas Eve the farm hands came in to greet the lady of the house, who had a special word and gift for each; and there was much singing and visiting, a Christmas service in the village church, and a goose for Christmas dinner, and on New Year's Eve the traditional carp.

During the two years I spent in Germany I heard all the music I could. The Cologne opera house, which had been built about 1900 in Art Nouveau style, was not beautiful, but the performances were of the highest quality. Besides numerous performances of *Figaro,* I heard *Rosenkavalier, Magic Flute, Don Giovanni,* and *Freischütz,* among others. There were concerts of the Cologne orchestra under Eugen Jochum in the fifteenth-century Gürzenich. And in the spring came the Beethoven Festival in Bonn, where one year I heard, besides much Beethoven, Bach's *Art of the Fugue,* played by the organist of the Thomas Church in Leipzig. I went to Munich a number of times, and particularly remember a performance on a perfectly clear, beautiful evening of the Schubert "Trout" quintet in the Renaissance court of the Royal Palace, with the piano part played by Elly Ney, who came from Bonn and was always queen of the Beethoven Festival, and *Don Giovanni* in the eighteenth-century Cuvilliés Theater conducted by Richard Strauss. I was given the opportunity to play in a small orchestra connected with the university—the others played much better than I, but they were most friendly, as musicians usually are, and we enjoyed each other's company. At a special holiday performance we played a Christmas cantata of Heinrich Schütz and one of the Bach Brandenburg concertos.

The purest music I heard while in Germany, because it was intended for God rather than man, was the singing of the Gregorian chant by the monks of Maria Laach. I went there a number of times with my friend Hermann and later with an English and American friend from the university. It is a beautiful, most impressive place—a thirteenth-century Romanesque church on a strangely somber, isolated lake in the Eifel hills west of the Rhine. We would always go at least part of the way on foot, which seemed the most appropriate manner to approach such a place, and would spend the night in a small hotel near the monastery and come back the next day. The singing and the liturgy of the Mass in that austere, beautiful church were of an unforgettable purity and dignity.

In the foregoing account little has been said of the other side of the Germany of those years, the side that ended in the suicides in the cellar of the burning Reich Chancellory in Berlin, in death for millions, and in destruction on a scale unparalleled in history. As foreign students we were well aware of the Hitler regime, but it seemed far removed from us, and the university, so far as we could tell, intact and largely unaffected. It is true that Karl Barth, the distinguished Protestant theologian, had resigned from the Bonn faculty the previous spring rather than take the new oath of allegiance that was required of all professors, and we heard rumors of concentration camps. But although the ugly business of anti-Semitism had started it was not then particularly evident, and life on the whole seemed quite normal. The cities were clean and orderly, much more so than those we came from. We were always courteously treated by professors and students, and most of the people, indeed nearly all I knew, were either indifferent to National Socialism or strongly opposed to it. The best-known professor in Bonn in those years was Ernst Robert Curtius, a distinguished critic of contemporary literature and the German translator of Eliot's *The Waste Land*. He made no secret of his strong aversion to National Socialism. The professor of economics was Arthur Spiethoff, a sincere man and good teacher, who was widely respected for his original work in the field of business cycles and much admired by his students. Alois Dempf, one of the great authorities in the field of medieval philosophy, was still in Bonn and was director of the Meister Eckhardt Institute; he was a popular professor, so much so that his lecture course, Introduction to Philosophy, had to be held in the largest room in the university. He was forced to leave a year or two later, but that was in the future. To us the university was still a center of disinterested scholarship.

We are now so much aware of the hideous consequences of National Socialism that it is difficult to imagine how it may have appeared in its early stages and to recall the circumstances that made Hitler's rise to power possible. Hitler became chancellor on January 30, 1933; Franklin D. Roosevelt became President a few weeks later. A significant factor in the electoral victory of both was the economic crisis and the unemployment that went with it: in Germany, at the peak of the crisis nearly 30% of the working population was unemployed. Both Hitler and Roosevelt—each in his own way—were masters of the art of manipulating the masses, and by a strange quirk of fate they died within a few weeks of each other. In the early days, it should also not be forgotten, Hitler represented himself as the man of peace, as the simple, front-line soldier of the Great War who knew what war was. Whether he made a specific promise to the mothers and fathers of Germany not to send their sons into a foreign war I do not know, but he certainly gave them the impression that to do so was farthest from his thoughts, and they believed him, as we always believe what we want to hear.

Hitler had the good fortune to come to power just at the moment that production and employment were beginning to revive. His regime supplemented this revival by a massive program of public works such as the *Autobahnen,* work camps for young men, and rearmament. We must face the fact, which is easy to forget now, that within less than two years from Hitler's accession to power Germany changed at least superficially from a situation of economic stagnation, despair, and profound social unrest to one of confidence, direction, and national purpose. Where it would all lead was not then so apparent to most people as it is now. One of our Scottish friends predicted that he would be killed in the war that would be an inevitable consequence of the Hitler regime, and this very sadly is exactly what happened, but most of us, unfortunately, did not take the situation so seriously.

One of the first German words I learned was *Arbeitsbeschaffung* —job creation—and I must admit that I was enormously impressed in those years by the efforts to put people to work, all the more so in view of the almost total failure of our own government's measures to solve the unemployment problem. A German program I learned something about was one by which industrial workers were helped to acquire individual houses with plots of land large enough to give them attractive surroundings and to grow a substantial part of their own food. This seemed to me to offer a solution to one of the basic problems of industrialism: a chance for those who bear the brunt of the industrial process, who do the work, to lead a decent life.

I came back home in the summer of 1936. The presidential campaign was just getting under way, with Alf Landon as Roosevelt's opponent. I was all for Roosevelt and his New Deal, but the spectacle of the campaign was not particularly inspiring. It was also the year of the drouth, which made the countryside, especially in the Middle West, look particularly raw, flat, and uninviting. The main subject of conversation seemed to be baseball, which had never interested me, and which at that point of my life I thought especially trivial. After the stimulating, privileged existence I had been leading, America seemed terribly dull and matter-of-fact. I was simply making the adjustment that many young Americans have gone through after such an experience as I had had, and whatever I may have thought at the time, it was doubtless much less of a strain for me than for the other members of my family.

Having made a start with economics, I thought I had better go on with it, and in the fall of 1936 I entered the Graduate School at Harvard. By far the most distinguished man in the Harvard Department of Economics at that time was Joseph Schumpeter, who was a product of the Austrian school, from which have come some of the outstanding and most far-seeing economists of this century: others were Böhm-Bawerk, Menger, Mises, and Hayek.

Schumpeter gave the basic course in economic history in the Graduate School. There were not more than twenty-five students in his lecture course, and to be one of them was a great privilege.

14

Schumpeter was not only a fine scholar but also a consummate lecturer, and a good actor as well. When he came into the room he would slowly take off his hat, gloves, and coat, looking at us in the meantime as though he were rather surprised to see a roomful of students and had no idea what was expected of him. He would then proceed to deliver one of his beautifully organized lectures, each a work of art in itself and part of a coherent whole. At an early lecture he gave us a reading list, with the remark, "If one of our professors at the University of Vienna, Böhm-Bawerk, for example, had given us a reading list, we would have thrown it back at him." The author of one of the books we were expected to read was the English economist Joan Robinson. Being young men, we indulged in a certain amount of discussion about what a lady economist might look like, how old she might be, whether she was married, and so on. One day in class, when her book had come up, one of the students surrendered to his curiosity and asked, "What does Joan Robinson look like?" Schumpeter considered a moment, his head a little to one side and a finger against his nose, as though deep in thought, then with a twinkle in his fine brown eyes answered, "I would give her about a B plus."

Schumpeter was no narrow, academic economist, but a thoroughly educated, cultivated man, who viewed the world with a certain amused detachment, but who saw it as a whole, and the limited place of economic considerations within it. Whether he thought of himself as a conservative I have no idea, but he had the quality, which I think is an essential element of the true conservative, of being able to view the present in the long perspective of history, of seeing the present not as the end product or purpose of history, which I think is a typically liberal fallacy, but as a link connecting a long past with a limitless future. One day in class there was some discussion of the relative productivity, and therefore desirability, of various economic systems, whether capitalism is more or less productive than socialism, and so on, to which Schumpeter remarked, "It all depends on what you want. If I had the choice, I would take the society that produced the cathedral at Chartres."

It was during my first year at Harvard that John Maynard Keynes's famous *General Theory of Employment, Interest, and Money* was published. This was the book that gave the politicians a theoretical justification, and one with the whole weight of the liberal intelligentsia behind it, for unbalanced budgets, for the "spend and spend, elect and elect" syndrome, the ultimate effects of which the present inflation is making drastically evident. A group of us read the book together, discussing each chapter as we went; my principal recollection of it is its awkward style and the fact that it ends with Mandeville's *Fable of the Bees.* Keynes was much too intelligent a man, I am sure, to attach the seminal importance to his theories his followers did. He offered a prescription for a specific economic situation, extreme deflation, which the Keynesians, because it gave them a useful weapon, elevated into ultimate truth.

There were some outstanding students in the Graduate School's Department of Economics at Harvard in those years; two, in fact, became presidents of two of the country's largest banks. But many had come to the university only as a steppingstone to a government job. During my second year, there were also a number of younger government officials who had been given fellowships for a year or two of graduate work. It was during those years that many government agencies and bureaus were rapidly expanding, particularly the Department of Agriculture. It was widely believed, probably with justification, that a Harvard professor of agricultural economics, John D. Black, exerted a great influence on appointments. The Graduate School, therefore, had a large quota of aspiring agricultural economists, all thirsting for a job in Washington. It is a tribute to the resourcefulness and productivity of American agriculture that after two generations of the ministrations of all those agricultural economists we still have enough to eat.

It was during the years I was at Harvard, 1936–37, that Marxist socialism was particularly fashionable with the intellectuals. Many students in the Graduate School followed the trend, as well as some members of the faculty. Two students proclaimed themselves to be Communists; how many others may have been I have no idea. I had come to Harvard a rather convinced admirer of Franklin D. Roosevelt and the New Deal; but the left-leaning New Deal students and bureaucrats I met at Harvard began to change my mind, a process that was helped by what I was learning of the realities of the world from such teachers as Schumpeter, and by the mere process of growing up. The Marxist students and bureaucrats, filled with illusions of their own importance and immensely sure of themselves, were an unattractive, intellectually shabby lot. They loved to use such unoriginal phrases as "the workers must take over the system," meaning, of course, that in this case they would be running it, and to denounce the exploitation of wage earners by their employers; but their chief immediate objective was a soft job in Washington. My commitment to the New Deal, to the idea that the solution of the obvious economic and social ills of the country was to be found in Washington, was given its final blow by a summer spent there, working in the very epitome of a New Deal agency, the Resettlement Administration.

The Resettlement Administration was, I believe, a product of the fertile imagination of Rexford Guy Tugwell, who was also its first administrator. Mrs. Roosevelt was most interested in it in its early days, and had considerable influence on its policies. The basic idea was to establish small communities where people whose chief source of income was industry would have room to raise at least part of their own food, thus making them more independent and giving them a better life. I wanted to learn more about the project, and for the summer of 1937 was able to get a temporary job in the administrative office in Washington. I went off at the end of the academic year in June full of illusions and anxious to have a small part in what seemed to me to be a great and promising program to give some of the people who had been left behind a better chance.

The Resettlement Administration was supplied with large amounts of public money, directed by people who were full of zeal for reform and convinced that they knew exactly what was needed, but badly administered and almost completely unrealistic in its objectives. New communities were established in various parts of the country; in some cases small factories were also set up to provide jobs, in others the residents were expected to find work in nearby existing industry, and in still others rather large-scale farming operations were to be the main source of income. In all the new communities co-operatives were established—co-operatives were a basic part of the liberal ideology of those days—which were to operate the local store, the factory, the poultry farm, or whatever. The co-operatives, however, like everything else, were managed and financed by the government agency: complete control, in other words, remained in Washington.

One such community was established near Hightstown, New Jersey, for needleworkers from New York. Besides the usual houses and garden plots, a dress factory was provided to give employment to the residents. The whole thing was totally unrealistic and a complete failure. The clothing workers knew nothing about gardening, and soon discovered that life in a rather isolated community in the country had many disadvantages they had not heard about; furthermore, the factory had difficulty competing with better-managed ones located in New York.

Among the more ambitious projects was Arthurdale, in the mountains of West Virginia, which was a particular favorite of Mrs. Roosevelt's. Attractive, well-designed houses and a well-equipped furniture factory were built, together with the inevitable co-operative store. For a time, under the guidance of an expert cabinetmaker, the factory turned out well-designed and beautifully made furniture, but it could exist only so long as the government subsidy continued. There was another large project, intended for coal miners, near Greensburg, Pennsylvania, which was provided with a dairy and a poultry operation.

One of the jobs assigned to me was to go over lists of residents of the various communities who were behind in their rent, and then recommend whether or not they should be evicted. We would get a report from the manager of a project in the state of Oregon, for example, of those who were delinquent in their payments, together with financial information, family problems, and so on, and on this basis decide who should be evicted. The whole thing was a bureaucratic nightmare, which the employees, especially those on the lower levels, did their best to make work in some sort of orderly fashion.

By the time I was becoming acquainted with the workings of the Resettlement Administration in 1937, the initial enthusiasm of those who started it had perceptibly waned: Tugwell had resigned, and Mrs. Roosevelt was taking up other causes. None of the projects had sufficient vitality to stand on its own feet, nor was there evidence that any of them would ever be able to do so. There was much dissension, and the usual scandals were beginning to turn up. The whole enterprise had lost its glamour. Before long, Hitler and the prospect of a foreign war would give the New Dealers a far bigger and more appealing cause than homestead communities, as well as a sure cure for the problem of unemployment, which was beginning to increase again, and which none of the nostrums of the New Deal had been able to do much about. The Resettlement Administration was taken over by the Department of Agriculture, and the various projects were gradually liquidated. It was a pattern that many similar programs, announced with great fanfare, have followed since: the War on Poverty, Model Cities, Appalachia—who can remember them all?

It had been an interesting and illuminating summer for me, and also an enjoyable one. Washington was not too large in those days, and still had the air of a relaxed, charming, southern city. I lived in a house in Chevy Chase with a group of young men who were good company, I enjoyed the people I worked with in the government, and I made some friends. More important, I went back to Harvard with fewer illusions about government than I had brought to Washington.

After three semesters at Harvard I had completed the course requirements for a Ph.D. and passed the general examinations, which entitled me to an M.A. To get a Ph.D. I would have had to write a thesis, which, since I had no intention of going into college teaching, I saw no reason to do. In any case, I felt that it was about time I got out into the world and did something. In the meantime Clarence Pickett, who was executive secretary of the American Friends Service Committee, asked me if I would like to take part in the development of a community project they had started in western Pennsylvania. I had visited the community while working for the Resettlement Administration, and felt that the task he offered would give me the chance to do something useful and to gain some valuable experience; so I accepted.

The community was located about forty miles south of Pittsburgh, in the bituminous-coal region, and was intended for coal miners. The basic plan was exactly the same as that for many of the government projects I had learned something about the previous summer. Those behind it felt that the failure of the government communities was not the fault of the basic idea, but of the way it was carried out. Money for the new venture was raised from private foundations, a two-hundred-acre farm near Brownsville was bought, fifty families from nearby mining communities were selected, and the work of building houses began. My specific assignment was to establish some sort of industry in the community to provide employment.

I went to Philadelphia to start to work immediately after taking the general examinations at Harvard. At some sort of Service Committee supper I went to I met Eleanor Scattergood, which was doubtless the most advantageous event, for me, to come out of my association with the Quakers. We were married the following November in the Germantown Meeting House in the Quaker fashion. One elderly cousin of my wife's recounted for how many generations members of her family had been married in the same place. Rufus Jones and Clarence Pickett, both friends of my wife's family, also spoke. There was much family present, it was a beautiful day, and altogether a happy, auspicious occasion.

When the Service Committee project, soon named Penn-Craft, had been started in 1936, there was much unemployment among coal miners, which it was thought at the time would be permanent. The objective of the project, therefore, was not only to provide a better life and a more secure economic existence for those directly involved, but also to point to a way by which the problem of unemployment in the coal fields could be solved. With the war boom that was to come only a very few years later, there was soon a shortage of coal miners, but it is a human weakness to regard the existing situation as one that will go on indefinitely, and the planners of Penn-Craft were no exception. All these resettlement projects, of course, contained a large element of back-to-the-land romanticism. In this case people were to be taken out of the mining camps and given the opportunity to live in a small, rather self-contained community where they would have gardens, fruit trees, and chickens. Part of the land was set aside for a community farm, which was to supply milk; the original farmhouse was made into a community house, and there was a co-operative store; for a time there was even a hand weaver in residence, who, it was hoped, would teach the homesteaders, as they were called, to make their own cloth.

The members of the community probably represented a good cross section of the coal miners in the area. Many were of Anglo-Saxon background and had come originally from West Virginia and Kentucky; others were descendants of the immigrants from Eastern Europe who had come during the boom years before World War I. They were self-reliant, hard-working, realistic people, proud of their profession—"It takes a good man to dig coal," they used to say—and had strong ties to their families. They were all fiercely loyal to the miners' union, which was not then the bureaucratic organization it has since become, well versed in parliamentary procedure, and able to speak out when they felt the occasion demanded it.

Fayette County lies on the western edge of the Appalachians, and is quite rolling. The Monongahela River goes through it, and it was once heavily wooded, mostly with oak. It must have been an unusually beautiful area, and parts of it still are. The settlement of that part of western Pennsylvania began soon after the Revolution, and the first settlers must have been substantial people, judging from the well-built, fine old stone houses one can still see in the area. The Presbyterian influence among this element of the population was strong, and still is among their descendants. Exploitation of the coal deposits, which are or were among the richest in the world, began at about the time of the Civil War and by the 1920's dominated the whole region. Houses for miners were built around the mine entrance. They were typically owned by the company, and were neither esthetically pleasing nor particularly desirable places to live—such communities were locally referred to either as "patches" or "camps." Until the development of the by-products coking process, most of the coal was converted into coke at the mine, in what were called "bee-hive" ovens. At one time there were more than 25,000 active bee-hive ovens in Fayette County, filling the sky with smoke and sulphur by day and making a spectacular sight by night. At every mine there was also a huge pile of slate, which had been cleaned from the coal. There was enough coal left among it so that such piles eventually caught fire by spontaneous combustion, adding to the smoke and sulphur created by the coke ovens.

By the time we came to Fayette County nearly all the bee-hive coke ovens, which required large amounts of labor, had been shut down, as were many of the mines. During the worst of the Depression more than half the working population of Fayette County was unemployed, and there was much distress. The Friends Service Committee had first come into the area at the request of the federal government to distribute food. The desolate mining camps, abandoned coke ovens, smoldering slag dumps, and the hillsides made barren by the sulphur smoke presented a dismal, hopeless picture, all of which renders the back-to-the-land romanticism of those responsible for Penn-Craft, nearly all of whom came from Midwestern farms, more understandable.

By the time we reached Penn-Craft, construction was well under way. The families had all built temporary houses, which theoretically were later to be used for chickens or small animals. The permanent houses, which were attractive but perhaps not as well suited for the people who were to live in them as they might have been, were built of limestone, which was readily available from the facings of the abandoned coke ovens. All labor was performed by the homesteaders on a mutual-help basis: when a man worked on someone else's house he was given a credit for the hours he put in and the other man debited; when all was finished, everyone was to come out even. There were disputes, understandably, but the Quaker manager, who came from an Indiana farm and was a thoroughly practical, honest man and enjoyed the complete trust and confidence of the homesteaders, made it work. The Service Committee advanced the cash that was needed for tools, equipment, plumbing, wiring, and so on, which was to be repaid, along with the cost of the land, over a period of years, at which time the homesteaders got full title.

My contribution to the project, as I have said, was to be some sort of industry to provide employment and cash income. I soon discovered that establishing a factory at such a place was far more difficult than it had appeared when I discussed it with Clarence Pickett in the comfortable surroundings of the Harvard Faculty Club. Coming from a textile family and having some familiarity with a modern cotton mill, I could see no future in hand weaving. We looked into mechanized carding, spinning, and weaving equipment an English firm was then making for small-scale, specialized operations, but that seemed impractical also. After investigating literally dozens of possibilities, we finally decided to establish a knitting mill to produce low-priced boys' and men's sweaters of the kind that would be sold in that area. We bought used machinery in New York, hired a highly skilled knitter-mechanic, and early in 1939, in a building the homesteaders had built with volunteer labor, we began to make sweaters. To train the help we turned a rather large quantity of yarn I had bought at a bankruptcy sale into caps and sweaters, which we gave away. When we started to operate, the standard wage was twenty-five cents an hour, and people literally fought for the jobs.

I worked under a special subcommittee that was made up of four or five successful and experienced businessmen from Philadelphia, who were generous with their time, and most kind and helpful to me, which I appreciate all the more as I recall how inexperienced I was but how sure of myself I must have been. We had many problems getting our small venture started—all of the employees, including me, were completely inexperienced, with the exception of the knitter-mechanic and his wife, who was an expert sewing-machine operator—but within a few months we were producing salable merchandise. Although I was able to get orders from some of the chain stores in New York, and we made arrangements with a distributor to place our sweaters in stores in the Pittsburgh area, we found it very difficult to operate efficiently or profitably. By the end of the second year I decided that to be successful we would need to find an experienced man to run the business. In the meantime the war in Europe had broken out, my father had become ill, and my wife was expecting her first child, all of which made me feel that we should be thinking about more permanent arrangements, and particularly that it was time for me to get back to Chicago and to help, if I could, with the family business. Fortunately, after considerable searching, I was able to find a young refugee, who had learned the knitting business in Vienna, to take over the Penn-Craft knitting mill. He was energetic and competent, and within two or three years, with the help of his wife, made it into a successful business. It became so successful, in fact, that it eventually outgrew Penn-Craft and was moved to Uniontown, a rather ironical end to our attempt to establish a small industry for a homestead community.

After nearly forty years, what has happened to the community launched with so much idealism and the hope that it might point the way to a different and better way of living? With its well-constructed stone houses, its planting, and the obvious care with which it was laid out, the community is not only attractive but gives the impression of solidity, of being a part of the landscape. All but five of the houses are owned and lived in by descendants of the original families, which suggests that working together in the construction of the community has resulted in a strong sense of loyalty to it. On the other hand, it is a miners' village, better planned and built than the usual "patch," but far from the self-contained subsistence community that was to lead the way to a new style of life for the people of the area. The community house is boarded up, the co-operative store and the community farm no longer function, the factory building is empty, the hand weaver is long since gone, and the temporary houses, which were to be used for chickens and small animals when the permanent houses were finished, are still used to house families, and many have been made quite attractive. The residents have made a community that fits their needs and habits instead of following the pattern that had been imposed from outside.

It is instructive also to consider what has happened to Fayette County in the intervening years. The hillsides made barren by sulphur smoke are covered by trees again, and the coke ovens are gone, as are the slag dumps, which, after they have burned out, are useful for building roads. Much new industry has come into the area, and farming has returned. The great threat to the landscape now is strip mining, which will cause, where it takes place, even worse devastation than the underground mining did. But if the land is restored afterward, as is now required, nature will take over again after a generation or two, as it did after the earlier mining and bee-hive coke ovens were gone.

No planner, no sociologist, no economic adviser to a government agency could have predicted in the 1930's what has since taken place in Fayette County. The well-intentioned people from the Resettlement Administration and the Friends Service Committee who thought that there was a permanent surplus of coal miners and that their subsistence homesteads were a workable solution to the problem completely overlooked man's ability to adjust to changing conditions. They forgot, if they ever knew, the truth Heraclitus pointed out long ago, that life is not being but becoming.

The much deplored company coal camps were built to meet an immediate need—how else would thousands of new arrivals from the southern mountains and Eastern Europe without means of any kind have been housed? They came to the mines seeking higher wages and a better life; and although the company houses no doubt seemed appalling to a college girl from Bryn Mawr, and in many ways were, they were a change for the better to those for whom they were built. In the meantime the company towns have disappeared or become ordinary communities and the houses in them privately owned, not because of the social workers who found them objectionable, but because the circumstances that made them necessary no longer exist. Some of them have become attractive communities, again not because of what the sociologists may have thought about them, but because the people who lived in them have made them so. There can be no real progress in human affairs, however, without standards, and perhaps the greatest contribution that the people from the Friends Service Committee made to Fayette County was not in trying to impose their idea of a community on a group of coal miners, but by their example of orderly, unselfish living.

When we left Penn-Craft in June, 1941, I felt that a definite phase of my life had ended. It was also a difficult parting. We had become strongly attached to our small, very simple house and garden, which had been a shambles when we took it over, but which under our care had become, for us, pleasant and attractive. We had made many warm friends, and we had grown to like and appreciate the area, its people, and its contrasts; the miners and the old inhabitants, the mining camps and the handsome old farmhouses, the mountains, the Monongahela, and the sudden, violent storms. It was hard to leave, but the time had come to settle down.

My formal education was behind me. It had been a rather incoherent education in many ways, and the time I had wasted on engineering, mathematics, physics, and chemistry could have been put to better use. But I did learn something about three of the most influential forces of our time: science, technology, and organized social uplift—enough, in any case, to regard them all with skepticism. I had also learned enough about history to know that civilization had not begun with the invention of the steam engine and to appreciate the role of order in human affairs. After a rather brief period in the family textile business, I found myself, almost imperceptibly, sliding into publishing.

2

FROM PAMPHLETS
TO BOOKS

As World War II drew to a close, the world, or at least its leaders, seemed to have gone mad. The sole objective of the nations at war, it appeared, was destruction, destruction for its own sake, with no thought of where it might lead. Although it was evident at least by the middle of 1944 that the Axis powers were beaten, Hitler was obsessed with the idea of fighting to the last gasp, regardless of the consequences; and Roosevelt, on the same level of irresponsibility, announced the policy of unconditional surrender: "The only terms on which we shall deal with any Axis government or any Axis faction are the terms proclaimed at Casablanca: 'Unconditional surrender.' " *

There were the mass air raids on German and Japanese cities, which could have had little or no military purpose, and there were Teheran, Yalta, and the Morgenthau Plan, which last, it was announced at the Quebec Conference, would become official American policy. Among the provisions of the Morgenthau Plan were:

Removal from Germany of all industrial machinery which any liberated country wants; obliteration of the rest of German industry.

Permanent closing of all German mines, if any are left after territorial changes.

* *Time,* Feb. 22, 1943.

Cession of the Saar and other Rheinland industrial areas to France, of East Prussia to Poland.

Withholding of any economic aid whatever to Germany; no food, clothing or other relief supplies to be furnished to the German people; no reconstruction of factories or railroads to be permitted.*

As if all this was not disillusioning enough, there was the fate of the Atlantic Charter, which vividly portrayed the vast gap between promise and reality. The Atlantic Charter had been proclaimed August 17, 1941, following a meeting in the Gulf of St. Lawrence on board the cruiser *Augusta.* It was headed "Joint Declaration by the President and Prime Minister," and began with the words: "The President of the United States of America and the Prime Minister, Mr. Churchill, representing His Majesty's Government in the United Kingdom, being met together, deem it right to make known certain common principles in the national policies of their respective countries on which they base their hopes for a better future for the world." Among the principles set forth in the Charter were: "no territorial changes that do not accord with the freely expressed wishes of the peoples concerned"; "the right of all peoples to choose the form of government under which they will live"; "the enjoyment by all states, great or small, victor or vanquished, of access, on equal terms, to the trade and to the raw materials of the world." There were similarly pious declarations about the establishment of "a peace which will afford to all Nations the means of dwelling in safety within their own boundaries, and which will afford assurance that all the men in all the lands may live out their lives in freedom from fear and want"; and "the establishment of a wider and permanent system of general security," and of lightening "for peace-loving peoples the crushing burden of armaments."

After the President's return from the Teheran Conference, where it was obvious that in determining the fate of the nations and people of Eastern Europe, the "Big Three" had not been even slightly concerned about the "principles" proclaimed on board the *Augusta,* the question was asked at a press conference: "Mr. President, did Mr. Churchill ever sign the Atlantic Charter?" The President's answer was reported in *Time* as follows: "Nobody, said the President, had ever signed the Atlantic Charter. Then where is it now? This is what comes of thinking in banal phrases and banal

* *Time,* Oct. 2, 1944.

27

thoughts, he said. There isn't any copy of the Atlantic Charter. The nearest thing would be the notes given to the radio operators of the U.S.S. *Augusta* and H.M.S. *Prince of Wales* (aboard which Roosevelt and Churchill traveled to the Gulf of St. Lawrence in August, 1941). The agreement consisted of little scraps of handwriting. Some of it was the President's, some Mr. Churchill's, some Sir Alexander Cadogan's, some Sumner Welles's. Anyway, it was signed in substance, and four and a half months later, 26 of the United Nations (including Russia) had endorsed it."

On the day after that account appeared, at the beginning of January, 1945, what had been represented as a replica of the Atlantic Charter, bearing the signatures of Franklin D. Roosevelt and Winston Churchill, disappeared from the main lobby of the Smithsonian Institution in Washington, where it had proudly hung for all to see. According to the Chicago *Tribune*, the director of the Institution, Alexander Wetmore, said that it had been taken down "to avoid confusion after several visitors had asked if it was the original Atlantic Charter." He added that the original "facsimile" copy of the Charter had been supplied by the Office of War Information, which informed the *Tribune* that it had printed 244,900 copies of the supposed Charter for the public institutions and schools it supplied with information.

An incident that occurred at about this time stands out clearly in my memory. The papers had been full of glowing accounts of great American victories, of massive air raids that had "flattened" Berlin, Tokyo, Hamburg, or some other unfortunate city, and there had been a particularly bombastic statement by the President of how the "peace-loving nations" would rearrange the world when the fighting had finally stopped. As I thought about these things, and especially the attitude they represented, it occurred to me that it must be much easier for those who could accept all this at face value, and I was tempted for a moment to wish that I could. There were some, however, who kept their heads, and, perhaps, because the means of communication were largely closed to them, more than we realized.

It was at this time that I met Frank C. Hanighen, who had been active in America First, had spent some time abroad as a foreign correspondent, and had recently started a Washington newsletter called *Human Events*. He was originally from Omaha, had graduated from Harvard in the early twenties, and after working for a time as an editor in a New York publishing house was associated with various newspapers and magazines. He was co-author of *Merchants of Death*, a book that had attracted wide attention, and had contributed substantially to the enactment of the neutrality legislation of the thirties, which, it was hoped at the time, would keep us out of the next European war. Hanighen was a tall, impressive-looking man, characteristically had a rather amused and quizzical look in his eye, and was a good listener. He had the experienced newspaperman's ability to win the confidence of anybody he dealt with, was thoroughly familiar with the ins and outs of the power structure of Washington, and harbored no illusions whatever about those who manipulated it.

As an associate in his venture he had brought in Felix Morley, who at the time was president of Haverford College. Morley came from an English Quaker family and was born on the Haverford campus, where at the time his father was a professor of mathematics. Felix Morley graduated from Haverford, studied at Oxford for two years as a Rhodes scholar, and at the London School of Economics for one. After having worked on the editorial staff of the Baltimore *Sun* for six years, he went to Geneva, where he served as representative of the American League of Nations Association and as a correspondent for the *Sun*. In 1933, shortly after buying the Washington *Post*, Eugene Meyer invited Morley to become its editor, a position he filled with great distinction. He resigned from the paper in August, 1940, because his views on the crucial issue of American intervention in the war were diametrically opposed to those of its owner, and returned to Haverford as its president. He was a man of broad experience with a fine, cultivated mind, and he had strong convictions and great moral courage. Hanighen's views were always influenced by his native Midwestern nationalism and skepticism about "foreign entanglements"; Morley's, though he was not a doctrinaire pacifist, by his Quaker heritage and his association with the League of Nations. But both were realists, and they respected each other. During the six years of their association they made *Human Events* a most distinguished publication, which had a considerable influence in spite of its limited financial resources and circulation.

The first issue of *Human Events*, which appeared February 2, 1944, consisted of a four-page, closely reasoned, and carefully written essay by William Henry Chamberlin entitled "Stalin, *Pravda* and Churchill." The publishing office was Hanighen's small bachelor apartment, and the financial backing consisted of a few hundred paid subscriptions, many of them from former supporters of the America First Committee. During the entire time of Morley's association with *Human Events* its focus was a four-page essay, usually devoted to foreign policy. Morley contributed more of these essays than anyone else, but William Henry Chamberlin, who was listed as a "contributing editor," wrote a good many, as did Hanighen. Oswald Garrison Villard, Norman Thomas, Hugh Gibson, Henry Beston, John T. Flynn, Constantine Brown, and Alexander Boeker were among the other authors of those well-written, reasoned essays, which have stood the test of time remarkably well—a tribute to the honesty and realistic good sense of the two founders and editors of *Human Events*.

After the first few issues Hanighen added a supplement called *Not Merely Gossip*, for which he assumed the responsibility. This was made up of "inside" information of the sort that did not appear in the regular press and which he picked up through his many close connections in Washington. Readers of *Human Events* were given the truth about the precarious state of President Roosevelt's health during the last years of his life, which the regular press carefully concealed.

My association with *Human Events* began sometime during its first year, and consisted at first largely of helping to put its affairs on a more formal basis. We incorporated the venture in June, 1945, with Morley as president, Hanighen as vice-president, and me as treasurer, each of us putting in $1,000 and taking one-third of the voting stock. We also issued some preferred, which provided a little more solid financial basis than had been available before. At the end of the war Morley resigned as president of Haverford, and in July, 1945, moved to Washington. Through his friendship with the Pews of Philadelphia, who had acquired the old *Path-finder* magazine, *Human Events* was able to get adequate if very modest office space in the *Pathfinder* building, a renovated residence, in return for which Morley provided some much needed editorial help to the magazine.

When I first became associated with *Human Events*, we hoped we could develop it into a national magazine, but it was never possible to find the necessary financial backing. Our model was Albert J. Nock's the *Freeman*, which came out in the early twenties, and which some consider the best magazine ever to have been published in this country. One of the names we thought about was *The Federalist*, but that is about as far as we got. It would seem that those on the left are much more successful at raising money for such ventures than those of us on the right.

Not having the financial means to publish a magazine, we resorted to the pamphlet, a form that has played a great role in the spreading of ideas. I believe it was first used during the Reformation: Milton's *Areopagitica* was published as a pamphlet, as were Burke's *Reflections on the Revolution in France*, Thomas Paine's *Common Sense*, and *The Federalist Papers*. My first pamphlet consisted of two speeches Robert M. Hutchins had given as president of the University of Chicago, the first at a special convocation on the day the war in Europe ended, and the second, called "The New Realism," at the convocation for the graduating class in June, 1945. They were noble, courageous statements. The following is from the second:

So we call Japanese soldiers fanatics when they die rather than surrender, whereas American soldiers who do the same thing are heroes. We prove that all Germans are murderers and all Japanese apes, and at the same time insist that we are going to have one world in which all men are brothers. We say we are going to re-educate the Germans, and adopt a policy of non-fraternization. We hate slavery and propose forced labor. We want Europe rebuilt, but will have no heavy industry in Germany. We want order in Europe, but not if we have to sacrifice to prevent starvation. We are against dictatorship, but the dictatorship of the proletariat is an exception. And the new day dawns by the light of the burning homes of Tokyo and Yokohama.

Hutchins reminded his listeners that we could not attain peace with vengeance, that however strongly we may have felt about our recent enemies the time had come for reconciliation. With his permission, I had several thousand copies printed, and sold them with little or no difficulty. Many people, apparently, were longing for the spirit of generosity and Christian charity that had inspired these speeches, and shared my gratitude to their author for having made them.

There was a second Hutchins pamphlet soon after the first, *The Good News of Damnation*, in which he argued for some form of world government as the only possible way to protect mankind from eventual destruction by the atomic bomb; this, however, aroused little enthusiasm from my associates in Washington, particularly Hanighen.

A lecture sponsored by the Chicago Council on Foreign Relations was instrumental in getting us into the pamphlet business in earnest. The speaker, Karl Brandt, was a professor of agricultural economics at Stanford University and had just returned from Germany, where he had spent several months as an adviser to the U.S. military government. His subject was the catastrophic consequences that would ensue, not only for Germany but also for all of Europe, if the Draconian policies then being followed there were continued. Henry Morgenthau's *Germany Is Our Problem* had recently been published by a leading New York house, and a group of distinguished professors from several American universities, including Brandt, all of whom had left Germany during the Hitler years, had asked the same publisher if it would consider a book in reply, for which they would assume the responsibility. The answer was no. After Brandt's lecture, several members of this group, knowing my association with *Human Events* and the two Hutchins pamphlets, asked if I had any suggestions about how to make known the true facts of the hideous situation in Central Europe, where mass starvation and the complete collapse of civilized life seemed imminent. I got a copy of Brandt's lecture into Felix Morley's hands, and we decided to publish an enlarged version, which Morley agreed to edit, as a pamphlet—also to be entitled, at his suggestion, *Germany Is Our Problem*. This was very widely distributed, both by mass mailings and through newsstands. Whether reasoned argument has an appreciable influence on the conduct of nations seems questionable, but if it does, Brandt's pamphlet must have had some effect.

In the meantime Hutchins had made another speech that greatly appealed to me, "The Atomic Bomb versus Civilization." With this, the Brandt pamphlet, and the promise of a detailed, scholarly study of the United Nations Charter that Morley had made at the request of a foundation, we decided to launch a monthly pamphlet series. We published the Hutchins speech in December, 1945, the Brandt pamphlet in January, 1946, and Morley's study of the United Nations Charter, which also contained the complete text of the Charter, in February. Morley and I were to be the editors; although the publisher would be Human Events, Inc., I agreed to assume full responsibility for producing, distributing, and financing the series, and rented a small office in an old building south of Chicago's Loop for the purpose. With this step I disassociated myself, with my father's full approval, from the family business, and set out to establish myself in the uncertain but to me enormously alluring field of publishing, which in my case would carry the additional risk and also challenge—a challenge I found particularly appealing—of being in direct opposition to the dominant current of the time. A remark my father made to me sticks in my memory: "If you ever begin to make any money in that business you are going into, you can be pretty sure that you are publishing the wrong kind of books."

In our first pamphlet we boldly announced that we proposed to publish a series that would "consider educational, industrial, political and social problems, all from the viewpoint of the standards which are involved; all with a view to the clarification of issues in behalf of those 'Blessings of Liberty' which the Constitution of the United States was established to secure." The pamphlets were priced at twenty-five cents each and a one-year subscription at two dollars. There were forty-six issues in all, the last appearing in September, 1949. We covered a wide range of subjects, and I think I can say without exaggeration that, considering the times and my own lack of experience, the series achieved a remarkable degree of distinction and recognition.

Following Morley's study of the United Nations Charter, we published one on the nature of authority, called *Faith and Force*, by Joseph M. Lalley, whom Morley had brought to the Washington *Post* and who had for a number of years been its book-review editor. Lalley's essay begins with a careful distinction between authority and power, and goes on to describe some of the various forms of authority—of faith, language, and myth, among others— and its role as the cohesive force of society. It arrives at the conclusion that social revolution does not destroy authority, but that the destruction of authority makes social revolution possible. The next pamphlet was a collection of letters from Germany, chosen from many, which had reached various people in this country by some illegal means—it was still forbidden for Germans to communicate with the outside world—and which gave a graphic picture of what life was like in that broken country. There followed pamphlets by William A. Orton, John U. Nef, Milton Mayer, Oswald Garrison Villard, Douglas Steere, Arthur E. Morgan, Harold E. Fey, Montgomery Belgion, F. G. Juenger, Clare Luce, Raymond Aron, Clifford Manshardt, and David Dallin, among others—a distinguished company. Some of the subjects treated were Russian slave-labor camps, the failure of the high schools, the income tax, the role of the black market in a centrally controlled economy, the Potsdam Agreement, pacifism, Gandhi and Indian independence, the problem of technology, the basic conflict between Marxism and

Leninism, minorities. We broke new ground with our pamphlets, discussed issues, and brought out facts that the regular publications of the time had carefully ignored; we disturbed a few sacred cows; and we introduced to this country one author, Raymond Aron, who has since become a great figure.

Because producing, distributing, and promoting the pamphlets required an office and small staff, it seemed logical for us in Chicago to take over the printing, mailing, and promotion of the weekly newsletter, which we soon arranged to do. In addition, during the same period, we published three books. One was a collection of Communist documents under the title *Blueprint for World Conquest*, for which William Henry Chamberlin wrote an introduction, and the others were collections of the essays published in *Human Events* in 1944 and 1945.

The idea for *Blueprint for World Conquest*, as I learned some years later, had come from a long-time security officer of the State Department, Raymond Murphy, who also provided the copies of the documents it contained: the Theses and Statutes, the Constitution and Rules, and the Program of the Communist International. These documents were extremely rare and almost impossible to find, although they must have been generally available when they were first published in the early twenties—a change reflecting one of those mysterious shifts in Communist policy. Murphy was a most interesting man, and had acquired in his many years of experience an astonishingly thorough knowledge of the Communist conspiracy and of the Communist method of operating. During the time I knew him, however, he had been exiled by the State Department to a small office in one of the "temporary" buildings left over from the war; those in authority in Washington in those years preferred their illusions to such expert knowledge about Communism as Ray Murphy possessed.

Blueprint for World Conquest, my first experience in publishing a book, came out when the euphoria of the "good old Uncle Joe" period was beginning to wear off: it attracted some attention, was widely reviewed, and sold quite well. The documents it contained told in precise, unequivocal language exactly what the objectives of Communism were and the methods by which the Communists proposed to attain them.

My association with Hanighen and Morley was stimulating and enjoyable, and opened an entirely new world to me. They were both older and far more experienced than I was, both had a good sense of humor, and both were most generous toward me. Hanighen had a more relaxed attitude toward the world and other people than Morley, who could become impatient rather easily and was sometimes inclined to stand on his dignity, but Morley saw political developments from a broader perspective than Hanighen and with a greater understanding of history. To be closely associated with two men of their integrity, broad experience, and knowledge of the world was a great privilege. *Human Events* and the pamphlet series gave me invaluable experience in publishing and the opportunity to meet many people I would not have met otherwise, and some conception as well both of how ideas are communicated and of how they are suppressed, of what constitutes public opinion and how it is manipulated.

One man I came to know who was particularly helpful and kind to me was Frank Chodorov, whom I remember with respect and admiration. When I first met him in his dingy office, piled with books and magazines, in a decrepit old building near Brooklyn Bridge, he was publishing a four-page magazine called *analysis* (he would never capitalize the first letter), which he wrote entirely himself. It appeared at irregular intervals, cost one dollar a year, and was always beautifully written and full of fresh, original ideas. He was born and had spent all of his life in New York, the son of Russian-Jewish immigrant parents. He had begun active life as a knit-goods salesman, with a territory somewhere in the northwest, became a follower of Henry George, and then head of the Henry George School. He was an excellent, tireless talker, had a gentle, ironical sense of humor and a fine literary style, was a great admirer of Albert J. Nock, whom he regarded as his teacher, and firmly distrusted government in all its forms. Governments, he never tired of pointing out, are not an abstraction but are made up of individuals, whose first and foremost concern is to take care of themselves. By the power of taxation, governments can take money away from some people and give it to others, keeping some of it for themselves in the process, and they can wage destructive wars and can disrupt economic life; but by their nature, Chodorov always insisted, they are incapable of producing anything.

He was a born pamphleteer. When I first met him, which was soon after we had started our series, he was ecstatic about the idea, and helped in any way he could, by encouragement, by writing excellent promotional copy for me, and by contributing three sound and most successful pamphlets to the series: *Taxation Is*

Robbery, From Solomon's Yoke to the Income Tax, and *The Myth of the Post Office.* They were classic pamphlets: each treated a subject of general interest in a provocative way, was clearly and concisely written and argued, and came to a sharply formulated conclusion. When William F. Buckley, Jr., appeared on the scene a few years later, he and Chodorov became close friends, different though they were in almost every superficial way. Frank Chodorov was an honest and completely unselfish man, was helpful to many people, and by his life contributed something unique and of great value to the tradition of individual freedom.

It became apparent, as time went on, that Hanighen and Morley in Washington and I in Chicago, though pursuing the same general goals, were going about it in different ways, and the mere fact of the distance between Washington and Chicago created problems. Editing a small publication in one city and producing, mailing, and promoting it in another proved to be more difficult than we had anticipated, and both Morley and Hanighen, as the pamphlet series developed, began to feel that I was getting involved in something for which they had the ultimate responsibility but were less and less able to control. The publication of the pamphlets and three books, one of which had been moderately successful, had whetted my desire to get into publishing in a more substantial way, which would have created further complications if I had tried to do it as part of Human Events, Inc. It was decided, therefore, to set up a separate corporation to take over the pamphlet series and the rights and inventories of the three books we had published, and to transfer the printing and distribution of the newsletter to Washington. During the time we handled the producing and promotion of the newsletter we were able to improve its appearance, and we substantially increased its circulation, from some 2,500 copies weekly to about 5,000. With the most strenuous effort, however, we were never able to get much above this latter figure. Still, as with every publication, it is not how many readers it has, but who they are, that measures its effectiveness, and *Human Events* was read by an influential group of people, as the many editorials that would appear here and there following almost every issue testified.

Having learned something about the economic realities of publishing material that did not conform to the dominant opinion of the times, I decided it would be more realistic to face facts as they were and incorporate as a nonprofit organization. Accordingly, in

September, 1946, I set up Human Events Associates as an Illinois not-for-profit corporation. The pamphlet series was published from then on by Human Events Associates, and although Felix Morley continued to be most generous with editorial help and advice, the pressure of several other responsibilities he had assumed in addition to the newsletter made it impossible for him to participate as actively as he had in the beginning. Getting into book publishing in a more substantial way was very much in my mind, and the situation in Germany, where occupation policies were still under the influence of the Morgenthau Plan and the terms of the Potsdam Agreement, offered an opportunity.

During the first winter following the war, the English publisher Victor Gollancz made several trips to the British Zone of Occupation, which included Hamburg and much of the industrial north, and wrote a series of letters to London papers describing the situation. Malnutrition and actual starvation were widespread, plants that had survived Allied bombing were being dismantled, refugees who had been driven out of the former German territories in the east were pouring into the bombed cities, where housing was already hopelessly insufficient for the indigenous population, and economic life was virtually at a standstill. The present was dreadful and the future seemed utterly without hope. A correspondent from the London *Daily Mail* reported at the time, "Slowly, quietly, hygienically the Germans are moving toward death." Gollancz collected his reports, to which he added a large number of photographs he had had made during the course of his visits, and brought them out as a book under the title *In Darkest Germany*. He followed this factual account with a second book, *Our Threatened Values*, in which, in really passionate language, he denounced the whole conception on which Allied postwar policy was based. One of the central values of our civilization, he maintained, is respect for personality; it was this value that was being mocked by the Allies in Germany, and such disregard could not be without devastating results for all other values, and therefore civilization itself.

Victor Gollancz was a successful and distinguished publisher, of Jewish background, and a convinced and prominent socialist— he was the founder of the enormously influential Left Book Club. By no stretch of the imagination could he be accused of harboring sympathy for National Socialism; his concern for the hideous situation then existing in Germany derived solely from humanitarian considerations. He was also well known in New York. But no New

York publisher would consider the two books I have described. For some reason, probably as a result of our pamphlets, they were offered to me, and I made up my mind to publish them.

A third book, and one I thought was of the utmost importance, was made available to me at this time. In one of the first letters I received after the war from Germany, my old friend Hermann mentioned a book that he said would explain much of what had happened: *Hitler in Our Selves*, by the Swiss writer Max Picard. I got a copy from the Swiss publisher, Eugen Rentsch, and decided to publish it. The two Gollancz books, in a sense, were large pamphlets, and publishing American editions created no problem. The original editions were at hand and only needed to be photographed for offset reproduction, they were written in response to an immediate situation, and their author was fairly well known. The Picard book was something else again: it would have to be translated, it treated a complex problem in a way that would have little appeal to the reigning intellectual orthodoxy, and although Picard was well known in Germany and France, he was almost completely unknown in this country—most people, when they heard his name, thought of the man who went up in balloons. My decision to publish this book, therefore, was a decision to go into publishing in a serious way, as I was well aware.

Picard argued that the Hitler phenomenon was a result of the sickness of the modern world, a sickness that had taken its most virulent form in Germany, but one to which the rest of the world was by no means immune. We would do well, he implied, to regard the German catastrophe as a warning of what could happen to all of us. He described various aspects of modern life that were manifestations of its sickness, among them its discontinuity and fragmentation, its emptiness, its destructiveness. Modern man, he said, is inclined to regard nature not as the environment in which we live out our lives but as enemy territory to be conquered and occupied; language not as a gift of God for the discovery and communication of truth but as a tool for the subjugation of others; and art as a means of propaganda rather than a manifestation of the divine gift of creativity. Hitler, Picard said, represented all these symptoms of the modern sickness in their most extreme form; he filled the spiritual emptiness of his followers with his screaming speeches and his obsessive hatred. To put over a book with such a message, it was quite apparent, would not be easy.

The first thing was to get it translated. This proved to be a rather formidable task, because Picard wrote in a style, peculiarly his own, that was much better suited to the complexities and round-about quality of German than to the directness of English. A gifted and rather remarkable German, Heinrich Hauser, who had written two pamphlets for my series, offered to try his hand. He came from a prominent Weimar family and had been trained as a physician; but instead of practicing his profession he had gone to sea as a deck hand on one of the last large sailing ships, on which he made at least one voyage to and from Australia. He worked for a time as a publicity man for a traveling circus, wrote several successful books, and left Germany shortly after Hitler came to power. At least three of his books had been published in this country by the time I first met him. One was an autobiography, *Time Was: Death of a Junker*; the most recent, *A German Talks Back*, had appeared shortly before the end of the war and caused a great scandal, as well as the dismissal of the editor who had accepted it. The political scientist Hans Morgenthau was asked to write an introduction, notes, and a postscript, apparently with the purpose of protecting the American reader from contamination; in the light of what has happened since, Hauser's book makes far more sense than Morgenthau's additions. Amusingly enough, when he wrote the book, Hauser was working as a gardener at the University of Chicago, where Morgenthau was a professor. Hauser's translation of Picard was moderately successful—no translation, especially of Max Picard, is ever really satisfactory—and after extensive editing the book was ready for publication in the fall of 1947, when I planned also to publish the two Gollancz books.

It was apparent that I could not use the name Human Events for a book-publishing operation over which my two associates in Washington would have no effective control; so the decision was made to change the name of our not-for-profit corporation from Human Events Associates to Henry Regnery Company. This was done on September 9, 1947. Since the sort of publishing I planned to do would probably be controversial and of a more or less personal nature, I decided that people should know who was behind it. The first books to appear under the imprint of Henry Regnery Company were *In Darkest Germany* and *Our Threatened Values*, by Victor Gollancz, and *Hitler in Our Selves* by Max Picard; an auspicious beginning, it seemed to me, for a nonconforming Chicago publisher. I was most grateful to have an introduction from Rufus M. Jones for *Our Threatened Values* and from Robert M.

Hutchins for *In Darkest Germany*; to me these represented the stamp of approval for what I was doing by two men I greatly respected and admired.

Not surprisingly, none of my first three books appeared on best-seller lists, but they were all respectfully reviewed and may have had some impact, if only indirectly. *Time*, whose book-review section was then among the best and most influential in the country, gave *Our Threatened Values* a most intelligent, discerning review, from which the following excerpt is taken:

Though retaining his Jewish faith and socialist belief, Gollancz has here written a fiery, almost transported plea for a return to the ways of the early Christians. Political salvation is possible, he thunders, only if based on a union of traditional religious ethics and the secular humanist tradition of the West. A way of life based on unswerving devotion to love, mercy and respect for human personality is the only vision that can save modern man from total destruction.*

Victor Gollancz, needless to say, was a most interesting man, as I discovered, not long after I published his two books, when I spent an evening with him in New York. During its course, Gollancz told a story that had come out of the writing of these two books. "It is an important story, and for reasons you will soon understand, I decided not to put it into my book, but I want you to remember it." After returning to London from one of his trips to Germany, he had a call from Winston Churchill, then out of office, who said that he wanted very much to see him. Apparently Churchill had read some of Gollancz's reports in the London papers. When they met, Churchill questioned Gollancz closely about conditions in Germany and became visibly affected by what he told him. Finally Churchill asked, "Is it true, Mr. Gollancz, that five thousand civilians were killed in the British air raids on Hamburg?" Gollancz replied that the total was in fact many times that number, and then went on to say something about the bombing of cities, and particularly the great "saturation" raid on Dresden, with thousands of incendiary bombs followed by high explosives, from which the casualties may have been as high as 200,000—no one knows the exact number, because the city was crowded wth refugees from the east. Churchill, Gollancz said, paled, and then said, "Mr. Gollancz, they never told me we were bombing civilians." After waiting for this rather astounding remark to take effect, Gollancz

* March 1, 1948, pp. 91–92.

40

continued, "When I tell you this, your immediate reaction is to think that Churchill was lying. Of course he knew that we were bombing civilians, but that isn't the point: when he told me he didn't know, he was speaking the truth. Churchill is a romantic, and a romantic lives entirely in the present, so much so that he can be completely oblivious of a position he may have taken in the past, or of the consequences in the future of his present position. I can understand this, because I am just such a romantic myself. During the war Churchill would have been prepared to kill every man, woman, and child in Germany if he thought it was necessary to win—'I would make a pact with the devil to save Britain,' he once said, as you will remember—but when I saw him he could perfectly honestly say, 'Mr. Gollancz, they never told me we were bombing civilians.' "

Victor Gollancz was a romantic, as he said, and also had a rather theatrical quality. His socialism probably contained a large element of theatrics—he was, after all, a successful, well-to-do publisher—but he was also a man of courage and high principles. One of the last causes among the many he took up during his life was that of the Arabs made homeless by the establishment of the State of Israel.

Max Picard's *Hitler in Our Selves* was not a successful book, as success is usually measured, but it was treated with respect, some people read it, and it helped to establish the firm as one willing to take on a difficult, serious work. We were still receiving a few orders for it twenty years after its publication.

It probably was unwise, from a certain point of view, to launch my publishing enterprise with three books on such an unpopular subject as Germany. But it was the burning issue of the time, obviously no one else was anxious to take it up, and it seemed to me that if I felt strongly about it and had the means to do something, I had a moral obligation to publish the books I have described. It should also not be forgotten that these three were concerned not so much with Germany as with the upholding of the values and standards on which civilization rests. Looking back, after more than thirty years, I have no regrets, nor do I feel the need to apologize for having identified myself at the beginning of my publishing career with books by two men of the moral integrity, perception, and high-mindedness of Victor Gollancz and Max Picard.

3

THE FIRST TWO YEARS

THE first, very modest catalog of the Henry Regnery Co. appeared in the spring of 1948. It announced the publication of six new books, all of which came out in a rather small, uniform format, not distinguished, but legible and well printed. We padded out our catalog by including descriptions of the three books we had published the previous year as well of those we proposed to publish the following fall. The last three pages were devoted to the pamphlet series, which by now included twenty-seven titles. The message "From the Publisher," with which our catalog opened, bravely proclaimed: "It is our purpose to publish good books, wherever we find them." We went on to say that we hoped to contribute to the re-establishment of the interchange of ideas and opinions that had been characteristic of the Western tradition and that was indispensable if civilization was to recover from the shattering experience of the war.

Probably the most important, and certainly the longest-lived, of the six books we published that first, hopeful spring was Hans Rothfels's *The German Opposition to Hitler*. Rothfels, a distinguished and well-known historian, was at that time professor of history at the University of Chicago. He later returned to Germany to become a professor at the University of Tübingen and head of the Institute for Contemporary History. His book was the first fully documented historical analysis of the German opposition. It was a work of considerable importance, and although it did not receive the immediate attention from the reviewers it deserved—according to the official line there had been no German opposition—it gradually established itself as one of the major source books on a phenomenon of the greatest importance. "The ruthless police state, equipped with all the weapons of modern science and industry," as our catalog description put it, "is a new but not unique historical phenomenon: the possibilities of civil resistance to such a state become, therefore, of more than academic interest."

Of the remaining five books in that first announcement, one was written by a Scot, two by Germans, and two by Swiss.

Edmund Whittaker, professor of mathematics at the University of Edinburgh, wrote on medieval philosophy, particularly that of Thomas Aquinas, from the vantage point of modern science. By showing that its philosophical basis derives from classical and medieval philosophy, *Space and Spirit* demonstrated the continuity of the Western tradition.

The two Germans were Ernst Juenger and Ernst Wiechert, both well-known German writers; Juenger, indeed, is a major figure of modern literature. The Juenger book, *The Peace*, had been written during the war and was secretly distributed in thousands of copies, many handmade. It was not of great significance except for the circumstances under which it was written and the fact that when our edition appeared publication was still forbidden in Germany, this time by the Allied military government. The book by Ernst Wiechert contained three speeches, two given at the University of Munich, in 1935 and 1945, and the last after the war in Switzerland. The 1935 speech, in which he admonished his hearers "not to keep silent when conscience bids you speak, because nothing in the world so eats away the marrow of a man as cowardice," resulted in Wiechert's arrest and confinement in Buchenwald.

Hans Zbinden, whose book *Whither Germany* was one of our six, was well known in Switzerland as the author of a biography of Benjamin Constant and as a public-spirited man who had been associated with various international endeavors. "The disappearance of Germany as a political and spiritual force," Zbinden asserted, "would probably mean the end of European history." The last book, *From Versailles to Potsdam*, by Leonard von Muralt, professor of modern history at the University of Zurich, was an analysis of the basic assumptions of the Versailles Treaty and their influence. It was written in the vain hope that those who were to determine the further course of European history in the arrangements they would make following World War II might learn something from the mistakes their predecessors had made following the first war. Leonard von Muralt and Hans Zbinden represented the best of the Swiss tradition: they were Swiss through and through, but at the same time civilized Europeans, and not afraid, in the chaotic atmosphere of the time, to assert the primacy of reason.

One of the more satisfying results of the publication of those six books was the response to them of the more serious reviewers. Asher Byrnes, for example, devoted a long review in the *Saturday Review of Literature* to five of them, in which, speaking of the Rothfels book, he said, "His monograph has all the scholarly virtues. It is comprehensive, detailed and judicious in the treatment of conflicting materials." Henry Sowerby, in the *Christian Science Monitor*, spoke of the Muralt book as "an extremely able dissertation . . . worthy of careful study by all students of this issue," and H. S. Quigley, in the *American Historical Review*, wrote, "In his concise but clear analysis of the crowded years since the end of World War I, Muralt displays a masterly grasp of events and a comparably impressive literary style." There were equally positive and understanding reviews of several of these books in such publications as the *American Political Science Review,* the *Annals of the American Academy,* and the *Catholic World.* In the climate of 1948, when the response to such books was frequently either hostile or indifferent, reviews like these were all the more remarkable.

After the printing and distribution of the *Human Events* newsletter was transferred back to Washington, I had moved from the building in Chicago where we had taken space to a small office above a drugstore in Hinsdale. By the fall of 1948, as our publishing program began to increase, it became evident that I would need both more help and more space. I therefore hired Philip Starbuck as an editorial assistant and William Strube and Eugenia Fawcett for sales and promotion, the latter two from the University of Chicago Press, and took space in an old building on Jackson Boulevard in Chicago. We were young, worked hard, and enjoyed the association with a new venture.

As I have mentioned, the Henry Regnery Company was originally organized as a nonprofit corporation, not because I had any ideological objection to profits, but because, as it seemed to me then and does still, in matters of excellence the market is a poor judge.

The books that are most needed are often precisely those that will have only a modest sale. It was my original plan to operate more or less in the manner of a university press, trying to break even when we could, but prepared if necessary to face deficits, which I thought it would not be too difficult to make up if we had tax exemption and could keep our publications on a high level of excellence. The Internal Revenue Service, however, thought otherwise. Since we were engaged in a business that is normally conducted for profit, the I.R.S. ruled, there was no reason why we should have tax exemption, which was accordingly denied. There is no practical method of appeal from such a bureaucratic ruling, so there was nothing for us to do but to incorporate. The Henry Regnery Company, therefore, began business March 1, 1948, taking over inventories, publication rights, and other assets, as well as the liabilities, of the former nonprofit corporation. The name of the latter was changed to Human Affairs Associates, and continued to publish the pamphlet series until it was discontinued.

Our corporate entity was now established, we had taken on a modest but adequate office in the city, and we had the beginnings of a professional staff, with all that this meant in the way of expense. The I.R.S. ruled, in essence, that we could not operate as a nonprofit corporation, but that was not of much help in finding a way to operate profitably. By the end of 1949 our list of published books had grown from the ten included in our first catalog, of spring, 1948, to a total of twenty-six, and covered a broad spectrum. There was, for example, the symposium written in honor of T. S. Eliot on the occasion of his sixty-fifth birthday, which included essays by Wyndham Lewis, Clive Bell, Edith Sitwell, and W. H. Auden, among others. There were two books on education, *And Madly Teach* by Mortimer Smith and a new edition of Albert J. Nock's classic *Theory of Education in the United States*; a book on Gandhi's theory of nonviolence, *Satyagraha*, by R. R. Diwakar, and a collection of Gandhi's own writings on missions and the relationship between the various faiths, which Clifford Manshardt had put together and which appeared under the title *The Mahatma and the Missionary*; an essay on existentialism by Helmut Kuhn, *Encounter with Nothingness; Goethe's Image of Man and Society* by Arnold Bergstraesser; a previously unpublished book by Albert J. Nock, *Journal of Forgotten Days, 1934–35*; F. G. Juenger's *The Failure of Technology*; and two books on issues arising out of the war,

Montgomery Belgion's *Victor's Justice* and Freda Utley's *The High Cost of Vengeance,* the former on the war-crimes trials and the latter on Allied occupation policy in Germany.

A book we published in the fall of 1948 to which I felt particularly committed was *Great Saints,* by the Swiss Protestant theologian Walter Nigg. It had been recommended to me by an intelligent, sophisticated German Jesuit. Coming out in Europe immediately after the war, when many were looking for a renewal of faith and a source of meaning and order for their lives, the book attracted favorable and grateful attention, and was soon translated into French, Dutch, and Italian. An additional reason for its appeal in Europe was that, although written by a Protestant theologian, it treated, in a way that embraced the whole of Christianity, a subject usually associated only with Catholicism. None of these considerations, I was disappointed to learn, applied to the book in this country. Americans, in the confident arrogance of the postwar period, did not generally feel the need for inspiration from such self-effacing figures as St. Francis of Assisi or Nicholas of Flüe, the Swiss Brother Klaus. Protestants, in any case, were inclined to reject the book because all but one of the saints it described were Catholics, and Catholics because the author was a Protestant. Nevertheless, it was a beautiful and important book, and there were some who appreciated it. The purpose that inspired Walter Nigg to write it and me to undertake its publication appears in the following passage:

The true Saint belongs to all Christendom, and is not intelligible to one religious denomination only. The emphasis which we place on this in no way means that we propose to supplant the Saints from those Churches where they have taken root: rather would we point the way to them, so that their membership of one Church in the vault of Heaven can be extended to the others. Of the truth of the Saints as Christian manifestations the Apostles' creed has already spoken, when it employs the term "communion of Saints." As the true interpreters of the Gospel they embrace the whole of Christendom, for they represent that secret Christianity, which must not be allowed to disappear from modern religious consciousness.

The book by the German F. G. Juenger, which we published under the title *The Failure of Technology*—the original title, which we should not have changed, was *The Perfection of Technology*— has an interesting history, and one with some significance for our

46

time. It was written under the stress and sense of impending catastrophe engendered by the outbreak of World War II, and because of the reputation of the author, on the one hand, and of its message, on the other, could not be published in National Socialist Germany. At least two clandestine editions were attempted, and in both cases the printing shops were destroyed in Allied air raids before the book could be finished. By some quirk of fate, a copy of the manuscript came into the hands of the artist Victor Hammer, who at the time was working as a printer at Wells College, in Aurora, New York. Hammer was enormously impressed by what Juenger had to say, and fearing that the original might be lost in the chaos of wartime Germany, made up his mind to print a few copies on his hand press. The first edition of *Die Perfektion der Technik*, therefore, emerged from a hand press not very different from the one used by Gutenberg in the fifteenth century, from type set by hand, in a small college town in northern New York that was then still safe from the ravages of war and totalitarianism.

Juenger's attack is not against technology itself, which he recognizes as a necessary agent of human survival, but against the attitude that places the demands of technology above those of life itself. He argues that the consequence of what he calls the technological point of view, for which technological perfection becomes an end in itself, is the totalitarian state, in which all activity and the fulfilling of all human needs are controlled by a gigantic, perfectly functioning apparatus.

The two books on political issues published during 1949, Belgion's *Victor's Justice* and Utley's *The High Cost of Vengeance*, took positions decidedly in opposition to the accepted opinion of the time, and created a certain amount of controversy. Montgomery Belgion was well known in England as an essayist and literary critic, served as an officer in the British army during World War II, and was captured by the Germans during the Greek campaign. *Victor's Justice* was written in the form of a letter to a friend who had also been a prisoner of war in Germany, but at the time of writing was serving as an officer in the British Army of Occupation in Germany. Belgion, who knew his way in English literature, took the epigraph of his book from Dryden—"Ev'n victors are by victory undone."

Belgion objected to the war-crimes trials on several counts. They were based on ex post facto law, for one. And in spite of all that was said about the "international" character of the court at Nuremberg, it was not international at all, but in every respect a creature of the victors. He was furthermore concerned about the corrupting influence of the trials on the Western concept of justice, since, as he pointed out, the desire to punish predominated over the desire to do justice. Belgion's chief objection to the trials, however, was the hypocrisy of the whole miserable business—those sitting in judgment were guilty of the same crimes for which they were trying others. One of the crimes of which the Germans were accused was the murder of "11,000 Polish officers, who were prisoners of war . . . in the Katyn Forest near Smolensk," as it is stated in the original indictment. The number was actually about 4,200, and, when it became evident that the Polish officers had been murdered not by the Germans but by the Russians, the subject was quietly dropped and no further mention was made at Nuremberg of the Katyn massacre. "How then," Belgion asks, "can we believe that the Trial of the so-called 'major war criminals' was inspired by any desire to extend the dominion of justice?" Another crime of which the Germans were accused at Nuremberg was the use of forced labor; but, as Belgion points out, even while the trials were in progress both the French and the British, to say nothing of the Russians, were using as forced labor thousands of former German prisoners, many of whom had been turned over to them by the United States.

The reviewer for the San Francisco *Chronicle* accused Belgion of having said that "there was no moral difference between the victor and the vanquished." On the contrary, Belgion points out that by using the methods of Communist Russia and National Socialist Germany to exact retribution from our former enemies, we were destroying the very cause we had fought the war to defend. Milton Mayer, whose pronouncements often give the impression that he understands more about morality than anyone else, brushed off *Victor's Justice* in the Chicago *Sun* as a "mote and beam book." But have we not been told on the highest authority to cast out the beam in our own eye before we undertake to cast out the mote in our brother's? And whom, besides ourselves, did we deceive at Nuremberg? Howard Becker, in the *Annals of the American Academy*, recommended *Victor's Justice* to those "who are genuinely concerned about the nature and the possibility of justice among the nations." Those who are not seriously concerned about such matters, he said, had "better let it alone. It has the compacted heat and penetrating power of thermite."

Freda Utley was also English by birth and education, but by the time she wrote *The High Cost of Vengeance* she had lived for many years in the United States, and was soon to become an American citizen. Her father, who came from a family of Yorkshire black-smiths, was an early Fabian socialist and a successful journalist. In the early twenties she graduated with honors from the London School of Economics, where she attracted the attention of Bertrand Russell, with whom she remained on friendly terms for the rest of his life. But instead of following the secure academic career that lay open to her, she chose instead to become a Communist, married a Russian, and finally went to Russia to live. Like many thousands of Russian women, she watched as her husband was taken away in the middle of the night by the secret police, never to see him again. Long before this, however, she had come to understand Communism for what it actually was. She had a fine mind, enormous vitality, and, above all, a strong sense of justice—it was her sense of justice and her youthful idealism that brought her to Communism, and her sense of justice again, and her intelligence, that turned her violently away from it. She was always prepared to take the side of the oppressed, of the underdog, and in the immediate postwar period the Germans were decidedly the dogs at the bottom.

I published two more books by Freda Utley, and regard the friendship that grew out of them as one of the rewards for publishing books that take an unpopular position. She could be demanding and utterly unreasonable—she once called me collect from a small town in Alabama for an immediate explanation of why a recent book of hers was not on sale in the local drugstore—but she was at the same time wonderfully generous and warmhearted, and although she made no claim to being beautiful, she had great charm. She was a formidable person, with strong convictions, which she never hesitated to express, and she had many friends. She loved to give parties, which were always delightful affairs and were attended by people of the greatest variety. I particularly remember the one she gave in her Washington apartment in the summer of 1950 to celebrate having become an American citizen—a change of status that, for various reasons, required an act of Congress. Among the guests I remember, which would be only a small fraction of those who were there, were Senator Robert A. Taft, Senator Joseph R. McCarthy, Edith Hamilton, Frank Hanighen, Forrest Davis, General Albert Wedemeyer, Arthur Bliss Lane, the Ambassador from Free China, and Loy Henderson, Under Secretary of State and former ambassador to Russia. When I asked Freda about a rather shy man who didn't seem to know anybody, she replied, "Oh, he is a very nice Czech who lives upstairs and is awfully good at carving ham."

The High Cost of Vengeance resulted from a several months' stay in Germany during the latter part of 1948, a visit that had been made possible by a grant from the Foundation for Foreign Affairs and a commission from the *Reader's Digest*. The book was a frontal attack on Allied occupation policies, which, largely because of Russian intransigence, had made a turn for the better, but still had a long way to go. The notorious order JCS 1067, which established the policies to be followed by the U.S. military government when the war ended—among others that "Germany will not be occupied for the purpose of liberation, but as a defeated enemy nation," that "fraternization" of any kind with the population was prohibited, and that the army authorities must take no "steps looking toward economic rehabilitation"—had fortunately been suspended in 1947. But at the time Miss Utley visited Germany to gather material for her book, industrial plants were still being dismantled on a large scale, the massive "de-Nazification" program based on the theory of guilt by association was still in full swing, and arbitrary arrests and imprisonment by the occupation authorities, though declining, were still frequent.

Miss Utley based her book on personal observation, and on interviews with the occupation authorities and with ordinary Germans. In addition, she made herself familiar with the relevant documentary material. She knew what to look for and what questions to ask, went everywhere, and was intimidated by no one. She put down what she saw and heard, gave credit where she thought credit was due, and criticized where she thought criticism appropriate. The era she describes and the attitude it represented are now, fortunately, long behind us, but her account, as the work of an intelligent observer and a high-minded, courageous woman, is an important part of the historical record, and can well be read as a warning about the effects of policies based on emotion rather than reason and that are the work of people who have no knowledge or understanding of history or historical forces.

In the concluding chapter of *The High Cost of Vengeance* there is a paragraph that I think sets the tone of the whole book:

The roles of oppressors and oppressed change with the times. Yesterday's arrogant victor is today's vanquished, and those who fought for liberty now deprive others of freedom. It seems as true today as when Thucy-dides wrote his history of the Peloponnesian War that "right as the world goes is only a question between equals in power, while the strong do what they can and the weak suffer what they must."

The High Cost of Vengeance was the first book I published to have the distinction of being reviewed in the book-review section of the Sunday New York *Times*. The reviewer, Delbert Clark, had been the *Times* correspondent in Berlin and had an established repu-tation as a German hater. He could be relied on, therefore, to excori-ate the book, which is exactly what he did: "Such a compilation of half-truths, rumors and demonstrable untruths that it is difficult to make an appraisal of Miss Utley's thesis." There were also a number of highly favorable reviews, some from people of far greater moral authority than Delbert Clark: Reinhold Niebuhr, for example, in the *Nation,* George N. Shuster in the *Political Science Quarterly,* and Paul Hutchinson in the *Christian Century*. The book sold reasonably well, but may have had a greater immediate impact, which is often the case, because of the reviews it received than through the copies of the book itself.

During those first two years our most successful book from the standpoint of sales was Mortimer Smith's *And Madly Teach*. Mr. Smith undertook to write it after a term or two as a member of a Connecticut school board, during which he first became aware of the gigantic apparatus that largely controls public education in this country, and of its appalling results on education itself. The book is written in clear, idiomatic English, with a touch of wry, engaging humor, in striking contrast to the hideous, garbled language of the educationists. That wonderful old fighter for good causes Bernard Iddings Bell, Canon of the Episcopal Church and long-time friend of Albert J. Nock, wrote an appropriate introduction, and to my great delight *Time* devoted a three-column article to the book in its Education section. It began to sell immediately and went through several editions; judging from the hundreds of letters and postcards we received from teachers, it was those faced with the responsibility of educating the young who particularly welcomed and appreciated Mr. Smith's attack on the educational establishment and its stultify-ing influence on public education.

Finally, there were the two books by Albert J. Nock we published during those first two years. Having long been an admirer of Nock,

I thought it particularly noteworthy for a young, new firm to have two of his books on its list. I had read some of Nock's essays, in *Harper's* or the *Atlantic Monthly,* while still in school, but it was his *Memoirs of a Superfluous Man,* which I read soon after it came out in 1944, that made me a confirmed Nockian and was probably one of the influences that led to my publishing books. The first of our two works by him was a journal from the years 1934 and 1935, the only unpublished mansucript, except some letters, that Nock did not destroy before his death in 1945. This came to me from his son Samuel A., who had written two pamphlets for our series. The journal covers only a brief period, May 1934 to October 1935, but it was the period during which the lines were being drawn that led to the catastrophe of World War II, and Nock was a shrewd, keen observer, well aware of what was going on. Roosevelt and Hitler, for neither of whom Nock had any use whatever, had come into power the year before the journal begins; Mussolini was preparing for his Ethiopian adventure; and the politicians were helplessly wrestling with economic and social problems completely beyond their powers of understanding, with armaments and war in the background as the simple and inevitable solution. Nock comments on it all with his usual directness and relentless realism, and always in his admirably clear, classic English—advertising, newspapers, the weather, women's fashions, the opera and the theater, Mencken's latest book, the income tax, and, of course, personalities and politics. Whatever interested Nock he also made interesting to his reader. A rather typical Nock observation is the following:

Reading some outpourings in favour of the Child Labour Amendment sharpens my sense of the dreadful havoc worked by the unrestrained ascendency of the 'moral element' in society. I remember a wise saying that I think covers the case, though I do not know who said it. 'Virtue is more to be feared than vice, because its excesses are not subject to the regulation of conscience.' There seems no doubt about it.

Nock's *Theory of Education in the United States* was made up of lectures he had given at the University of Virginia in 1931, and was first published the following year. When we brought out our edition in 1949 it had long been out of print, and now it appears to be out of print again. That a book of the quality of this one should not be generally available provides eloquent confirmation of Nock's strictures on the results of the American educational system. Trash is available in abundance and the market for it seems insatiable, but with the millions of supposedly literate people turned out every year by our colossal educational establishment, the market for a classic book on one of the most basic issues facing our society is too small to keep it in print.

The thesis of Nock's book, simply stated, is that the American theory of education is based on three fallacies: the idea, derived from a false understanding of the doctrine of equality, that everyone can be educated; the idea, derived from a false understanding of democracy, that no one has a right to anything that is not accessible to everyone; and, finally, the idea that good government and a generally wholesome public order are conditioned upon having a literate citizenry. The American theory of education, Nock says, contemplates a fantastic and impracticable idea of equality, a fantastic and impracticable idea of democracy, and a fantastically exaggerated idea of the importance of literacy in assuring the support of a sound and enlightened public order.

The theory that everyone is capable of being educated, and that nothing should be made available to some that is not accessible to all, degrades education, Nock insisted, into training, with the result that society is deprived of the services of the small minority capable of being educated. True education, in Nock's view of the matter, should be formative, and above all *maturing;* it should inculcate the views of life and the demands on life that are appropriate to maturity and that are indeed the specific marks, the outward and visible signs, of the inward and spiritual grace of maturity.

The sum and substance of Nock's book on education is probably contained in the following:

The educable person, in contrast to the ineducable, is one who gives promise of some day being able to think; and the object of educating him . . . is to put him in the way of right thinking. Now, the experienced mind is aware that all the progress in actual civilization that society has ever made has been brought about, not by machinery, not by political programmes, platforms, parties, not even by revolutions, but by right thinking. . . . It would appear, then, that a society which takes no account of the educable person, makes no place for him, does nothing with him, is taking a considerable risk; so considerable that in the whole course of human experience, so far as our records go, no society has ever yet taken it without coming to great disaster.

The first two years of my publishing firm were wonderfully satisfying to me; in some ways they were among the most satisfying of the twenty-five years or so I devoted to publishing. We published some good books, several, unquestionably, of outstanding quality, which were also well produced; we confronted conventional opinion with some questions it could not evade and found difficult if not impossible to answer; we received a considerable degree of recognition; and in the process the firm acquired a definite and recognizable face. We did not make any money, but that was not my primary objective, and the demands of our balance sheet were still manageable.

4

SOME PEOPLE AND PLACES

THE publication of the three pamphlets by Robert M. Hutchins and my subsequent acquaintance with him had several consequences: it opened the door to a number of people at the University of Chicago, several of whom, in one way or another, influenced the development of my firm, and it led to the publication of the quarterly magazine *Measure* and of the paper-bound books used in the program of the Great Books Foundation. Hutchins had been president of the university since 1929, and although some of his innovations proved of questionable value, there can be no doubt that through his influence a number of outstanding men were attracted to the university, which remained, under his administration, a place of great intellectual distinction.

One of the first people I met at the university was John U. Nef. His long association with it had begun with his father, who had established its department of chemistry. John Nef was a distinguished scholar and decidedly in the Hutchins camp, which of course was not true of all members of the faculty. He was the founder of the Committee on Social Thought, and when I knew him, its chairman. The Committee was an academic department, and had the authority to grant advanced degrees and to make faculty appointments. Its basic purpose was to provide a means of communication

55

and mutual stimulation among different scholarly disciplines, with the ultimate aim of adding to the understanding of man and society. Nef's own field was economic history. His innovative work on the history of the British coal industry, which showed that the rise of industrial society had been a slow and gradual process rather than a sudden "revolution," put the development of industry as a whole into new perspectives. He was a thoroughly civilized man, a good conversationalist, and a gracious host: dinner or lunch in his spacious apartment near the university was always an enjoyable occasion.

I soon discovered that Nef suffered from a malady fairly common among academicians: magazinitis. He often talked to me about the desirability of a journal to be sponsored by the Committee on Social Thought, with T. S. Eliot's *Criterion* as its model. He had enlisted the interest of several others, including three or four members of the Committee, among them—most important, to me—Robert M. Hutchins. After several discussions with Hutchins, I worked out a cost estimate and prepared a dummy, and submitted them to him along with a letter in which I expressed willingness to assume responsibility for getting the magazine out. We soon agreed that it would appear quarterly, that it would be called *Measure,* after a suggestion by Hutchins, and that an editorial committee consisting of Hutchins, as chairman, Daniel J. Boorstin, David Grene, John U. Nef, Robert Redfield, Henry Regnery, and Otto von Simson, as managing editor, would take on full editorial responsibility. Hutchins arranged to meet the editorial costs, including payment for articles, through a fund that he controlled. I in turn agreed to transfer the subscription list of the pamphlet series, which had by then about run its course, to the new journal.

The first issue appeared in December, 1949, and led off with an article by Hutchins, "T. S. Eliot on Education," which in effect would dominate the eight issues of the magazine that appeared. In the following academic year Eliot gave four lectures at the university in which he undertook to answer Hutchins's criticism and clarify his own position; and each of these lectures appeared, successively, in the last four issues. The immediate impression conveyed by the eight issues, considered after a quarter of a century, is their high level. *Measure* survived for only two years, but published articles of unquestionable quality and covered a broad spectrum of interests.

Its excellence was largely the work of Otto von Simson, who was secretary of the Committee on Social Thought. He was not only a competent and creative scholar, his field being the history of art, but he also stood up unflinchingly for his strongly held convictions, as his subsequent career has demonstrated. He is now a professor at the Free University of Berlin, and has taken a leading and courageous part in the fight to save the university from Communist domination. All the other members of the Committee but Boorstin wrote for *Measure* themselves, and further made their scholarship available by reading manuscripts. But because there was virtually no basic philosophical agreement among them, it was impossible to give *Measure* the definite character that might have helped to establish it as a lasting influence.

It did gain some recognition. The London *Times Literary Supplement,* for example, gave it favorable notice in May, 1951, specifically mentioning its "concern with the spiritual foundations of the West." But the renewal rate was no more than 30%, and we were never able to get our circulation rate much above the 2,000 acquired from the pamphlet series. By the middle of the second year it had become evident that *Measure* could not continue much longer as it had originally been set up. Nef made it clear that the Committee on Social Thought wished to withdraw. And Hutchins, in response to an offer to head the Ford Foundation, resigned from the university; this in effect removed the magazine's base, since it had been through him that the editorial costs had been met.

The last issue, which appeared in the fall of 1951, included, besides the fourth of Eliot's lectures on education, a wise and realistic essay on Churchill's memoirs by the Swiss historian and statesman Carl Burckhardt, and Chancellor Hutchins's farewell address to the students, which marked the end of his long and stormy career at the University of Chicago.

The end of *Measure* ended my association with Robert M. Hutchins. I had never been intimate with him, but I met with him frequently for a time, in varying circumstances, and had come to know him, I believe, fairly well. Whatever may be said about the public positions he took in his later years, we owe him a great debt of gratitude for his outspoken, courageous criticism of the superficiality of American education, for his eloquent statements of what education should mean, and for his attempts to find a solution to the problem of education in a democracy.

Through John Nef I came to know not only Otto von Simson, but others of those distinguished European scholars who found refuge and a place for creative work at the University of

Chicago, among them G. A. Borgese, Hans Rothfels, and Helmut Kuhn. There were also Arnold Bergstraesser, who was the motivating force behind the Goethe Bicentennial Convocation in Aspen in 1948, one of the first truly international scholarly meetings to be held after the war; Max Rheinstein, professor in the Law School and a leading authority in the field of comparative law; the theologian Wilhelm Pauck; and Kurt Riezler, who, after a diplomatic career, did important work in philosophy. Some I came to know better than others, and I published books by four of them—Arnold Bergstraesser's *Goethe's Image of Man and Society*, Kurt Riezler's *Man: Mutable and Immutable*, Helmut Kuhn's *Encounter with Nothingness*, and, as I have already mentioned, Hans Rothfels's *The German Opposition to Hitler*. These men were all distinguished scholars and strong personalities; having some association with them was stimulating and rewarding. Arnold Bergstraesser recommended one of the most successful books I have ever published, Romano Guardini's *The Lord*, and Wilhelm Pauck read the manuscript of James Collins's *The Mind of Kierkegaard* when it first came in and strongly recommended it for publication, as well as Collins's next manuscript, *The Existentialists*. Both books were successful, and more than twenty-five years later they are still in print.

G. A. Borgese was chairman of one of those projects that could have been thought of only by a group of intellectuals in the euphoria of postwar America, when everything seemed possible. This was the Committee to Frame a World Constitution, which Hutchins, himself a member, often referred to as the "Committee to Frame Hutchins." I got into a dispute with Borgese about a manuscript that the Great Books Foundation had ordered from him, at my suggestion, and then refused to use. Because I was publishing the books for the Foundation at the time, he threatened to sue me. After a long telephone conversation, which was interspersed with various threats that sounded more ominous than they were probably intended to be, Borgese suddenly said, "Come out and have lunch with us." This proved to be a most friendly and agreeable occasion—his wife, who was the daughter of Thomas Mann, was a charming woman and a good cook—and it led to several more. On one of them Borgese told me he wanted to discuss a book project. I can still hear his rolling *r*'s and those extra vowel sounds the Italians often add to English words, projected by his deep, resonant voice, as he described it, more or less as follows: "For the first generation or so after Christ, Christianity was nothing more than a small, dissident Jewish sect on the eastern shore of the Mediterranean. Paul, by putting the message of Christ into the language and concepts of Greek philosophy, made it the religion of the Roman Empire and finally of the Western world, but it has remained limited to the West by the fact that it is expressed in the terminology of Western philosophy." Then, raising his voice somewhat and focusing his full attention on me, he went on to say, "I, Borgese, will do for Paul what Paul did for Peter: by putting the message of Christianity into a universal philosophical language, I will make it the religion of the world!" So far as I know, he never wrote the book, but he was sufficiently persuasive to induce at least one New York publisher to give him a contract and a modest advance.

It was through Otto von Simson that I met Paul Scheffer, who was of great help to me in the early days of my firm. When Simson first introduced me to him, Scheffer was living in a rather dingy hotel on the south side of Chicago, not far from the university. He was badly crippled, and at first glance would have appeared to be just another elderly man, of no particular distinction, if it had not been for his wonderfully shrewd, intelligent eyes beneath rather heavy lids, which seemed to have seen everything and to be capable of taking in everything still.

He had been sent to Moscow in November, 1921, as the correspondent of the *Berliner Tageblatt*, then a leading European newspaper, and became, during his eight-year stay, one of the most influential foreign correspondents of his time. His reports to his paper, which are essays rather than the usual kind of newspaper story, are brilliant commentaries on Russian life under Communism, and are significant historical documents. An example of Scheffer's style is an account, which appeared in the *Tageblatt* on January 8, 1928, of the exile by Stalin of a number of the leading figures of the revolution. "This is the most extraordinary historical phenomenon that the Russian revolution has brought forth. It involves people who, as few others, incited and then led the revolution, who created the state that now sends them into the wilderness." Scheffer describes some of the figures involved: two former ambassadors, the former Minister of the Post, the former editor of *Pravda*, and, of course, Trotsky—"the hero of all the heroes of the revolution, the great man of the Battle of October and of Kronstadt, first

Foreign Minster and then Minister of War of the Soviet Union, dialectician and orator like no other." Scheffer goes on to observe:

It will be particularly interesting for all of these people to learn that for exiles of the present regime there is not even the 17 Kopeks of pocket money the Czar still provided. . . . They must all take the road they had already taken under the Czars, or would have taken had they been caught. There are revolutionaries among them, Smirnow, for instance, who have been in the party for almost thirty years [since 1898, therefore]. . . . History has never invented anything more ironical or cruel than the spectacle of these victorious revolutionaries who, under the system they destroyed and the one they led to victory, receive the same reward for their efforts—the silence of Siberia. . . . Europe watches the performance with the curiosity of the non-participant. It must, however, seem to us that besides the "permanence of the revolution" Stalin and Trotsky argue so much about, the "permanence of Siberia," as the symbol of the unchanging Russian method of dealing with political dissidents deserves some attention.*

Scheffer's career as a Moscow correspondent ended in 1928, when he was refused permission to return to Russia after a vacation, because, apparently, of his acount of the brutal, ruthless methods used to collectivize agriculture in the Ukraine, the reporting of which he regarded as the greatest achievement of his Russian career, and an article "Terror as an Expression of Raison d'Etat." In the early thirties he spent several years as a correspondent in New York, where the Foreign Policy Association invited him to lecture a number of times as an expert on Russia. He also contributed to *Foreign Affairs*.

Toward the end of 1933, after Hitler's rise to power, he returned to Germany, believing, as many did then, that the Nazi regime was only a passing phenomenon, and that the important immediate task was to preserve as much as possible of the national substance. The *Berliner Tageblatt*, which was Jewish owned, and in its general policy liberal in the European sense of the word, was closed almost immediately after Hitler came to power. In 1933 the owners managed to reach an apparent accommodation with Joseph Goebbels, Minister for Propaganda and Public Enlightenment, who promised the paper a degree of freedom. It was on the basis of this promise that Scheffer decided to become editor of the *Berliner Tageblatt* and to try to restore it as one of the great European newspapers. This was no easy assignment, but Scheffer brought with him several

* *Augenzeuge im Staate Lenins,* Muenchen, 1972, pp. 303–13 (my translation).

distinct advantages: he knew where he stood, he was far more intelligent and experienced in the ways of the world than his adversaries in the Ministry of Propaganda, and from his eight years in Communist Russia he knew what to expect from a totalitarian, ideological regime. In addition, his excellent connections in the Foreign Office and the respect he enjoyed both inside and outside Germany provided him with a considerable degree of protection. For some time he succeeded in maintaining the paper as what he called an anomaly, and by various subterfuges kept his readers informed of what was going on in the outside world, and made clear his own attitude toward what was going on inside Germany. Criticism of a speech by Hitler on foreign policy could be indicated with an appropriate quotation from Bismarck; Max Planck would be quoted on the necessity for independent research; other things one could not say oneself could be expressed by quoting Goethe, Kant, or the brothers Grimm.

The following, from a letter to Margaret Boveri from Dr. I. G. van Maasdijk written November 29, 1960, gives a most interesting account of the impression Scheffer made in those years on a neutral journalist:

From 1933 on I was on very friendly terms with Paul Scheffer, and regarded him as an important advisor on politics in Berlin and in Geneva (at the League of Nations) during the time I was diplomatic correspondent of the Amsterdam paper *De Telegraaf,* of which I am now Chairman of the Board.

For all diplomats and journalists stationed in Berlin before the war Paul Scheffer was one of the most respected editors, superbly educated and gifted with an almost prophetic vision of the future of the Hitler regime. From the very beginning he regarded the regime as a terrible adventure, and until 1935 or 36 was convinced that the outside world would intervene. After the militarisation of the Rhineland and the failure of the League of Nations action in connection with Abyssinia he became more and more pessimistic and discouraged. He constantly warned foreigners whom he trusted, among whom I had the honor to be, of the dangers of the Hitler regime.

Scheffer's situation finally became untenable, and on December 31, 1936, he resigned: principles and intelligence had finally to succumb to the power of the state. In October, 1937, he arrived in the United States, after a trip through China, Japan, and Java, and he spent the rest of his life in this country. When Adam von Trott arrived in the United States in October, 1939, shortly after

61

the outbreak of the war, to attempt to gain support for the opposition, and expressed a wish to see the President, it was Scheffer who wrote the memorandum requested by George Messersmith, then under secretary of state. It was not made possible for Trott to see the President, but he did have an interview, which proved to be highly unsatisfactory and fruitless, with Felix Frankfurter. Scheffer was strongly of the opinion that the names of some of the people involved in the opposition, which Trott was put under great pressure to disclose to prove his authenticity, were later communicated to the Nazi authorities by someone in Washington. Trott himself, who had been a German Rhodes scholar, was one of those executed for treason.

Scheffer was interned at the beginning of the war, along with the German diplomatic officials and other newspaper correspondents. The injuries he sustained as the result of a fall he suffered at the time were carelessly and inadequately treated; this was the misfortune that crippled him for life. When I first met him he was without employment of any kind, and was supported by various friends. It seemed to me that a man of his background, training, and enormous experience could be invaluable to me, and I soon invited him to work with me on an informal basis, which he was glad to do. He helped me with my pamphlet series, and read and reported on numerous manuscripts. It was through him that the Rothfels book on the German opposition, the Kuhn book on existentialism, and several others, including an important philosophical work by Kurt Riezler, were published under our imprint. He appreciated good writing, and his long experience reporting on politics gave him an almost infallible ability to judge a book in that field. He worked closely with both Rothfels and Freda Utley in getting their manuscripts ready for publication, and contributed substantially to the excellence of the books that eventually came out.

Especially interesting to me was Scheffer's account of the 1922 Conference of Genoa, which he attended as a correspondent, and which ended with the German-Russian agreement signed in nearby Rapallo. The purpose of the conference was to settle some of the economic problems resulting from the war, particularly reparations; it was the first such conference to which the Russians had been invited, whom the French naïvely hoped to use to squeeze more reparations out of the reluctant Germans. Conversations between the Russians and the Germans, in which Scheffer had had an important part, with a view to a trade treaty and the resumption of diplomatic relations, had begun the year before in Moscow, and were continued in Berlin, where the Russian delegation spent a few days on the way to Genoa. At this time it was agreed that neither party would make any agreement at the conference to the disadvantage of the other. After several days of maneuvering and fruitless discussion at Genoa, it was noticed that the Germans and the Russians had disappeared. Scheffer described the rising tension as the significance of their disappearance began to be realized. The return of the Germans and the Russians and the announcement of the agreement they had made had the impact of a bomb and broke up the conference. Scheffer wryly remarked that Lloyd George, who was head of the British delegation and himself had tried to lure the Russians into some sort of separate deal, was particularly incensed at the perfidy of his fellow man. Rapallo, which was probably the logical and inevitable consequence of the Versailles Treaty and the policies that followed it, marked a historic turning point; it was followed seventeen years later by the Hitler-Stalin pact and the catastrophe of World War II. In both cases, as again with Willy Brandt's *Ostpolitik*, the Russians skillfully exploited the German sense of isolation as a divisive weapon against the West.

It was a great privilege to come to know Paul Scheffer as I did, and to work closely with him for several years. He was of more help than I can easily describe in pointing my new, struggling firm in the right direction, and in establishing the reputation for quality that we acquired in a remarkably short time. When I knew him, he was living in the most modest circumstances, and suffered considerable pain and discomfort from his injuries. But I never knew him to utter a word of complaint or to feel in the slightest degree sorry for himself. He was always courteous, and intensely interested in what was going on, and never lost his ironical sense of humor or the manner of the *grand seigneur*, which he most definitely was. He was always ready to read any manuscript that came in, hoping and expecting to discover the Eliot or Hemingway of the post-World War II generation. This never happened, but it was through no fault of his. He was a rare person, and I am glad to have this opportunity to express my gratitude to him.

To carry out the assertion in our first catalog that it was our intention to publish good books, wherever we found them, required that we go out and hunt them up. In the fall of 1949, therefore, in the second year of our corporate existence, I made a rather extended trip to Europe for the purpose of meeting publishers and finding those good books I was sure were there, and for which I believed the American public was impatiently waiting. We would put ourselves in a position, I naïvely hoped, to become the representative American publisher of the creative outburst that I was not alone in believing would develop in the postwar period. On this trip, and on all those that followed in the twenty years I was active in publishing, I met many European publishers and authors. We did publish a number of distinguished books of European origin, but I was not fortunate enough to discover the Wyndham Lewis, the Thomas Mann, the Paul Claudel, or the Ortega y Gasset of the 1950's. One may point out that no comparable figures came along. But who can say that I would have recognized them if they had?

One of the first people I went to see on that first trip was Bertrand de Jouvenel, a friend of Frank Hanighen's, who very kindly invited me to lunch in his beautiful eighteenth-century house in the country outside Paris. Jouvenel had written a number of important books on politics, several of which, including *Power*, have been translated into English. He came from an influential conservative family and was thoroughly familiar with the currents and crosscurrents of French life. He talked at some length, and with great bitterness, about the virtual civil war that followed the German occupation and of the thousands who had been executed, often on the flimsiest evidence. Jouvenel was a strong believer in European integration and an end to the senseless feud with Germany. The one book he particularly recommended to me was a novel by a young Roumanian named Virgil Georghiu, *The Twenty-fifth Hour*, which had just been published and had much to say, Jouvenel thought, about the present plight of Western man.

During that stay in Paris, I also met Raymond Aron, who was not so well known in this country then as he has since become. He had written a pamphlet for our series we had published the year before, *France and Europe*. Aron had been recommended to me by George Pettee, who had spent some time in Europe after the war and had also written a pamphlet for our series, *Union for Europe*. Pettee described Aron to me as an influential writer who was not afraid to push the cause of European unity, which was an unpopular subject, particularly in France, but which seemed to many people, including me, the only salvation for Western Europe. We had a pleasant, long lunch together, which gave me an opportunity to become somewhat acquainted with this brilliant man. He told me that since he was of Jewish background he could advance the cause of European unity, which of course meant co-operation with Germany, without danger of being accused of Nazi or pro-German sympathies. It was through the influence of such people as Raymond Aron that French foreign policy after World War II did not repeat the disastrous pattern of the 1920's, as at first seemed likely, but culminated instead in the co-operation instituted by De Gaulle and Adenauer.

American rights to the Georghiu book, which several others besides Jouvenel had recommended, had already gone to Knopf, but I was determined to meet the author. I finally tracked him down in a small café near the university, where he was autographing books and basking in the warmth of his success and the admiration of a group of students. I found him to be a modest, friendly, outgoing man. Fortunately he spoke German, having studied theology in Heidelberg before the war. He came from a family that had produced orthodox priests for several centuries, a fact of which he was very proud. He had been in concentration camps, internment camps, and refugee camps, and had suffered many of the other indignities peculiar to our century before arriving penniless and friendless in postwar Paris. His book, which might be described as a last ditch, passionate defense of the dignity of man, came out of this experience, and was an immediate success, more so in Europe, where the things he described seemed closer, than in the United States. Knopf fairly soon let the American edition go out of print —on the mistaken idea, I was told, that it was anti-Semitic—and we reissued it more than twenty years after my first meeting with the author in a Paris café. We published several other books by Georghiu; he, in the meantime, had become an orthodox priest in the tradition of his family, and spiritual leader of the large Roumanian community in Paris.

Another great figure I met on that first visit to Paris was Gabriel Marcel, who is usually described as a Catholic existentialist. When I looked him up in the Paris telephone book I was impressed, coming fresh from Chicago, to notice that he was listed as "homme de lettres." He received me most cordially in an apartment so crowded with books that there seemed room for little else. He was a rather small man, with curly white hair that clung to the top of his head like a skullcap, a high-pitched voice, a round, pink, cherubic face, and intense, bright eyes. We eventually published four of his books: *Man Against Mass Society, A Metaphysical Journey, Homo Viator,* and the two volumes of his Gifford lectures, *The Mystery of Being.* Marcel seems largely to be forgotten in the confusion of the present world, but will be rediscovered by those looking for a realistic appraisal of our time and for thought that is ordered and developed from first principles.

Marcel's publisher, Fernand Aubier—whom I went to see to discuss publication arrangements—presided over his Editions Montaigne in a modest office on a picturesque street near the Institut de France. He was one of those cultivated, serious men who conduct rather small firms and whose books reflect their own taste and point of view. Such personal publishers play a far more important role in cultural life and the development of ideas than the size of their firms may suggest, but the task they impose on themselves is not easy, walking, as they must, on a narrow path between the abyss of bankruptcy and the temptation of complete submission to the demands of the market.

To meet such a publisher was always stimulating. Vittorio Klostermann, of Frankfurt, whom I also first met in 1949, was another. He was the original publisher of the book by F. G. Juenger we had brought out in translation, and also of the essays by Martin Heidegger we published later. He had founded his firm in 1930, during the Great Depression; he went through the economic crisis, the Hitler regime, and World War II and all that followed it without wavering from his determination to publish serious, scholarly books. His list concentrates on the fields of philosophy and jurisprudence, and includes such authors as Ernst Cassirer, Wilhelm Dilthey, Martin Heidegger, Edmund Husserl, Friedrich Georg Juenger, Vladimir Solovief, and Charles Peirce, as well as many of the classics. His books stand out not only by their substance and good design, but also by the fact that in an era infatuated with color, his covers are always printed black on grey paper.

Manya Harari, in London, with her Harvill Press, was another such personal publisher who maintained high standards. We did a number of books with her, including several of those by Max Picard and Gabriel Marcel, sharing composition and translation costs.

The European publisher I came to know best was Eugen Rentsch, together with his wife, Lenore, who is as much a part of the firm as he. Rentsch is the publisher of Max Picard, which was my reason for going to see him for the first time in 1949. Dr. and

Frau Rentsch conduct their business, which was founded in 1910 by Dr. Rentsch's father, in their house in Erlenbach, near Zurich. The first time I was there, orders were packed in the basement and taken to the post office by pushcart. The offices of the firm are on the first floor, and the family live above. The Rentsch list, which includes the definitive and complete edition of the nineteenth-century writer Jeremias Gotthelf, who is an integral part of the Swiss tradition, plus biography, history, philosophy, and literary essays, represents a cultural achievement of a high order. For such a publisher as Eugen Rentsch, a book is not a piece of merchandise but the expression of a creative act.

After my visit in Zurich with Picard's publisher, I took the train to Lugano to visit Picard himself. I have made this trip over the Gothard Pass many times since, and always find it intensely enjoyable—the train makes a long climb through beautiful alpine country to reach the entrance of the long tunnel, going through neat, typically northern European villages and towns with such names as Altdorf, Erstfeld, Andermatt; but the name of the first town on the south side of the tunnel is Airolo, the language has changed from Swiss German to Italian, and one soon sees vineyards, stone fences, and other unmistakable evidence of a different tradition. It is a striking example, which never fails to impress me, of the diversity of European culture.

From Lugano a branch line took me to Caslano, where Dr. Picard was waiting for me. It was my first meeting, but I had no difficulty distinguishing him in the small crowd of people waiting for the train. How he looked on that sunny fall day remains fixed in my memory. He gave the impression as he stood there of being immovable, rooted to the spot. He was rather short, solidly built, with a fringe of white hair around an otherwise bald head, intensely blue eyes, and a broad, ruddy, expressive face with strongly marked features. His movements were sure and deliberate, and his voice was rather high pitched; he had a warm sense of humor and told amusing stories very well, but there always seemed to be a distant look of sadness in his eyes. He was most cordial and friendly, but also reserved. We talked as we walked to his house; there was no barrier between us to be overcome, and no need of small talk to establish a relationship. I felt that I had always known him, and on future visits it seemed that there had been no break, that we simply took up where we had left off, without interruption.

Max Picard came from a Jewish family that had lived in Switzerland for generations, but he himself was born in Baden, at the southern end of the Black Forest, in 1888. He studied medicine in Heidelberg, and practiced for a time in Munich, very successfully, but gave up medicine, he said, because its orientation had become too mechanical, positivistic, Darwinistic. He moved to Tessin, or Ticino, the Italian-speaking canton of Switzerland, in the early 1920's for the sake of his wife's health, stayed on after her early death, and spent the rest of his life there. He was eventually converted to Catholicism, but he was more than either Christian or Jew; he was both, and, above all, a complete person. He was a wise man, had a deeply felt faith, and understood and appreciated, as few others do, the great works of the past. In a letter to André Gide, written in 1921, Rilke called Picard "the most unpretentious, purest man I know." He was not a systematic philosopher, but a critical thinker, specifically, a critic of modern civilization and all that goes with it. His most profound and prophetic book, perhaps, is *The Flight from God*, first published in 1934, and in our translation in 1951. Wyndham Lewis once said something to the effect that when Shakespeare wrote *King Lear* he must have been in a kind of trance; in another place he remarks that he found it difficult not to believe that the great artist is in possession of an experience the equal, at least, of the mystic. Picard's description of modern civilization as a gigantic flight from God could only have been the result of such an experience. It is, as one critic described it, a prophetic vision. Then there are those books of Picard's devoted to what he thought of as primal elements of man's basic structure, elements that were there before man existed, that were given to him in advance—language, marriage, and silence. It is such basic elements of the human condition, and these alone, he thought, that can restore the wholeness of life. These three books— *Indestructible Marriage, The World of Silence,* and *Man and Language*—perhaps encompass the essence of Picard's thought. The book on silence is particularly remarkable: for Picard, silence is not merely the absence of sound, it has a positive, creative quality, it is the counterpole of language. Without silence, language becomes nothing more than idle chatter, and for Picard, language has a sacred character: "When language is destroyed, man loses his relationship with the Original Word from which his own words and their measure are derived."

Picard felt strongly that one of the things lacking in modern life is the true encounter—people see and talk to each other but do not really encounter one another; the one gives nothing of himself to the other. To have met Max Picard was an encounter, and to meet him in his work is just as much so. He gave generously of himself; his heart is in his work, and if his reader meets him only part way, he will take with him something that will make him a more nearly complete and a better person.

From Lugano I took the train to Konstanz, in the southwest corner of Germany, where I had arranged to meet several people, including Ernst Juenger and his brother Friedrich Georg. Konstanz was under French occupation, but the city had not been much damaged in the war and life seemed quite normal. Ernst Juenger invited me to his house in a village on the opposite side of the Bodensee from Konstanz, from which he had a fine view of the lake. His brother was there, as well as the poet Rudolph Hagelstange and the Swiss writer Armin Mohler, who was then acting as Ernst Juenger's secretary. Mohler had attracted some attention to himself during the war, as well as the wrath of the Swiss authorities, by attempting to volunteer to fight with the Germans against the Russians. I had published Ernst Juenger's wartime essay *The Peace* and his brother's book on technology. But despite my respect for Ernst Juenger and my admiration for his wonderfully clear, polished, if somewhat cold style, I never felt inclined to publish another book of his. I read numerous essays and one novel, but decided that they were not for me; of all his later books I found his war diaries the most impressive—his account, for example, of the long columns of tanks, armored vehicles, and trucks of the American army coming into the town where he was living in Lower Saxony is unforgettable.

There was much discussion that rainy November afternoon in 1949 of what the future might bring: Europeans were not so accustomed then as they have since become to the presence of Russian troops less than forty miles from Frankfurt. During the course of the conversation Ernst Juenger remarked, "If the Allies persist in their present policy of driving millions of people from the east into this small, overpopulated country and depriving us of our only means of survival, our industry, another German explosion is inevitable." The two Juengers were impressive men, but Friedrich Georg, who had an easier manner than his brother, was the more appealing to me.

During that stay in southwest Germany I met two generals of the former Wehrmacht, Hans Speidel and Adolph Heusinger. I met

Speidel, who was then living in Freudenstadt, in the Black Forest, and lecturing on history at the University of Tübingen, through Truman Smith, who before the war had been U.S. military attaché in Berlin. Colonel Smith had sent me Speidel's book, *Invasion 1944*, with his strong recommendation that I publish it. Speidel had been Rommel's chief of staff, and at the time of the first landing of Allied troops in Normandy was in command of the German forces, since Rommel had been called to Hitler's headquarters. Speidel was very much involved in the opposition, as was Rommel also—Rommel was given the choice of suicide or execution for his part in the July 20, 1944 attempt on Hitler's life, and Speidel spent the last months of the war in the Gestapo prison in Berlin.

I did publish General Speidel's book, for which Colonel Smith wrote an excellent introduction. This had one amusing consequence, which is also not without significance. The book was reviewed in the New York *Times* by Drew Middleton, who was then the chief *Times* correspondent in Germany. Middleton was utterly contemptuous of the book, and, by implication, of its author. "This book is not history," he asserted. "It is propaganda for a lost cause." Not long after the book appeared, American foreign policy made a sharp change of course. The illusions about our "peace-loving" ally in the east finally gave way to a more realistic appraisal of Soviet Russia and the world situation we had helped to create, and in this reappraisal a German army appeared to be an essential element in the defense of Western Europe. The Middleton review of the Speidel book appeared November 5, 1950 in the *New York Times Book Review*. On November 18, 1951, following Speidel's selection as one of the two German generals to rebuild a new German army, an article on him appeared in the *New York Times Magazine* by the same Drew Middleton. "This tall, gray-haired, suave veteran appears to combine all the best characteristics of the German professional soldier plus a worldliness and ease which help him mix with all sorts of people. . . ." To conclude the story: when Middleton asked General Speidel for an interview, his request was refused.

General Speidel was strongly of the opinion that if the Allies had properly exploited their enormous advantage they could have ended the war in the west in the summer of 1944, an opinion which General Patton, as his wartime diary shows, held perhaps even more strongly. Speidel described the great Allied offensive at the end of August as a raging torrent that nothing could stem, and asserted that by the time the furious Allied advance was unexpectedly halted, the German forces were in a state of complete disorganization: "Had the Allies kept up their attack on their enemy, they could have pursued the German forces until they dropped from exhaustion, and could have ended the war half a year earlier. There were no longer any German ground forces worth mentioning, to say nothing of air forces." Whether the decision to halt the overwhelming Allied drive was made to give the Russians time to occupy the part of Europe that had been allotted to them at Teheran will probably never be known, but this seems highly probable. Patton was well aware of the political significance of the military decisions that were made during that fateful summer, but he received little credit or thanks for his foresight.

General Heusinger, when he spent a weekend with me in Konstanz, was then just another unemployed German general, without resources or any apparent prospects for the future. He had been taken into custody at the end of the war and held for some time for interrogation, but no charges were brought against him. A refugee literary agent in New York had somehow gotten possession of the written statements a number of German generals had been required to make in connection with the war crimes trials and had offered them to us for publication. Paul Scheffer read them all, and reported that only one had anything significant to say, and that the author of this document was obviously intelligent and might be worth looking up, with the possibility of a book in mind. This is how it happened that I arranged to meet General Heusinger.

Adolph Heusinger was a General Staff officer, and chief of operations during the Russian campaign. He was sitting within five feet of Hitler when the bomb exploded, almost under Hitler's chair, on July 20, 1944, and was soon after arrested and jailed for his part in the conspiracy. He had attended numerous conferences with Hitler, and described at great length Hitler's method of operation and his almost demonic ability to dominate the will of those around him. All this gave me some understanding of the dilemma of a professional soldier caught between the prospect of unconditional surrender and the dismemberment of his country, on the one hand, and the leadership of a megalomaniac, on the other, but shed little light on the question of why those in responsible positions permitted this man, no matter how demonic his inspiration,

71

to lead their nation to destruction. For the riddle of Adolf Hitler and the secret of his domination of a great nation there is no reasonable explanation.

The fall of 1949 was an interesting time to be in Germany. There was still evidence on every hand of the destruction left by the war, but after one had gotten used to railroad stations without roofs, temporary buildings in the cities, bomb craters here and there, and whole blocks of bombed-out buildings, life seemed quite normal. The rubble had been cleared from the streets, so that such traffic as there was moved normally. Trains ran slowly because of temporary bridges and the condition of the roadbeds, but those I rode in were clean and comfortable, and the service was adequate. Munich, in spite of having been terribly bombed during the war, still had much of its charm and liveliness: the principal churches had been rebuilt, and to my great surprise there were many quite elegant shops, some in temporary buildings. Every building around the great square in front of the opera house was in ruins except for the Spatenbräu restaurant, which looked exactly as I remembered it and served the same excellent food and beer. When I asked someone how it was that this one place survived of all the buildings on Max-Joseph Platz, I was told that it had been destroyed too; that it had been decided to rebuild the churches first, then the beer halls. The brick Gothic cathedral, the Frauenkirche, whose characteristically Bavarian towers have been a symbol of Munich since the fifteenth century, had been virtually destroyed; little was left of it except the outside walls and parts of the two towers. But by 1949 it had been completely rebuilt, in exactly the same style as the original.

West Germany, as reconstruction began and economic life revived, possessed a number of enormous advantages. As Nietzsche remarked after the German victory over France in 1871, the defeated always possess a great advantage. The millions of refugees who poured into West Germany from Czechoslovakia, Poland, the former German territory east of the Oder-Neisse, even from German communities as far away as Roumania, were an asset of inestimable value—they were energetic and anxious to work to re-establish a life for themselves and their families, and many were highly skilled. Another though perhaps less evident asset was the absence of ideologies in West Germany in the immediate post-war period—millions of Germans had experienced Communism at first hand, either as soldiers in Russia or under Russian occupation, and the war and its consequences had completely destroyed whatever attraction National Socialism may have had. Finally, postwar West Germany was fortunate in its leadership, perhaps again thanks to defeat and the policy of the victors.

Many if not most of those in positions of leadership in the immediate postwar period were men who had come to maturity in the years before 1914, in a stable society still largely influenced by the traditional values of Western civilization, and they had maintained their integrity during the Hitler years. Konrad Adenauer is a conspicuous example. As this generation was superseded by the one that had reached maturity during the 1920's, the quality of German life changed drastically, and, with its frantic prosperity, conspicuous consumption, and the revival of the influence of ideologies, not for the better. The contrast between the reserved, utterly realistic, sober Adenauer and his ascetic manner of life, and the voluble, posturing Willy Brandt, whose Marxist ideology did not interfere with a well-developed taste for luxurious sensuality, is a striking example of the change that had taken place.

Ludwig Erhardt is deservedly given much of the credit for the German "economic miracle" because it was he, as minister of economics, who at one stroke, and contrary to the advice and wishes of the American and British authorities, abolished rationing, as well as price, credit, and wage controls. This, however, was possible only because of the absence of the influence of ideology— the Germans had had enough of a centrally controlled economy and were willing to take their chances with the free market. Erhardt, under the influence of the economist Wilhelm Roepke, went on the theory that what Germany required was production; that if people were given the opportunity to earn, and to better their situation, production would be stimulated, and everyone from the bottom of the ladder to the top would benefit, as proved to be the case. The British, on the other hand, followed the theory that distribution deserved first consideration and that production would take care of itself. The Germans used their Marshall Plan money to rebuild their capital assets, to add to their productive capacity, whereas the British used theirs largely to finance welfare schemes. I was given a good example of the results of these two different approaches to economic life when in November, 1949, I took a British plane from Düsseldorf to London. Nearly all the other passengers were either British officials or officers from the Army of Occupation going home on furlough. All were taking their families packages of such things as bacon, eggs, and butter, which were readily available in defeated, occupied Germany, but in England still rationed, if available at all. Needless to say, there were many bitter comments about this rather anomalous situation.

I was in several cities on that trip—Freiburg, Tübingen, Stuttgart, Frankfurt, Munich, Bonn, and Cologne—and saw a number of publishers and many other people. My stay in Bonn and Cologne was particularly interesting. Besides the saturation bombing, Cologne had at the very end of the war been subjected to heavy shellfire. When it was all over there was hardly an undamaged building in the city. Its many beautiful and historically important Romanesque churches had been severely damaged, and several had been virtually destroyed, and although the cathedral was still standing, it had been hit many times by high explosives and incendiary bombs. Cologne offers graphic evidence that the Allied air raids were largely directed at civilian rather than military or industrial objectives. In contrast to the destruction inflicted on this old city, with its many treasures, a great power station beyond the city limits, which is one of the largest in Europe and can be seen for miles, was undamaged.

Since accommodations at that time in Bonn or Cologne were rather meager, my old friend Hermann arranged for me to stay in a castle near a village between the two cities, where the contents of the museum of which he was director had been stored for safekeeping. He and his family lived in an outbuilding of the castle; my room was on one of its upper floors and had a magnificent view of the Rhine valley. Because of the initiative of my friend and the assistance offered by the prince of the castle, this village had become a center for Cologne artists bombed out by the war. They were an attractive, lively group, and several have since become well known. In the years immediately following the war, when food was scarce, clothing and other ordinary necessities almost unobtainable, and cigarettes the usual medium of exchange, lectures, concerts, recitals, and art exhibits of the highest quality were held on a regular basis in the castle. In Cologne itself, where there were no newspapers, an enterprising book dealer arranged to give oral book reviews every week in the railroad station; they became quite famous and were well attended. With the revival of economic life following the currency reform in 1948 this sort of thing came to an end. It is interesting, though, how many Germans of the older generation speak of this time with nostalgia—they like to remember the imaginative improvisations, the lack of class distinctions, and the feeling of mutual sympathy and solidarity the necessities of those years brought forth.

The London I saw in the fall of 1949 was the London Wyndham Lewis described in *Rotting Hill*, which I was to publish three years later. His description of postwar, socialist England is unrelievedly grim, even if, as he said, the majority of the nation was highly stimulated by the great extravaganza put on by the new Labour government, as a result of which England became for a time, as Lewis said, "a brighter rather than a darker place," with the bill to be paid later. London, however, if somewhat shabby and run-down, seemed to me in its essentials to be quite normal, and I greatly enjoyed my visit. I saw people from many publishing houses, Faber & Faber, Eyre & Spottiswood, Allen & Unwin, Victor Gollancz, Burns, Oates, among others. In spite of my inexperience, they were uniformly courteous, and all of them seemed confident and busy.

Someone had called my attention to a book on the war crimes trials by Lord Hankey, *Politics, Trials and Errors*. The publisher, whose office was in Oxford, arranged for the three of us to have lunch at Lord Hankey's club, which proved to be a most interesting experience. As secretary for many years of the British Cabinet, Lord Hankey could be considered to have been the leading civil servant of England. He was a fine example of the competent, loyal, superbly trained civil service that held the vast empire together and made it work, that was one of the glories of England and in its great days a basic element of its wealth and power. Lord Hankey had been secretary of the British delegation at Versailles and at Genoa, and for a generation or more was intimately involved with the foreign and domestic policies of his country.

I arranged to publish a U.S. edition of *Politics, Trials and Errors*, which was quite respectfully reviewed—more, I suspect, because of the position of the author than because of any agreement with his position. As a man of enormous experience and few illusions, Lord Hankey viewed the trials as a political blunder of the first magnitude, which he predicted the Western powers would be among the first to regret.

While I was in London I renewed my acquaintance with Victor Gollancz. The office of his firm was in Covent Garden Market. To get to it one had to make one's way among carts, market men, and crates of fruit and vegetables. His firm occupied rooms on various levels, and when he wanted someone, there was no formal pushing of buttons, but simply a loud shout into the hall. All of this was refreshing, I thought, and in accordance with his love of the theatrical.

The publishing project I wanted to take up with him had been offered to me in Germany by Helmut Becker, the son of the famous Prussian Minister of Education of the 1920's, who had defended Ernst von Weizsäcker at Nuremberg. Weizsäcker was convicted and sentenced to imprisonment, but later released through the intervention of Thurman Arnold. He was now writing his memoirs, which Becker suggested I consider for publication. The Weizsäcker episode is an interesting one, and I think it sheds some light on the manner in which American policy was conducted in the first postwar years. Weizsäcker had had a distinguished career in the German foreign service, but had the bad luck to become state secretary of the Foreign Office during the Nazi period, an appointment that under normal circumstances would have represented the culmination of his career. The fact that he had taken a leading part in the German opposition, at great risk to himself, and that several prominent churchmen from England, Sweden, and the Vatican testified to that effect, made no difference. The American prosecutor, Robert Kempner, who himself had occupied a rather high position in Berlin before migrating to the United States, was determined to "get" Weizsäcker, and with the power of the United States government behind him he was able to do so. The shamelessness of this episode is somewhat mitigated by Thurman Arnold's later courageous and successful intervention.

Gollancz, who was familiar with the Weizsäcker case and felt strongly about it, agreed to publish the book jointly with us. It was not as successful as it should have been—at least partly, I think, because of Weizsäcker's reluctance to tell his story as fully and openly as he should have. Paul Scheffer, to whom I turned over the manuscript, made numerous suggestions for additions and modifications, but to no avail. The book remains a modest contribution to history, but it could have been much more.

There is a footnote to the Weizsäcker story that needs to be told. Although the American edition of the book was not published until 1951, six years after the ending of the war, the Alien Property Custodian in Washington saw fit to seize the modest royalties it had earned. The bureaucratic formalities involved in what can only be called "theft" of this money must have cost the American taxpayer several times the amount it brought it; but taking money from the family of a helpless former official of the German Foreign Office must have given satisfaction to someone in the rather notorious office of the Alien Property Custodian, even if it brought discredit to our country.

I came back from that trip loaded with books, manuscripts, publishing projects, and the conviction that I had made some notable discoveries. We live from our hopes, and if mine had been unrealistically raised by meeting a number of unusually interesting and stimulating people, it had been a great experience, and resulted in some lasting associations and in the publication of several significant if not notably successful books.

5

REVISIONISM–
WORLD WAR II

THE Japanese attack on Pearl Harbor on December 7, 1941, put an abrupt end to the great debate that had raged in Congress, the press, and public forums from one end of the country to the other, on whether the United States should become involved in what had begun as a European war. The America First Committee, which had been the largest and most effective organization opposing American intervention, was formally dissolved two days after war was declared, and its leaders—among them General Robert E. Wood, Colonel Charles A. Lindbergh, and Robert D. Stuart— loyally and unstintingly served their country at war. But when the war ended, the great question of American involvement again be- came a burning issue. The form the developing debate was to take between the "orthodox" historians, who supported the official ver- sion of events, and the "revisionists," who questioned it, was clearly foreseen by the distinguished historian and onetime president of the American Historical Association, Charles A. Beard, in a short article on the editorial page of the *Saturday Evening Post* of October 4, 1947.

The immediate reason for Dr. Beard's article was the announce- ment by the Rockefeller Foundation, in its annual report for the year 1946, that in order to forestall a repetition of "the debunking journalistic campaign following World War I" the sum of $139,000 had been granted to the Council on Foreign Relations, which the Council had agreed to use to support the preparation of a clear and competent history of World War II from 1939 to the peace settlements, a project that was to be entrusted to Professor William Langer of Harvard.

The report of the Foundation went on to say that Langer had been granted exceptional access to materials bearing on foreign relations. Beard pointed out that in the introduction to a previous book concerned with foreign policy, *Our Vichy Gamble,* Langer acknowledged that he had been furnished secret documents, or digests of such documents, by Roosevelt, Cordell Hull, William Leahy, and the War Department. Furthermore, the first draft of the book had been read by Hull, who had suggested the project to Langer in the first place, and by other government officials, who had made suggestions for revision and who had finally approved publication. To all this Beard commented:

Duly blessed by Secretary Hull, the War Department and Admiral Leahy, the professor's book was issued by a private publisher with an official fanfare valuable to all parties of interest. Presumably, in carrying out the new Rockefeller commission, Professor Langer will again enjoy special favors denied to others—favors from the State Department, the War Department, Admiral Leahy, President Truman and the guardians of the Roosevelt and other papers.

Who is to write the history of World War II? Some person or persons well-subsidized and enjoying access, under Government patronage, to secret archives? Or is the opportunity of inquiring and writing the story of this critical period to be open to all talents on the same terms, without official interference or favoritism? There is the choice before us, and if tested methods of truth-seeking are to be followed in the business of history writing, the answer seems rather obvious.

What might be called the intellectual establishment of the country—the most eminent universities, the great foundations, the established publishers, and the influential press—was predominantly on the official "orthodox" side of the controversy, as Beard's article indicates. But those not afraid to look behind the accepted version of events or to take an independent position were by no means reduced to silence. What they lacked in foundation grants, academic prestige, official support, and recognition by the influential press, they made up for in conviction, resourcefulness, and energy.

The first revisionist book on World War II was George Morgenstern's *Pearl Harbor: The Story of the Secret War,* published in 1948 by a small New York firm, Devin-Adair Company. It was the thesis of the Morgenstern book that the Roosevelt administration had deliberately provoked the Japanese attack as a means of getting into the European war; that the fleet had been kept at Pearl Harbor against the advice of the admirals directly involved; and that information concerning the probability of a Japanese attack had been withheld from the military commanders for fear that if the proper moves to protect the fleet were taken, the plans of the Japanese might have been changed. Morgenstern's thesis had been succinctly stated for him by Secretary of War Henry L. Stimson in a passage in his diary describing a meeting of the war cabinet in the White House on November 25, 1941, thirteen days before Pearl Harbor: "The question was how we should maneuver them into the position of firing the first shot without allowing too much danger to ourselves."

The Morgenstern book presented the defenders of the Roosevelt foreign policy with a formidable challenge: it was skillfully written and meticulously documented, and its jacket carried the endorsement of two highly respected men, Charles A. Beard and Norman Thomas. The intellectual establishment responded to it by various evasions: they ignored it completely, or treated it as the work of an anti-Roosevelt crank not worthy of serious consideration, or questioned the propriety of writing such a book at all, or admitted that there might be something, in a very limited way, in the author's presentation of facts, but denied its significance with the assertion that he was incapable of grasping the larger issue.

Such publications as the *Atlantic Monthly, Harper's,* and *Saturday Review* chose the first alternative and ignored the book completely. The *New Yorker* ended a very brief paragraph with the neither relevant nor particularly witty remark "Mr. Morgenstern is a Chicago newspaperman, and you have only one guess as to which paper he works for." The New York *Times* review, which appeared on a back page and was headed "Mythology for the Critics of F.D.R.," was written by Gordon A. Craig, a young assistant at Princeton, who, after pointing out that Morgenstern was "an editorial writer for the Chicago *Tribune*," contented himself with the assertion that Morgenstern is propagating "mythology" and "nowhere seriously considers the possible consequences to the United States of an axis victory."

In his review in the New York *Herald Tribune,* which was headed

"Twisting the Pearl Harbor Story," Walter Millis, after the usual references to the Chicago *Tribune,* argued that in all his actions supporting Britain and Russia, President Roosevelt was "repeatedly sustained . . . by Congress as well as by public opinion." If this was true, why were so many of the President's actions—the joint staff talks with the British and the Dutch, and the North Atlantic naval patrol, for example—carried out in secret? Why were such measures as the destroyer deal and "Lend-Lease" represented as means to "keep us out of war"? And why, if public opinion favored war, did Roosevelt, on October 30, 1940, during an election campaign, assure the mothers and fathers of Boston, "again—and again —and again," that "your sons are not going to be sent into any foreign wars?" *

The longest, most serious, and probably most significant critical review was that of Samuel Flagg Bemis, Professor of Diplomatic History at Yale, in the *Journal of Modern History.* Bemis began with a condemnation of the revisionism that followed World War I: it resulted, he declared, in complete repudiation of Woodrow Wilson's foreign policy, and in the neutrality legislation of 1935–37, which "assisted the rise of Hitler's power and his onslaught on western civilization." After implying the dire consequences of a new campaign of revisionism, he carefully warned the reader "not to be prejudiced against the author because he is not a professional historian or because he is a journalist and on the editorial staff of what is considered by many to be a notoriously isolationist newspaper, the *Chicago Tribune.*"

Bemis accepted Morgenstern's carefully documented thesis that the officials in Washington were responsible for the disaster at Pearl Harbor, not the military commanders General Short and Admiral Kimmel, who were made the scapegoats. But he was not willing to agree with the second thesis of Morgenstern's book, that the failure to alert the commanders at Pearl Harbor was deliberate and the final act of the plan to provoke a Japanese attack, in order to give the President the *causus belli* he needed. Bemis, rather, asserted that with Lend-Lease we had deserted American neutrality in the At-

---

* Robert E. Sherwood, one of President Roosevelt's speech writers on the subject of this speech was later to remark: "I burn inwardly whenever I think of those words 'again—and again—and again' . . . unfortunately for my own conscience, I happened at the time to be one of those who urged him to go to the limit on this, feeling as I did then that any risk of future embarrassment was negligible as compared with the risk of losing the election." *Roosevelt and Hopkins: An Intimate History,* New York: Harper & Brothers, 1948, p. 874.

lantic, and were, therefore, in fact if not in name, already at war. This is doubtless true, but after such election promises as "Your boys are not going to be sent into any foreign wars," President Roosevelt needed such an incident as Pearl Harbor to get a formal declaration of war and to mobilize the country behind him. Although unwilling specifically to admit this, Bemis argued that, confronted by "the most awful danger that ever faced our country," Roosevelt was justified in taking the actions he did.

The Morgenstern book was followed by Charles A. Beard's *President Roosevelt and the Coming of the War, 1941*, which was published in 1948 by Yale University Press. This was a sequel to Beard's *American Foreign Policy in the Making, 1932–1940*, which Yale had published two years before. The first book was a documentary account of the foreign policy of the first two Roosevelt administrations, which marked a distinct break from that of the previous three administrations, and of which three wars were the immediate consequence. In the second book, Beard uses his unequaled mastery of documentary material and his long experience in the writing of history to bring to account those who were responsible for the decisions that led to the war with Japan and intervention in the European war.

Charles A. Beard was a man of great independence of mind and strong convictions, as he had demonstrated by resigning his professorship at Columbia to protest the dismissal of two professors during the hysteria of World War I and supporting himself and his family for some years thereafter as a dairy farmer. He felt strongly that President Roosevelt not only had deceived the American people and betrayed their trust, but also, by abrogating unto himself complete control of foreign policy, including the power to make war, had subverted the Constitution and the orderly process of government. In addition, he objected to the habit of certain American presidents of moralizing on an international scale, of proclaiming that "it is the duty of the United States to assume and maintain 'the moral leadership of the world.' " As a rather old-fashioned American, Beard felt that moral leadership began at home, and was best exerted by example.

In the *New York Times Book Review*, Arthur Schlesinger, Jr., characterized the book as a "philippic against Franklin D. Roosevelt," loftily suggested that it could not fail to provoke criticism on grounds of historical method, without specifying what such grounds might be, and remarked that as a devotee of reality against appearance, Beard should have inquired into the realities of alternatives. The alternative to going to war, obviously, is not going to war, one that Beard was quite willing to accept, and had unhesitatingly recommended. There were equally strong and sometimes more unrestrained objections to the book from Harry D. Gideonse, Max Lerner, Quincy Wright, Percy Miller, and Peter Levin, among others.

Commenting on the reviews in the professional journals of *President Roosevelt and the Coming of the War*, Howard K. Beale observed in an article in the *Pacific Historical Review*: "There are in the profession people of standing who agree with Beard's interpretation, and others who disagree but feel the book has much of the impressive quality of the early works on the Constitution and Jeffersonian democracy that made Beard's great reputation. Curiously, no editor could find any of these people to review the book."

It remained for Samuel Eliot Morison, Professor of History at Harvard and official historian of the United States Navy in World War II, to return the final verdict of the orthodox historians on the Beard thesis.

Morison's long review, which appeared in the *Atlantic Monthly* of August, 1948, began with a tribute to Beard's generosity and independence, as well as to his great achievements in the writing of history; but it soon degenerated into a personal attack. Morison made much of Beard's belief that no historian can write truly "objective" history; that he must make choices from the vast mass of historical evidence, and that in so doing he consciously or unconsciously acts in accordance with some frame of reference. On the basis of this quite logical, straightforward, and honest conception of objectivity in historical writing, Morison asserted that Beard's standards of truth and objectivity differed from those of any other professional historian and that this was the source of his "inconsistencies and tergiversations." Morison admitted that President Roosevelt did perhaps mislead the American people and "utter soothing phrases in 1940 in order to be re-elected," but he thought this was justified in view of the "isolationist" campaign against intervention, that throughout modern history Western nations in danger of war have chosen to await the first blow rather than give it, and that maneuvering the Japanese into firing the first shot was entirely comparable to Captain Parker's command at Lexington: "Stand your ground. Don't fire unless fired upon, but if they mean to have a war, let it begin here." To compare all that was involved at Pearl Harbor with the command of an honest captain at Lexington green is pure sophistry. Is it any wonder, then, that in a letter to George Morgenstern about the reviews of the latter's book, Beard remarked, "Such, my young friend, is life in the 'intellectual world' "?

It was into this intellectual world, in the fall of 1950, that we launched our own first revisionist book, William Henry Chamberlin's *America's Second Crusade*.

Chamberlin was a distinguished and respected writer—he had been Moscow correspondent of the *Christian Science Monitor* from 1922 until 1934, after which he served as a correspondent in the Far East and in France—and the author of eleven previous books. His *History of the Russian Revolution*, published by Macmillan in 1935, is recognized as one of the authoritative books on the subject. But none of his former publishers, including Macmillan, Scribner's, Knopf, and Little, Brown, expressed interest in his new book, and on March 10, 1950, he wrote to ask if we would like to see it. It was a manuscript, he said, of some four hundred pages; its subject was "the origins, course and final results of our involvement in the last war." Harry Elmer Barnes had been instrumental in arranging for publication with one of the university presses, but because of its vigorous criticism of the Roosevelt foreign policy, Chamberlin had been given clearly to understand that they would not let their contract stand in the way if another publisher might wish to take it on.

His research, Chamberlin said, had included "careful examination of the more important books about the diplomatic and political side of the war . . . and . . . private talks with a number of men who were active in making policy." These had included former Ambassadors William Bullitt and Joseph Grew; George Kennan, Charles Bohlen, and Philip Mosley of the State Department; former Assistant Secretary of State A. A. Berle, and William Donovan and Allen Dulles of the OSS. Former President Hoover had been helpful to him by giving him access to unpublished, private material in his possession.

He finished the letter with the remark that the book logically and irresistibly culminated in a proposition he thought must appeal to more and more thoughtful people, "that the late victorious war was a colossal political and moral failure." He realized that such a book was "strong meat for the average publisher," but he hoped, in view of our having published the books by Freda Utley and Montgomery Belgion, that we might be willing to consider his.

Within a few weeks we had agreed to publish the book, and on the terms of a contract. We were able to send page proofs to reviewers in July and bound copies in late August, and to publish the book in October. Chamberlin was well known through his years as a correspondent and his previous books, and he had built up a following, particularly among conservatively inclined businessmen, with his column in the *Wall Street Journal*. In addition, he was a regular contributor, and listed as "associate editor," of the socialist but strongly anti-Communist *New Leader*. We had the great advantage, therefore, of an established and respected author, whom the reviewers would have to take seriously, however strongly they might disagree with him.

Like Charles A. Beard, Chamberlin was a man of strong convictions, and his years in Soviet Russia had made him even more critical of the manner in which the war and its objectives were represented to the American people by the administration and the liberal press. Chamberlin had seen both forms of totalitarianism in action and had himself experienced the fall of France and its consequences. He had no illusions whatever about Nazi Germany, but the claim that peace, freedom, and the brotherhood of man were to be secured by an alliance with Communist Russia was for him the rankest form of misrepresentation. The Beard book was the work of an experienced, highly skilled historian who, by the nature of his profession, relied heavily on official documents. Chamberlin was also a historian, but his approach was broader: he was able to supplement the ample documentation of his book by information and knowledge acquired from his many years of experience as a correspondent.

His book began with a brief account of the manner of our intervention in the first great war, the glowing promises, the hysteria aroused in its behalf, and the disillusionment that followed. "By no standard of judgment," Chamberlin wrote, "could America's First Crusade be considered a success. It was not even an effective warning. For all the illusions, misjudgements, and errors of the First Crusade were to be repeated, in exaggerated form, in a Second Crusade that was to be a still more resounding and unmistakable political and moral failure, despite the repetition of military success."

Having thus disposed of Wilson's war at the beginning of his book, he concluded it with the following unequivocal judgment on Roosevelt's:

It is scarcely possible . . . to avoid the conclusion that the Roosevelt Administration sought the war which began at Pearl Harbor. The steps which made armed conflict inevitable were taken months before the conflict broke out.

Some of Roosevelt's apologists contend that, if he deceived the American people, it was for their own good. But the argument that the end justifies the means rests on the assumption that the end has been achieved. Whether America's end in its Second Crusade was assurance of national security or the establishment of a world of peace and order or the realization of the Four Freedoms "everywhere in the world," this end was most certainly not achieved.

America's Second Crusade was a product of illusions which are already bankrupt.

Such statements, more than a generation after the end of World War II, may not appear to say anything that is not fairly obvious and generally accepted. But in 1950, only five years after an overwhelming military victory, when American power and influence seemed to dominate the world, and when the memory of Franklin D. Roosevelt was still cherished, such assertions were regarded as a particularly repulsive form of blasphemy. In spite of his years of experience in the "intellectual world," even Chamberlin was taken aback by the violence of the attacks on his book.

The reviewer in the New York *Post* called Chamberlin a "totalitarian conservative" and implied that he justified or apologized for things done in Germany and Japan that he found execrable in Russia. J. M. Minifie, in the *Saturday Review of Literature*, commented, "To anyone who had to endure over a number of years the daily dose of Virgilio Gayda or Dr. Goebbels, it comes as a shock to find Mr. Chamberlin ladling out the same dish." Harry D. Gideonse, in the *New Leader*, called the book "another rehash of the 'Chicago *Tribune* history of World War II,'" and was "not surprised to discover" that Robert M. Hutchins was "Chairman of the Editorial Board of the publishers of the volume," a discovery, I must say, that came as a great surprise to me.

The New York *Post* failed to print Chamberlin's reply to their slanderous suggestion that he had justified or apologized for Nazi behavior. In this letter, he reminded the *Post* that he had been "one of the first American writers who pointed out the many common traits of Communism and Fascism," and in his book had listed ten "deadly parallels between Fascism and Communism." The *New Leader*, to its everlasting credit, did reprint a long "Reply to My Critics" from Mr. Chamberlin. In this letter, he remarked that he was not discouraged by the fact that the reception accorded the book was largely critical—"there is endless room for difference of opinion"—but that "all but a small minority of the reviewers [failed] to face the challenge of the book head-on, to debate specific points of fact and opinion instead of flying into fits of stratospheric emotionalism or lapsing into vague generalities."

We published two further books by William Henry Chamberlin. For all his strong convictions, he was a thoroughly reasonable man, and, unlike some authors I published, easy to get along with. He was by no means the swashbuckling, trench-coated foreign correspondent sometimes depicted in novels, but quiet, reserved, completely without pretensions of any kind, and of uncompromising integrity, as he demonstrated many times during his career.

After the publication in 1947 of the editorial in the *Saturday Evening Post* in which Charles A. Beard objected to the policy of granting access to official papers only to those who supported government policy, the historian responsible for the State Department archives, I was told, informed Beard that if he would submit a list of historians he considered competent and independent, one of them would be given permission to work with the State Department papers. From this list Charles C. Tansill, Professor of Diplomatic History at Georgetown University, was selected. Tansill later told me that he was given complete freedom to see and copy anything he wanted in the State Department archives. He did not gain access to the Roosevelt papers at Hyde Park, and had no idea if certain papers had been removed from the archives, but he felt that he saw enough, with what he knew and could learn from other sources, to put together a fully documented diplomatic history of the events that led to World War II and of American participation in it.

Tansill had first become seriously interested in the causes of World War I and of American intervention when he prepared a special study on the subject in the early twenties for the Foreign Relations Committee of the Senate. One result of this study was his book *America Goes to War*, published by Little, Brown in 1938, which Allan Nevins, in the *Atlantic Monthly*, called "absolutely indispensable to an understanding of three critical years in our history." And no less a figure than Henry Steele Commager described it in the *Yale Review* as "the most valuable contribution to the history of the pre-war years in our literature, and one of the notable achievements of historical scholarship of this generation." But when Tansill completed his book on World War II, which represented a detailed, carefully documented study of years that were even more critical to our history, and which was an achievement of historical scholarship on the same level as *America Goes to War*, none of the large eastern publishers was interested. The manuscript came to me, and we brought it out in 1952 under the title *Back Door to War*. It made a book of nearly seven hundred pages, and in every respect is a formidable work of historical scholarship. After twenty-five years it still stands as the fullest and most thoroughly documented account of American participation in World War II by a revisionist historian.

Back Door to War begins with this provocative sentence, which was characteristically Tansill: "The main objective in American foreign policy since 1900 has been the preservation of the British Empire." A few pages later, so that there might be no mistake about where he stood, he added, "American intervention in World War I established a pattern that led America into a second World War in 1941. . . . Our intervention [in World War I] completely shattered the old balance of power and sowed the seeds of inevitable conflict in the dark soil of Versailles. We had a deep interest in maintaining the political structure of 1919. Thousands of American lives and a vast American treasure had been spent in its erection. . . . The bungling handiwork of 1919 had to be preserved at all costs, and America went to war again in 1941 to save a political edifice whose main supports had already rotted in the damp atmosphere of disillusion."

Tansill gives a detailed account of the decisions—in which stupidity, arrogance, pride, selfishness, and lack of vision played their customary role—that led to the outbreak of war in Europe in September, 1939. He displays mastery of the documentary material and skill in putting the pieces together, but the greatest original contribution of his book, perhaps, is its account of Japanese-American relations, of the long chain of events that culminated in an unnecessary war, of which Hiroshima and Nagasaki are the most appropriate symbols, and the rise of Communist China is the most conspicuous result. Tansill shows that the his-

tory of American economic and diplomatic pressure against Japan
went back at least to the Wilson administration, but he ascribes
a major role in this tragic episode to Henry L. Stimson. "Some
scholars like Charles A. Beard," Tansill wrote in his preface,
"have pointed out that presidential pronouncements from 1933 to
1937 gave scant encouragement to ardent one-worlders, but they
underestimated the importance of the Chief Executive's conver-
sion to the explosive non-recognition doctrine so strenuously ad-
vocated by Henry L. Stimson. This was the bomb whose long fuse
sputtered dangerously for several years and finally burst into the
flame of World War II. It was entirely fitting that Stimson became
Secretary of War in 1940; no one deserved the title quite as well as
he."

The last chapter of *Back Door to War* is devoted to Pearl
Harbor. Tansill's conclusions concerning the causes of this disaster
are generally the same as those of Morgenstern and Beard, but
he was able to add some important details confirming the thesis
from official sources that had not been available to his predecessors. He ends his book as provocatively as he began, with the
following paragraph:

But the President and Harry Hopkins viewed these dread contingencies
with amazing equanimity. In the quiet atmosphere of the oval study of
the White House, with all incoming calls shut off, the Chief Executive
calmly studied his well-filled stamp albums while Hopkins fondled Fala,
the White House scottie. At one o'clock Death stood in the doorway.
The Japanese had bombed Pearl Harbor. America had suddenly been
thrust into a war she is still fighting.

The Tansill book did not arouse the violent condemnation
aroused by the Morgenstern, Beard, and Chamberlin books. It was
given a quite fair review in the New York *Times*, for example, by
Dexter Perkins: "When he is at his best, he is unfolding a diplomatic narrative with considerable skill, and with an excellent command of his sources. Unfortunately, however, Mr. Tansill is not
always at his best. . . . Yet let it be cheerfully conceded that
speculative though Mr. Tansill's judgments must be, the discussion which he will stimulate will be useful." The *Library Journal*
recommended "caution as to his conclusions . . . since he is
sometimes as unjust as Charles A. Beard was in his last works,"
and suggested that the book "should be read in conjunction with
William Langer's recent *Challenge to Isolation*, which does more

justice to F.D.R. and his collaborators." In the *Yale Review, Back Door to War* was reviewed, together with Langer and Gleason's *Challenge to Isolation*, by Charles Griffin. Tansill, in Griffin's judgment, "adds nothing convincing to those whose minds are not already disposed to uphold his theory of Rooseveltian rash irresponsibility." On the other hand, after remarking that Langer and Gleason, like most men of our age, were awed by Roosevelt's towering personal force, Griffin declared that "they chronicled events and policies with conscious and sober restraint," which reminds me of Roy Campbell's famous verse

> You praise the firm restraint with which they write—
> I'm with you there, of course:
> They use the snaffle and the curb all right,
> But where's the bloody horse?

Tansill doubtless opened himself unnecessarily to criticism by the rather strident tone his book sometimes assumes, but this must be considered together with the circumstances in which it was written. He was fully aware that his position was in complete opposition to the views of those who largely controlled opinion, and therefore doubtless felt that to make himself heard he would have to raise his voice. Langer, writing with the self-confidence of a Harvard professor and the comfort of a $139,000 grant from the Rockefeller Foundation, was in a quite different situation and could afford to be more restrained. Tansill's access to the archives had to be opened by a vigorous assault; Langer was greeted as a friend and collaborator, and offered every possible official assistance. Tansill was not in a position even to hire a secretary; with his Rockefeller grant, Langer could employ a staff. In the case of the Tansill book, however, no one will ever have to ask Roy Campbell's question about the whereabouts of "the horse."

Charles C. Tansill, as his book makes clear, was a man of decided opinions, which he never hesitated to express. He was born in Texas, and was the grandson of a Confederate general, a fact of which he was inordinately proud. Through some hideous misunderstanding he was invited, sometime in the thirties, to give the Lincoln's Birthday address at the Lincoln Memorial in Washington. Facing "Arlington," General Lee's old mansion on the other side of the Potomac, Tansill took full advantage of the situation to deliver a ringing defense of the Confederacy, with appropriate oratorical flourishes. In the ensuing scandal—people probably took such things more seriously then than now—Tansill, he told me, might well have lost his Georgetown professorship had it not been for the intervention of an influential southern bishop. In getting the manuscript ready for publication we tried hard to induce him to remove some of the rather overblown metaphors with which he adorned his pages—"the dark soil of Versailles" and "the exotic wench of collective security," for example—but to no avail. He loved and was proud of his metaphors. In any event, Charles Callen Tansill was a man of courage and integrity and a tireless and resourceful searcher for historical truth; he wrote history as the facts led him.

Although American involvement in World War II did not begin at Pearl Harbor, it was the attack on Pearl Harbor that led to formal declaration of war; Pearl Harbor marked the transition from a nation legally and formalistically at peace to one mobilized for total war. It is for this reason that Pearl Harbor occupies a central place in any account of American involvement in World War II. Having published two books that went into the Pearl Harbor disaster in considerable detail, I was pleased to be able to give one of the central figures and victims of the great drama, Husband Kimmel, a chance to present his view of it. We published *Admiral Kimmel's Story* in 1955. It is always gratifying to publish a book one can feel is honest and has something to say that needs to be said; in the case of Kimmel's there was the further compensation that it was successful—it even appeared on some of the national best-seller lists.

The two commanders at Pearl Harbor at the time of the Japanese attack, Admiral Husband E. Kimmel and General Walter C. Short, were both summarily relieved of their commands a few days later. A commission, with Owen J. Roberts, of the Supreme Court, as chairman and including two retired officers from the navy and two from the army, was immediately appointed by President Roosevelt to make an investigation. The report of the Roberts Commission was released to the public January 24, 1942, with the comment by Stephen Early, the White House Press Officer, that the President had spent two hours over it with Justice Roberts and had expressed "his gratitude for a most painstaking and thorough investigation." It charged Short and Kimmel with dereliction of duty and errors of judgment, and held that the latter were "the effective cause for the success of the attack." Their superiors

91

in Washington were found blameless. A further element of guilt was implied by the announcement that both commanders would be tried by courts-martial. In spite of Admiral Kimmel's repeated request for such a trial, however, it was never held. His account of all this is factual, straightforward, and without self-pity; it leaves the reader with the distinct impression that those in responsible positions in Washington were determined to use every means at their disposal to hide the true facts, and to make the two commanders, Short and Kimmel, appear responsible for a disaster that cost the lives of more than 2,000 men, for which later investigations held them to be blameless.

Admiral Kimmel's requests for a trial, or for an extension of the statute of limitations so that it could not be invoked later to preclude a trial after the war, finally led to a Joint Resolution of the House and the Senate on June 13, 1944, directing the Secretary of War and the Secretary of the Navy "to proceed forthwith with an investigation into the facts surrounding the catastrophe . . . and to commence such proceedings against such persons as the facts may justify." These investigations, in contrast to that of the Roberts Commission, were conducted in proper legal fashion, with cross-examination of witnesses, presentation of evidence, and full reporting, and led to the complete exoneration of both Short and Kimmel. As Charles A. Beard put it, "Besides bringing Secretary Hull, General Marshall, General Gerow, the War Department, Admiral Stark, and the Navy Department into the network of responsibility [they] did more. They placed on the public record numerous facts about transactions in Washington relative to Pearl Harbor which were hitherto unknown to the American public." Although the reports of the army and navy boards were filed with the secretaries of the army and navy in October, 1944, no information concerning their findings was made public until after the November, 1944, elections, and the full reports were not published until after the 1946 elections, and then only after persistent prodding by members of Congress and the press.

The publication of Kimmel's book caused a sensation. The various investigations and several previous books had made the facts concerning Pearl Harbor generally available, but Kimmel's account, presented within the compass of a slim book and with the conviction of a brave man who had been unjustly treated by the highest officials of government, had an impact all its own. *U.S. News & World Report* reprinted a large part of the book on the thirteenth anniversary of Pearl Harbor, and the Chicago *Tribune* ran a front-page story with a banner headline—it was still Colonel McCormick's *Tribune*. There were news stories, editorials, reviews, and letters to the editor in literally hundreds of papers in all parts of the country. The reviews, especially in the less "sophisticated" publications, were generally favorable; those more or less committed to administration policy were often sympathetic to Admiral Kimmel but were not willing to accept his contention that vital information had been purposefully withheld from the commanders at Pearl Harbor. The Columbus *Dispatch* called the book "convincing"; the *Wall Street Journal*, besides running a long and favorable review, suggested in an editorial that it was time for a full and honest investigation of Pearl Harbor. The New York *Times* review ended with the remark that Kimmel's allegations "must remain conjectural," but the one in the San Diego *Union* concluded: "It is impossible . . . to read the chapter 'Suppression of Evidence' in this book without a shudder and a blush of shame for the honor of the country." A long review in *Time* remarked that "the admiral has presented his case with brevity, restraint and a quarter-deck command of facts," but was not willing "to go along with him when he concludes: 'I cannot excuse those in authority in Washington for what they did. . . . In my book they must answer on the Day of Judgment like any other criminal.' "

With the publication of the Roberts Report in 1942, those in control in Washington doubtless felt that Pearl Harbor had been safely buried, and it seems probable that such facts as we know now—and we do not yet know them all—would still be hidden had it not been for the courageous and persistent demand by Admiral Kimmel for a fair trial. His book is a testament to a brave man, who, despite the most shameless calumny, never lost his dignity or confidence in his own integrity.

We published many more books on foreign policy, but only one other specifically concerned with American intervention in World War II. The author of this book, George N. Crocker, appeared in my office one warm spring day in 1959 and told me that he had come from San Francisco to bring me a manuscript he thought might be of interest to me. He proposed to stay at the Drake Hotel, where he had taken a room, until I told him whether or not we would publish it. As it worked out, he had to spend only two or three days in Chicago. We published *Roosevelt's Road to Russia* the following September; it was without doubt one of the most effective of all the revisionist books, and it was successful.

George Crocker received his education at Stanford University and Harvard Law School and served as an officer in the army in World War II. After practicing law, and experience as an assistant U.S. attorney and dean of a law school, he devoted several years to the study of the diplomatic history of World War II to discover, if possible, why, after overwhelming military victory, none of our professed war aims had been achieved. He was not willing to accept the argument that it had all been in accordance with the iron logic of events, as though it had been a gigantic Greek tragedy. He did not believe that the destruction of the geographical unity of Europe, the expulsion of millions of people from their homelands, and the expansion of the power and influence of Communist Russia to the Yalu River in Korea and in Europe to a line fifty miles from Frankfurt were necessary. These things had come about as the result of decisions made by powerful men. It was his purpose to describe what went on at the meetings that brought them together, to discover how the fate of millions had been determined by a few men. It is not a pleasant story or one that gives us as Americans reason for pride in those who then guided our country, in us as a people for having chosen them, in our educational institutions for preparing the way, or in our sources of information and means of communication for having so thoroughly misrepresented not only what went on, but also its fateful consequences.

For the participants, however, the great conferences were pleasant occasions, in luxurious surroundings and a generally relaxed and friendly atmosphere. The weighty business of determining the future of the world, the fate of nations, the location of boundaries, the movement of armies of men and fleets of ships was interspersed with sumptuous banquets, lengthy toasts, and hearty camaraderie. Following a dinner at the Casablanca Conference, to which "the President had invited the British and American chiefs to dine with him and Churchill and Averell," Harry Hopkins reported, there was "much good talk of war." * Elliott Roosevelt, writing of the same occasion, remarked, "I busied myself filling glasses." † It was at the Teheran Conference that Stalin offered a toast as a salute to the execution of 50,000 German officers and technicians. Churchill was appalled, and instantly protested "the cold-blooded execu-

---

* Robert E. Sherwood, *Roosevelt and Hopkins*, p. 678.
† *As He Saw It,* New York: Duell, Sloan & Pearce, 1946, p. 68.

tion of soldiers who had fought for their country." * Roosevelt, with his customary aplomb, suggested a compromise, that "we should settle on a smaller number. Shall we say forty-nine thousand five hundred?" † The Russians and Americans present found this amusing; Churchill left the table, but by this time it was too late: British power no longer counted in the world.

At the Teheran Conference the division of Germany, the annexation of eastern Poland by Russia and of eastern Germany by Poland, and the complete expulsion of the populations involved were settled, and with these decisions the fate of Eastern Europe. As Crocker described it:

History knows that on the afternoon of December 1, 1943, in the Russian Embassy at Teheran, the Polish Republic was secretly partitioned by a Russian, an Englishman, and an American. Forty-eight percent of the land of Poland was to be torn away and given to the Soviet Union.

No Pole was present. There was no talk of plebiscites, of the will of the people, of justice, of compensation to the inhabitants, of legal rights, of moral rights. It was a naked power deal. Roosevelt did not lift a finger to prevent it and must be deemed to have acquiesced. Reading Churchill's memoirs, one is struck by the casualness—and the callousness—with which these Moguls of the twentieth century wielded the cleaver. Ancient cities were picked off like the wings of butterflies. "I was not prepared to make a squawk about Lvov," and "Stalin then said that the Russians would like to have the warm water port of Koenigsberg."

The State Department account of the Teheran Conference reports President Roosevelt's opening remarks as follows: "He said he wished to welcome the new members to the family circle and to tell them that meetings of this character were conducted as between friends with complete frankness on all sides with nothing that was said to be made public." (Robert Sherwood's account in *Roosevelt and Hopkins* omits the phrase "with nothing that was said to be made public.") With an election coming up the following year, and several million Polish-Americans among the voters, it was of the utmost importance that the details of the Polish agreements be kept secret. Rumors, however, began to circulate, and there was the obvious fact of Russian behavior toward Poland. When Congressman Joseph Mruk asked Roosevelt whether any

* *The Conferences at Cairo and Teheran, 1943,* Department of State Publication 7187, Washington, 1961, p. 554.
† *Ibid.*

secret agreements regarding Poland had been made at Teheran, he received in reply the following letter, dated March 6, 1944:

I am afraid I cannot make any further comments except what I have written to you before—there were no secret commitments made by me at Teheran and I am quite sure that other members of my party made none either. This, of course, does not include military plans which, however, had nothing to do with Poland.

A few weeks after the Teheran Conference, on a world-wide broadcast on Christmas Eve from Hyde Park, President Roosevelt characterized Stalin with these words:

He is a man who combines a tremendous, relentless determination with a stalwart good humor. I believe that he is truly representative of the heart and soul of Russia; and I believe that we are going to get along very well with him and the Russian people—very well indeed.

The second Quebec Conference is memorable chiefly as the occasion when the Morgenthau Plan became official Allied policy. Churchill vehemently objected, as did Secretaries Stimson and Hull, but the promise by Secretary of the Treasury Henry Morgenthau of $6.5 billion in the form of postwar credits to Britain brought Churchill around. In describing his futile efforts to dissuade the President from accepting Morgenthau's proposal, Stimson quoted Morgenthau as having written, in a memorandum to the Cabinet Committee, that in the Ruhr and surrounding industrial area, comprising some 30,000 square miles, "All industrial plants and equipment not destroyed by military action shall either be completely dismantled or removed from the area, all equipment shall be removed from the mines and the mines shall be thoroughly wrecked." * This was bad enough, but events soon overtook the Morgenthau Plan and left it little more than an embarrassing memory. It was the Yalta Conference, when an American President went halfway around the world to meet the Russian dictator on Russian soil, that will be remembered as one of the most shameful episodes in modern history. The suffering and bitterness caused by the Morgenthau Plan are now largely forgotten, and the dismantled industrial plants have long since been rebuilt. The decisions made at Yalta, which resulted in the death of millions and the enormous increase of the power and influence of Communist

* Henry L. Stimson and McGeorge Bundy, *On Active Service in War and Peace*, New York: Harper & Brothers, 1948, p. 574.

Russia, will plague mankind for generations. Yalta, as Crocker put it, was a moral debacle of unimaginable evil to the world.

Crocker argued that World War II was not one war but three: the British, French, American, and Russian war against National Socialist Germany, the American war against Japan, and the war of Communist Russia against the non-Communist world. The wars against Germany and Japan, from the Russian standpoint, were only a necessary prelude to the much bigger third war. Crocker further argued that although the American people may have been deceived about the nature of the war they were in, their President was not:

In this third war, which was to be the longest and most crucial one of the twentieth century, we find Franklin D. Roosevelt almost invariably charging ahead on the side of Soviet Russia. In fact, his support was the *sine qua non* of its successful launching. His mission, which he performed implacably, was to put weapons in Stalin's hands and, with American military might, to demolish all of the dikes that held back the pressing tides of Communist expansion in Europe and Asia. Meanwhile, everything was done to prevent the average American citizen from becoming conscious of this war; his mind was kept preoccupied hating Hitler and Tojo. And since Roosevelt was concealing the war itself, a fortiori he did not reveal his own sympathies in it.

There may be room for disagreement with Crocker's emphasis or interpretation, but the facts and their consequences speak for themselves, and no amount of glossing over with arguments of historical necessity or such pretty phrases as "doing good by stealth" will make them go away. The big question, however, remains: Why did it all happen? Why did the American President acquiesce in almost any Russian demand? Why, to bring Russia into the war against Japan when his military commanders had told him that Japan was beaten, did he make concessions to Stalin that betrayed a loyal ally, Chiang Kai-shek, and led inevitably to the loss of China? Crocker did not accept the argument that Roosevelt was deceived, that he was not aware of the true nature of Communism or of Stalin's rapacity and ruthlessness. But neither did he believe in the theory of ideological motivation. There were without doubt many Communists and Communist sympathizers in the Roosevelt administration, but Crocker asserted that Roosevelt himself was no more a Communist than he was a Jeffersonian. As Jesse Jones put it, he was a total politician. The State Department report on the Teheran Conference quoted Roosevelt as remarking to Stalin, on the question of India, that "the best solution would be reform from the bottom, somewhat along the Soviet line." * This rather indicates admiration for the Soviet way of getting things done, which, as he must have known, included mass extermination; but although he may have loved to exercise power and admired the ruthless exercise of power by others, for Roosevelt it was power for its own sake. It is with Roosevelt's complete surrender to politics, Crocker believed, that the "psychobiographers of the future will probably start in their quest for the 'Why?'" Crocker himself, however, let the matter rest there.

The response to the Crocker book, not surprisingly, was of two kinds—warm approval from those who agreed with it, and stony silence from those who did not. The one exception to the latter was a brief review in the New York *Times* (December 6, 1959) which ended, "neither history nor scholarship—it is sheer nonsense." By the time of the publication of the Crocker book, however, both *National Review* and *Modern Age* had come into existence, so that there were at least two serious publications in which such a book could be given fair and adequate consideration. Forrest Davis, in *National Review*, suggested that President Eisenhower would do well to include *Roosevelt's Road to Russia* in his knapsack as he reconnoitered the Communist empire's southern frontiers from New Delhi to Rome. He said that Crocker expertly marshaled the familiar sources, although he faltered when it came to motive. Davis, who had known Roosevelt well, and in the early days of the New Deal had been a White House insider, remarked that Crocker minimized Roosevelt's "essential frivolity, his empiricism, his vindictiveness and his one-dimensional mind." Harry Elmer Barnes, in *Modern Age*, called *Roosevelt's Road to Russia* the "most brilliantly written and felicitously expressed of all revisionist books yet published on the second World War." Except for the excellent reviews in the Chicago *Tribune* and the Boston *Herald*, there were few others, but two widely syndicated and respected columnists, Lyle Wilson and Holmes Alexander, each devoted a column to the book and so brought it to the attention of people in all parts of the country. Largely as a result of their interest, *Roosevelt's Road to Russia* went through five large printings within a year after publication, and in 1961 we brought out a revised edition in our paperback Great Debate series. George

* *The Conferences at Cairo and Teheran*, p. 486. In Sherwood's account, it is worth noting, the phrase "somewhat along the Soviet line" is omitted.

Crocker, unfortunately, did not live to write the second book he had planned, but his one book is a worthy memorial to a man of conviction who searched for the truth and did not shrink from telling what he found.

No account of revisionism would be complete without an expression of gratitude and respect to Harry Elmer Barnes. Barnes wrote the first fully documented revisionist book on World War I, *The Genesis of the World War*, which was published by Knopf in 1926, and following World War II devoted much of his time and incredible energy to encouraging and helping those willing to try to penetrate what he correctly called the "historical blackout," the well-organized practice of "ignoring or suppressing facts counter to war-time propaganda." It was Barnes who found the financial support that enabled William Henry Chamberlin and Charles C. Tansill to take time from their regular work to write their two revisionist books. He found similar help for others, not all of whose proposed books were ever finished, and in such pamphlets as *The Struggle Against the Historical Blackout* and *A Select Bibliography of Revisionist Books*, which he published and distributed himself, he carried on a relentless campaign for the historical truth as he saw it. He believed that American intervention in each of the two world wars had been an unmitigated disaster, and that if such disasters were to be avoided in the future it was essential that the true facts be known.

Revisionist historiography was doubtless the cause that absorbed the major part of his talents and energy, but was by no means the only one; he was completely in the tradition of the liberal reformer. In the Summer, 1973, issue of the *Wisconsin Magazine of History*, in an informative article on Barnes, Justus D. Doenecke wrote: "He opposed prohibition and censorship, assailed capital punishment, pushed for prison and court reform . . . liberalization of divorce laws, abolition of sexual taboos, planned parenthood, compulsory health insurance, revision of drug legislation, and far greater equality for women and blacks."

Barnes's commitment to revisionism was in no way related to sympathy for Germany or German culture—by temperament, he said, he was more inclined toward the French than the German tradition—but derived entirely from his firmly held belief that if the truth concerning American involvement in the two World Wars could be made generally known, such disasters would not recur.

It may have been a naïve faith, but it was a sincere one, and Barnes unhesitatingly sacrificed a brilliant academic career in its behalf. His commitment to revisionism was a reflection of his belief in the primacy of reason; he firmly believed that if "the American people" could only be correctly informed, they would act in a way that is in accordance with their own best interests.

It is interesting and instructive to reflect that Barnes's *Genesis of the World War*, which challenged the whole basis of American intervention in World War I and of the punitive peace that followed it, was not only published by Alfred Knopf, but that Knopf himself had suggested that Barnes write it, Knopf having read and been impressed by the series of articles on the causes of the war Barnes had written for the *Christian Century*. Although not every reviewer agreed with Barnes's book, it was widely and seriously reviewed. Sidney B. Fay's monumental *The Origins of the World War* was published by Macmillan, C. H. Grattan's *Why We Fought* by Vanguard, C. C. Tansill's *America Goes to War* by Little, Brown, and Walter Millis's *Road to War* by Houghton Mifflin. The revisionist books on World War II, by way of contrast, were nearly all published by small publishers or, in the case of the two books by Charles A. Beard, by Yale University Press, and for the most part were either ignored by the influential reviewers or treated as irresponsible assaults on public order. George Morgenstern's *Pearl Harbor*, Admiral R. A. Theobald's *The Final Secret of Pearl Harbor*, and F. R. Sanborn's *Design for War* were all published by Devin-Adair in New York, and the authoritative collection of essays Harry Elmer Barnes put together, *Perpetual War for Perpetual Peace*, was published by the Caxton Press in Caldwell, Idaho. The four revisionist books we published all sold well—more than 20,000 copies in each case, which is quite respectable—and several of the other revisionist books did considerably better, so that it cannot be said that the large New York publishers rejected them on the grounds of lack of public interest.

For all his strongly held convictions, Barnes was an amiable man, with an excellent sense of humor, and I enjoyed his friendship. We made a trip to Texas on one occasion to try to arouse interest on the part of some of the Texas oil tycoons in books that in our opinion undertook to "set the record straight." It was an enjoyable experience but produced no tangible results—there were a number of pleasant lunches and dinners and many good conversations, but little else. The oil barons commended us for our efforts but were not willing to risk a commitment. One of the Texans I met on another occasion had a fine library, of which he was justly proud, and had given substantial financial support to one of the left-liberal magazines in New York; but although he was temperamentally fully in agreement with the position of the books I was publishing, he was not willing to support them financially—a left-liberal magazine was more fashionable, offered greater recognition, and was certainly less controversial.

In his fight against the "historical blackout," Barnes became argumentative, strident, and at times rather bitter. Having been an extremely successful and sought-after teacher, author, and lecturer, he now found himself literally stifled, and reduced to writing for obscure publications or having to publish his writings himself. "Short of some monstrous crime," he once said, "I could have chosen no line of activity less likely to be of material benefit to myself.* His stridency becomes understandable in view of all this, as does his enthusiasm for one or two books that were not worthy of his support. One of these enthusiasms led to a period of distinct coolness on his part toward me, an episode that also had its comic aspects. Barnes became quite angry because I rejected a manuscript he had been most insistent that I publish, but he finally agreed that my reasons for rejecting it had been well founded. In one of the last of many letters on the subject he wrote that the author in question "appears to be breaking down mentally, and the only reason that one cannot truthfully say that he is breaking down ethically is that I have discovered far too late that he apparently never had any ethics at any time."

Was the fight for what we thought was the historical truth worthwhile? I find it difficult to believe, as much as I would like to believe it, that telling the true story of what happened when Roosevelt and Churchill met in the Gulf of St. Lawrence on board the cruiser *Augusta*, or the true story of Pearl Harbor, Teheran, or Yalta, will prevent such occurrences in the future. Men and politics, ambition and power are what they are and will remain so to the end of history. Nor will the consequences of the decisions made at Teheran and Yalta be in any way changed because that rather abstract collective, the American people, is given the means to find out what actually happened. The vast literature that set the

---

* Quoted by Marguerite J. Fisher in "Harry Elmer Barnes: An Overall Preview," from *Harry Elmer Barnes, Learned Crusader,* Colorado Springs: Ralph Myles, Publishers, 1968, p. 25.

record straight concerning the lies, misconceptions, blunders, and misrepresentations involved with the first World War did not, obviously, prevent their recurrence on a much larger scale during the second. One of the most effective revisionist books on the manner in which America was brought into World War I was *Road to War*, but this did not prevent even its author, Walter Millis, from becoming one of the most ardent interventionists the second time around.

Whether writing and publishing the historical truth brings any immediate practical results or not, if we believe in anything we must believe that the truth is worthwhile for its own sake. If the free society is to survive, is to have any meaning, men must be made accountable for their actions. We must know what our leaders did, said, and agreed to in our name. The alternative is the society described in George Orwell's *1984*.

6

COMMUNISM AND
FOREIGN POLICY

BY the early 1950's the fatuous, utterly uncritical attitude toward Communist Russia represented by President Truman's characterization of Stalin as "good old Uncle Joe" had been swept away by the harsh reality of events, but there was still a large store of illusion that needed only a slight hint of warmth from the direction of Moscow to reassert itself, and again to influence attitudes, decisions, and policies. Revelations of slave-labor camps, mass arrests, and the brutal suppression of the least evidence of independence might dampen, for a time, the longing of certain intellectuals to see Communism as the hope of the future, but they were soon forgotten. Illusions, especially of ideological origin, die hard.

It was not difficult for me, in the environment of the postwar period, to convince myself that one of the obligations of our firm was to do what we could to publish the truth concerning Communist Russia. Through Eugene Davidson, who while editor at Yale University Press had published David Dallin's books, I met that stalwart, courageous old Menshevik. Dallin had been a member of the 1918 Provisional Assembly and had afterward devoted his life to the study of Soviet Russia. He was another of those who saw things as they were, and with Boris Nicolaevsky he had written the first authoritative account of the Soviet system of slave labor, *Forced Labor in the Soviet Union*, which Yale published in 1947. At Davidson's suggestion, the Foundation for Foreign Affairs (a small organization to which I belonged) made a modest grant to Dallin in 1948 to enable him to spend a summer in Europe visiting camps for fugitives from Eastern Europe. He was sure that in such places he would be able to find people who had had direct experience with the slave-labor system, with what Solzhenitsyn was later to name the "Gulag Archipelago."

After his return, Dallin gave those associated with the Foundation a long, detailed account of the results of his journey. His expectations of finding people who had been in the slave-labor camps were more than fulfilled: when it became known, he said, that someone had come to a displaced-persons camp who wanted such information, lines would form of people anxious to relate their experiences so that the world might know of the gigantic Soviet slave-labor system. Dallin, a scrupulously careful scholar, used whatever new information he obtained to check against and add to what he already knew.

With his large head, broad forehead, strong features, and the straightforward look of his intense blue eyes, Dallin was an impressive man, but the thing I remember best about him is his deep, resonant voice, made all the more impressive by his habit of speaking slowly and deliberately. When he said something, one had the impression that he had thought about it for a long time. To hear his account of his visits to the displaced-persons camps of World War II was an unforgettable experience.

One result of my meeting with Dallin was the publication in our pamphlet series, in May, 1949, of *The Economics of Slave Labor*. There was another result. When a Swiss publisher, not long after, called my attention to a book he was about to bring out, *Eleven Years in Soviet Prison Camps*, one of the first descriptions of the Gulag Archipelago by someone who had been there, I took it almost at once, and arranged to have it translated into English. The author, Elinor Lipper, was born in Brussels, came from a comfortably situated German-Jewish family, and had become a Communist while studying medicine in Berlin in the early thirties. In 1934 she went to Russia, and was arrested only a few weeks later during the great purge. Sentenced without trial to five years' imprisonment for counterrevolutionary activity, she was not released until after she had spent eleven years in various prisons and labor camps, under the most degrading conditions. She had acquired

Swiss citizenship not long before going to Russia, and her release was brought about by the firm intervention of the Swiss government, which seems far more willing to protect the interests of its citizens than our government, in spite of the great disparity in the military forces available to each.

Elinor Lipper's book, with its straightforward, rather terse account of the fate that has befallen millions of people, is a great human document. Despite all the cruelties, unimaginable horrors, and pitiless disregard for the suffering of others her book described, she never lets us forget that an indomitable spark of humanity, of the divine gift that makes some men at least more than beasts, still survived. There was always, for instance, the storyteller, "the only person in camp who is loved and respected by all prisoners equally, no matter whether they are contriki or criminals. For every prisoner wants to forget reality, and the storyteller gives him forgetfulness. When the storyteller speaks, the barracks no longer seem so dark and cold; the loneliness of the forest is no longer so hostile and oppressive. . . . It is altogether remarkable that these prisoners, who endure all the suffering that men can think of to impose upon other men, who have before them years of daily torment—that these prisoners can still weep over the fictional tragedy of a fictional love."

It happened that Miss Lipper was in the camp that Vice President Henry Wallace visited in 1943 in the company of Owen Lattimore. Wallace described his visit in his book *Soviet Asia Mission*, which appeared three years later. A report by Lattimore had appeared in the December, 1944, issue of the *National Geographic*, which often seems ready to lend its services for the propaganda purposes of whatever cause is momentarily in the ascendancy. In the tradition of the Potemkin villages, great preparations were made for the visit of the two prominent Americans—watchtowers were taken down, good clothing was issued to the prisoners the visitors might see, even a theatrical performance was arranged, as though this was a regular feature of prison-camp life. The most fantastic rumors went through the camps, Miss Lipper tells us, one of the most persistent being that the visit of the Vice President was in connection with the demand of the United States for the annexation of eastern Siberia in return for its help in the war against Germany, in consequence of which all the prisoners would be freed. The ecstatic account of the two visitors to Kolyma is rather different from that of our former prisoner. To his credit,

Henry Wallace, who was a naïve man, later regretted what he had written about the prison camps, and when Elinor Lipper came to the United States in 1952, the year after her book was published, he asked her to come to visit him, so that he could express his regret to her in person. But there is no evidence that Owen Lattimore, who was not a naïve man, ever expressed regret for his part in this inexcusable case of deception.

Eleven Years in Soviet Prison Camps was reviewed widely and, without exception, favorably. The review in the *Nation* spoke of the book's vividness and humanity, and, like almost every other, mentioned the report of the Wallace-Lattimore visit to Kolyma. A condensation of the book appeared in *Reader's Digest*, the United States Information Agency distributed more than 300,000 copies in sixteen languages, and through the intervention of Sidney Hook, who never misses an opportunity to let the truth be known concerning Communism and Soviet Russia, Miss Lipper made a lecture tour under the auspices of the International Rescue Committee. She was a trim, bright, and attractive woman, and with her sincerity, conviction, and ability to rise to any occasion was a great success, whether she spoke before the executive board of the AFL-CIO, to an American Legion auxiliary, or at a New York press conference.

Communism, it must be freely admitted, is not an inspiring subject, nor is Soviet Russia to be compared with, let us say, Renaissance Italy as an object of study, but they are two of the great determining factors of our times, and we ignore them at our peril. However I may have felt about it, in the twenty years or so I was active in publishing we brought out a long series of books about Communism and Soviet Russia. In looking back, I am surprised myself at their number and variety. Among several on Communist methods of subversion there were Louis Budenz's *The Cry Is Peace,* Stefan Possony's *A Century of Conflict*, and James Atkinson's *The Politics of Struggle,* all concerned with Soviet theory and methods of warfare. There was a book on political warfare and the particular vulnerability of Soviet Russia to external subversion, Oleg Anisimov's *The Ultimate Weapon,* for which General William J. Donovan wrote an introduction; and one on how the Communist Party functions and is organized, *The Communist Party Apparatus,* by Abdurakhman Avtorkhanov. It was we who published, only a few weeks after its tragic end, the first eyewitness account of the 1957 Hungarian revolt, *No More Comrades,* by Andor Heller, and the American edition of Wolfgang Leonhard's *Child of the Revolution*, a chronicle of the author's education and training for membership in the upper echelons of the party apparatus, and his eventual disillusionment. I should also mention our publication of the history of Soviet foreign policy, *Peaceful Co-existence*, by the distinguished Polish scholar and former diplomat W. W. Kulski, and David Dallin's *From Purge to Co-existence*, essays discussing the critical issues that influenced Russian foreign and domestic policy during the period from the Pyatakov-Radek trial of 1937 to the ascendancy of Khrushchev. We published paperback editions of Whittaker Chambers's *Witness* and Freda Utley's *Lost Illusion*, *The Communist Manifesto*, the Russian Diary of the Marquis de Custine, and *Das Kapital*, and selections from the works of Nicolai Lenin, the last edited by Stefan Possony. Two other books in this general area were Stefan Possony's authoritative biography of Lenin, which had as its subtitle *Compulsive Revolutionary*, and the memoirs of William Reswick, *I Dreamt Revolution*. Reswick had emigrated from Russia as a young man, went back immediately after World War I as an interpreter for one of the American relief missions, and then stayed on as Russian correspondent of International News Service. His friendship with many of the original revolutionaries, most of whom were later liquidated by Stalin, made this a particularly interesting and revealing book.

The books we published on Communism and Soviet Russia represented a serious, coherent attempt to come to terms with one of the great facts of our time, to view it in every possible aspect. Our reputation became such that when we published an English translation of the novel *The Thaw*, by Ilya Ehrenburg—who without doubt was one of the most shameless opportunists of all time—the *Daily Worker* called us "the most reactionary publisher" in the United States. Considering the source, I took this as a great compliment.

Besides *The Cry Is Peace*, we published one other book by Louis Budenz, *The Techniques of Communism*. As a fairly representative figure of the ideological wars of the 1940's and 50's, Budenz deserves more than a passing reference in any account of what went on during those tumultuous years. He created a great sensation when, in October, 1945, he abruptly announced that he had resigned as editor of the Communist *Daily Worker* and gone back to the Catholic Church. As editor of the leading Communist newspaper, president of the corporation that published it, and member of the National Committee of the Communist Party, Budenz was well versed in every detail of its operation, and knew much about the make-up of its membership and support. In the two books we published for him he made no attempt to exploit the sensational aspect of what he knew; it was his purpose to show how it is that in any encounter with Communism, whether on the level of ideas, political power, or influence, the United States almost invariably gives up something; in short, makes itself appear the weaker, less resolute nation despite its vast military and industrial power and its vaunted idealism. Then, writing in 1951, Budenz could point to Poland and the other countries of Eastern Europe, to China, to the great wartime and postwar conferences, and to Alger Hiss. Reading *The Cry Is Peace* twenty-five years later, with Vietnam, Cambodia, and Angola behind us, and Rhodesia and South Africa just ahead, it becomes easier to understand why Whittaker Chambers once remarked that when he left the Communist Party he felt he was leaving the winning side to join the losers.

What is one to say about such a man as Louis Budenz, who gave the best years of his life to the cause of a great conspiracy, and then devoted himself—tirelessly, unselfishly, and to the great disadvantage of his own situation—to unmasking it, to warning his countrymen of the danger it posed to the institutions, even the survival, of his own country? I have known five people who have been active, committed members of the Communist Party and have turned violently and wholeheartedly against it: Freda Utley, Louis Budenz, Whittaker Chambers, Paul Crouch, and Frank Meyer. They were strikingly different in personality and background: Freda Utley, aggressive and outgoing, with a fine mind and the best education her native England could give her; Louis Budenz, a lawyer and journalist by training, of Midwestern, Catholic, rural background; Whittaker Chambers, introspective, enormously gifted, with the instinct and sensitivity of a poet, a New Yorker in upbringing and education; Paul Crouch, with generations of fundamentalism and Appalachia behind him; and Frank Meyer, son of a New York Jewish lawyer, possessor of a keen, well-trained mind. But they all had in common a deep sense of commitment. They did not play with Communism by joining front organizations, peace sit-ins, protest demonstrations, and the like; they went all the way and joined the party, not because they saw it as a path to power and influence, but because, in their youthful idealism, they believed it offered the only way out of the dilemma of modern life. When they realized that they had made a hideous mistake, their commitment to anti-Communism was also total.

The path of the ex-Communist is not an easy one. When he leaves the party, he gives up not only the psychological security of belonging to a tightly knit group with a strong sense of mission, but economic security as well—the party and its friends see to it that its influential members are well taken care of. He must confront not only the violent hostility of his former comrades, which can involve physical danger, but the distrust of those uncomplicated fellow citizens who can have no comprehension of why anyone in his right mind would become a Communist in the first place, and the distinct animosity of the liberal intellectual establishment, with its great influence and power in the universities, publishing, and the press. The liberal will forgive a Communist, but never the Communist who leaves the party and openly fights it—for Alger Hiss the liberal can have compassion and understanding, but for Whittaker Chambers only distrust and animosity.

The books published by the Henry Regnery Company in the area of foreign policy, about a dozen of them, were nearly all concerned with the Far East and the Middle East, the two parts of the world where American interests were involved most critically—and most emotionally. The two that aroused the widest discussion were Freda Utley's *The China Story*, which we published in the spring of 1951, and Alfred Lilienthal's *What Price Israel*, which came out two years later.

Freda Utley was eminently qualified to write on the consequences of American policy in Asia. She had written her doctoral dissertation at the University of London on the Japanese textile industry and its impact on Lancashire. During her Communist days, when her husband was an official of the Soviet government, she had lived in Japan for a year; one result was her successful book *Japan's Feet of Clay*, published in 1937. She had spent six months in China in 1938 as a correspondent of the London *News Chronicle*, and returned there, again as a correspondent, in 1946. The prophetic book that came out of this visit, *Last Chance in China*, published in 1947, was unfortunately largely ignored. Freda Utley was a shrewd, tireless observer who knew what to look for, and with her outgoing personality she was able to establish a relationship with almost anyone, all of which gave her books, whether on China, the Middle East, or occupied postwar Germany, a unique quality of immediacy, informed judgment, and humanity.

In *The China Story,* which we published in 1951, she undertook to describe not only the course of American policy, which in her judgment contributed substantially to the fall of the Nationalist government and the triumph of Communism, but also the influences that determined policy and underlay the crucial decisions. At the end of the introduction to her book she set forth her position with characteristic directness:

> In presenting an analysis of Communist influence on American policy, I take account of the mixed motives of men in all parties and of all political persuasions. Only the historian of the future will be able to pronounce a definitive judgment. I have attempted to evaluate from such evidence as is now available the degree to which Communist influence, as distinct from incompetence, ignorance, and ambition, determined the disastrous course of America's Far Eastern policy.
>
> One thing is certain, Communist conquest of a large part of the world since the defeat of Germany and Japan, and the threat of even greater conquests, was not unavoidable.

It has become fashionable, not to say absolutely *de rigueur,* to condemn "McCarthyism" as the epitome of irresponsibility and "anti-intellectualism" and McCarthy himself as a ruthless, unprincipled demagogue. Such people as John Stewart Service and John Paton Davies are represented as innocent victims of a wave of terror, and the triumph of Communism in China as an inevitable historical development. It is, then, worth the effort to reread such a book as *The China Story* and find out what people did in fact say, write, and recommend; to discover for one's self what actually happened at one of the great turning points of history, as the fall of Nationalist China undoubtedly was. We can read, for example, that on November 15, 1944, John Paton Davies, who was General Joseph Stilwell's political adviser and later an influential member of the State Department's Planning Committee, reported to Washington as follows:

> We should not now abandon Chiang Kai-shek. To do so at this juncture would be to lose more than we would gain. We must for the time being continue recognition of Chiang's government.
>
> But we must be realistic. . . . A coalition Chinese Government in which the Communists find a satisfactory place is the solution of this impasse most desirable to us. . . . If Chiang and the Communists are

irreconcilable, then we shall have to decide which faction we are going to support.

In seeking to determine which faction we should support we must keep in mind these basic considerations: Power in China is on the verge of shifting from Chiang to the Communists.

Miss Utley came to know Davies well during her stay in China in 1946, and liked him personally however much she may have disagreed with him. She said his dispatches did not reveal that he ever was a Communist, but did prove that he had no scruples in arguing on opposite sides at different times to gain an advantage for the Chinese Communists, and that he was, at best, totally unaware of what should have been obvious to any informed and intelligent man, that Communist control of China would endanger the security of the United States. She never knew John Stewart Service, but asserted that his reports displayed ignorance and naïveté rather than a definite Communist orientation. She believed he was typical of the "liberals" who fell easy victims to Communist propaganda because they had little or no experience of totalitarian methods, and did not know what the Communists' real aims were.

One of the most revealing chapters in *The China Story*, particularly in retrospect, is "How the Communists Captured the Public." It was not, of course, the "public" that was captured by the Communists, but those who speak for the public, the writers of books, articles, and reviews, and the editors who published them. There were, for example, Edgar Snow, author of *Red Star over China*; Agnes Smedley, correspondent of the Manchester *Guardian* and author of *Battle Hymn of China*; Theodore White and Annalee Jacoby, authors of *Thunder Out of China*, which became a Book-of-the-Month Club selection; Gunther Stein, author of *The Challenge of Red China*. And there was Owen Lattimore. It was, as Miss Utley showed by many striking examples, a well-organized, smoothly functioning group—they reviewed each other's books, published each other's articles, and built each other up; each was a Far Eastern expert because the others had proclaimed him so. As Owen Lattimore, in his review in the New York *Times* of Israel Epstein's *Unfinished Revolution in China* put it:

From Edgar Snow's *Red Star* to Theodore White's and Annalee Jacoby's *Thunder Out of China* the list of names is distinguished. Israel Epstein has without question established a place for himself in this distinguished company. It is noteworthy that the recent trend of good books about China, well documented and well written, has been well to the Left of Center.

The China Story was published not long after President Truman's dismissal of General MacArthur, which put the whole question of American policy in the Far East at the center of public discussion. The Korean War, which was grinding toward its inconclusive end, had demonstrated that the administration in Washington was quite prepared to sacrifice American lives in what Truman called a "police action," but that beyond the restoration of an uncertain *status quo* it had no policy or ultimate objective. For pointing out this embarrassing fact, MacArthur was abruptly relieved of his command.

The China Story did not presume to set forth a course of action, but it clearly and unabashedly showed how we had gotten where we were, and its publication could not have been better timed. It was widely and favorably reviewed, appeared on the national bestseller lists for weeks, went through many printings, and was later published as a paperback. *Time* described it as "a tellingly documented account of the errors and confusions which lost the U.S. its last chance to save free China," the Los Angeles *Times* pronounced it "our best book on the Chinese-Korean situation," and although the author was sharply critical of the New York *Times* for its favorable treatment of books by Owen Lattimore, Gunther Stein, and Edgar Snow, it gave her book a long and very fair review. Miss Utley remarked at the time, I remember, that in 1947, when she had published *Last Chance in China,* in which she had recommended a positive course of action, there was still time to do something, but no one paid any attention to what she had to say. Such books as Lattimore's *Solution in Asia* held the center of the stage then; now that it was too late, everyone wanted to read how it had all happened.

Before leaving *The China Story* I should mention two people who contributed substantially to its success. When I saw the manuscript in its original, rather disorganized state, I despaired of ever making a book out of it—we were all devoted to Freda, but she was not what one would call a neat worker. It was Florence Norton, then associated with *Reader's Digest*, who volunteered to put the manuscript into shape for publication, and she did so with great skill. When she had finished, Howard Ellis, a distinguished Chicago lawyer, went over the manuscript line by line and eliminated, rephrased, or insisted on further documentation for passages that might have been subjected to question. Freda was incensed, and stormed that he had "emasculated" her book, but in fact he made it far more effective. We had a threatening letter or two from Owen Lattimore, but no libel suits, for all of which I remember Howard Ellis with gratitude and esteem.

The year after *The China Story*, we published a firsthand account of the American occupation of South Korea, John C. Caldwell's *The Korea Story*. The book ends with a graphic description of the impact of the invasion from the north of June 25, 1950, on the completely unprepared, unwieldy, and marvelously incompetent American mission, by then under the State Department, which had taken over control of all American activities in Korea from the army on January 1, 1949. Under this arrangement the last American troops were withdrawn on June 29, 1949. Exactly one year later to a day, American troops were back in Korea, this time engaged in fighting President Truman's "police action."

John Caldwell was born in South China of American missionary parents, attended Chinese schools, and spoke fluent Chinese and adequate Korean. His wife, who came from an American missionary family stationed in Korea, was completely fluent in that language. Caldwell returned to China during World War II on a military mission, and after the war became director of the United States Information Service in China, which was then under the State Department.

His book describes an incident that reveals much about the attitudes determining American policy in China at the time. Late in 1946 he received a cable from the State Department directing him to prepare a report, originally requested by a member of the House Foreign Affairs Committee, on the propaganda activities of the Russians and the Chinese Communists in China. Caldwell set to work immediately, listening to Russian radio programs, visiting Russian information centers, seeing Russian films, and reading the Russian-subsidized, Chinese Communist newspapers. His report was sixty-four pages in length, and no one who read it could fail to realize how viciously anti-American the Communist line in China had become, or to see that the propaganda lines of the Russians and the Chinese merged, "as in one slanderous tirade." The report was sent to Washington as directed, but, despite its being highly classified, a copy got into the hands of the United Press, which released it. Before long Caldwell heard himself denounced by Radio Moscow as a warmonger, but that was by no means the end of the incident. He subsequently received an insulting telegram from Walton Butterworth, the U.S. Minister in Shanghai, who had passed on the original cable ordering him to make the study, which accused Caldwell of insubordination and of maliciously adding to the friction between the United States and Russia. Then came a cable from General George Marshall, who was then secretary of state, relieving him of all authority to make further studies or reports, and virtually ending his career in China. Caldwell had become the victim of the illusion that the Chinese Communists were "agrarian reformers" and, as such, independent of Moscow and of the policy advocating their participation in a coalition government. Early in 1948, after a period in Washington, he went to Korea as a civilian information specialist.

Caldwell's headquarters were a few miles south of the infamous thirty-eighth parallel, which divided Korea in two. In his book Caldwell made us realize what such a division of a country means to the people who live in it. When the decision to divide Korea was made at the Yalta Conference, the thirty-eighth parallel was only a line on the map to the great personages who agreed to it; but to the people of Korea the division was the cause of bitter tragedy from the beginning, and soon led to a long, bloody, and hideous war, which ended only in another uncertain, precarious truce between the two superpowers.

During the first year of his assignment Caldwell worked for the U.S. Army of Occupation. The army was not exactly a model of efficiency, but in its own way it got the job done. Men in Caldwell's position were expected to use their own initiative, and to deal with situations and people as they found them, not as someone in Washington thought they ought to be. Caldwell had only respect and admiration for the ability, devotion to duty, and purposefulness of General John R. Hodge, the army commander in Korea during the first phase of the occupation. But administration by the State Department, which soon established an enormous mission in Korea —the largest, according to Caldwell, of all U.S. diplomatic missions at the time—appears to have been something else again: highly bureaucratic, unwieldy, ineffective, wasteful, and in its results often destructive of the aims of American policy.

Caldwell describes, for example, how under the army his group prepared a film entitled *The People Vote* to explain the methods and purpose of democracy, in preparation for the first Korean election, which was held, with a very high participation by the eligible voters, on May 10, 1948. The film was made in Seoul in a few weeks and cost a few thousand dollars. With the help of portable army generators and jeeps, it was shown wherever a screen could be set up and a crowd gathered, and it was enormously effective. For another example, the army had maintained small information centers in towns all over Korea, but the State Department concentrated everything in Seoul. There it established an information center, occupying a four-story building, that required the services of more than one hundred Koreans, and a large American library, where American magazines, including *Atlantic*, *Vogue*, and *Railway Age*, were made available to Koreans, very few of whom were even slightly familiar with the English language. And there were photographic displays showing American life—neat New England villages, housing projects, superhighways—none of which was of much use when the invasion from the north began.

To read all this is depressing enough, but most devastating of all is Caldwell's account of the behavior of the American mission when the invasion began. There had been rumors of troop concentrations in the North, but all was optimism in the mission. "It was common knowledge in Seoul," Caldwell reported, "that the embassy, and therefore the United States, considered communist morale low, their military equipment poor, and their aims not too inimical to ours. Just three weeks before, *Time* (to all other nations the official news organ of the States) in no uncertain terms had told of the embassy's splendid work in training the South Korean Army. . . . And everyone knew that Harold Noble, First Secretary of the American Embassy, had stated publicly that the South Korean Army could not only stop an attack but could move north and take over the communist capital in two weeks' time." At four o'clock on Sunday afternoon, twelve hours after the beginning of the invasion, in a public statement broadcast over the embassy radio, Ambassador John Muccio announced that the South Korean army had contained the attack, although there had been no real contact between the forces and the North Korean tanks were advancing at will.

An evacuation plan had been worked out, but the Ambassador insisted that this be abandoned, because it provided for evacuation by air and he was afraid, with Russian and North Korean planes aloft, that this might cause an international incident—as though the invasion itself had not been an incident of some significance. Instead, 682 women and children were sent to Japan on a small Norwegian freighter that happened to be in the harbor at Inchon, was loaded with a full cargo of fertilizer, and offered accommodations for only twelve passengers. It was General MacArthur, as Caldwell remarked, who finally put an end to the embassy's dilemma by telling its staff what to do.

Most shameless of all was the abandonment of the 5,000 South Korean employees of the embassy, with their personnel records, which, since no one had thought to destroy them, remained as a ready-made list for the Communist invaders. A persecution began three days after the invasion, and continued through the summer months of 1950. Caldwell asserts that the number of drivers, houseboys, translators, interpreters, and secretaries who were killed, and where and how they perished, will never be known. They simply disappeared, as did hundreds of Methodist and Presbyterian ministers and church workers. Vyvyan Holt, the British Ambassador, more realistic and professional than his American counterpart, had seen it all coming and advised his compatriots three weeks before to evacuate; but he himself remained at his post, and he too disappeared. Ambassador Muccio, however, was honored by the Truman administration upon his return to Washington.

Caldwell devotes one chapter of his book to an account of the work of the American missions in the Far East, which gives the reader some appreciation of what a great achievement the establishment of Christian churches, and of schools, hospitals, and universities was. It has become fashionable to say that we never "lost" China because it was never ours. In a literal sense, of course, this is true; but the deliberate sacrifice of the good will, the cultural ties, and the bonds of friendship that had been built up over generations, to say nothing of the murder by Communists of thousands of Christians, Western and native alike, is tragedy on an enormous scale, which no amount of sophistry can hide.

The Korea Story was widely reviewed, and sold moderately well, but despite its rather sensational account of ineptitude, waste, and outright incompetence, it did not attract anything like the attention the publication of *The China Story* had aroused only a year before. This was no doubt partly because Freda Utley was better known as an author than John Caldwell; but the national mood had also gone through one of its sudden shifts between the spring of 1951 and the fall of 1952. *The China Story* was published when the

country was still in the state of shock that followed the collapse
of Nationalist China, the invasion of South Korea, and the dismissal of General MacArthur; in addition, the Hiss case and the
McCarthy hearings had put the liberals temporarily on the defen-
sive. By the fall of 1952, China was receding into the background,
the Korean War was coming to an end, and there was the diversion
of an election campaign. The liberals had regrouped, and soon
recovered their customary self-confidence, as is evident in the
rather airy way the Caldwell book was dismissed in the New York
Herald Tribune: "a disappointment . . . written in a dismal combination of military, bureaucratic and journalistic jargon . . .
narrow . . . superficial . . . lacking in objectivity." The New
York *Times* said, "Mr. Caldwell has not, of course, told the Korea
story. . . . He has told a lively tale of small accomplishments,
personal hardships and bumbling bureaucracy." But the less
ideological *Christian Science Monitor* called it "colorful and well-
written, and one of the most devastating attacks on the State Department's record in Korea that has yet been published."

Two other books on the Far East that we published, both in
1956, were based on the personal experiences of Americans who
went through the ordeal of Communist imprisonment. *Four Years
in a Red Hell* was by the Reverend Harold W. Rigney, a Catholic
priest of the Society of the Divine Word. As rector of Fu Jen
University in Peking, he tried to come to a working arrangement
with the Communists after they captured Peking, but the attempt
ended when the Communist authorities seized the university on
October 12, 1950. He was refused permission to leave China, and
on July 25, 1951, was arrested as an American spy. Released from
prison in September, 1955, he wrote his account almost immediately, when the memories of days and nights of brutal interrogation, of weeks of wearing iron shackles on his ankles and wrists
with his arms bound behind his back, of lack of sleep, poor food,
filth, crowded prison cells, sickness, and cold, were all still fresh
in his mind.

Justice in the People's Republic of China, Father Rigney was
told over and over again, is different from justice in the "imperialist" countries, where prisoners are punished for what they confess:
in the People's Republic of China they are punished only for
what they do not confess, which was somehow felt to be a great
advance. Since prisoners were usually not told for what crime they

had been arrested, they would confess to almost anything—murders, misdeeds, wrong thoughts, anything that might offer release from imprisonment and torture. Father Rigney, however, was accused of being an agent of the F.B.I. or, still worse, of the C.I.A. There was no evidence whatever that he was or ever had been a spy or an agent, which made it necessary for the Communist authorities to spend days, weeks, months, and finally years, with the help of the most sophisticated methods of physical and psychological torture, to force him to confess, to break his will, and to make him see the error of his ways. Whatever its larger purpose in the strategy of world Communism may be, the fact that organized mistreatment of people on this scale can happen at all is a reflection of the pernicious belief that men are subject to no rules of conduct not of their own making, and that it is within their power to force other men to conform to their will and preconceptions.

In *A Ride to Panmunjom* Duane Thorin describes the response of a number of Americans to Communist imprisonment. Thorin grew up on a Nebraska farm, the eighth son of Swedish immigrant parents. He became a chief petty officer and then a naval flyer in World War II, and as a helicopter pilot during the Korean War had the mission of rescuing fellow Americans from behind enemy lines. On one of these missions, early in 1952, he was taken prisoner; he was released in August of the following year.

The story Thorin tells has been largely forgotten, but for many reasons should be remembered. Some of the men he describes are no credit to the society that produced them—weak, improperly trained, with little or nothing in the way of standards, beliefs, or resourcefulness to help them. But there are others we are glad to meet and to know about. As in the case of Father Rigney, one cannot help but ask: What was it all for? What purpose did it serve to devote days and weeks to "brain washing" and interrogation, to subject these young men to the most brutal physical and psychological pressure to obtain confessions to crimes that both sides knew had never happened? The collaborator was useful to the Communists, not as an individual, but as a symbol of the weakness of the society that produced him—to break his will was to break the will, in a sense, of American society also—and in the same way the prisoner who refused to give in, no matter what the provocation, maintained not only his own self-respect and integrity as a person, but that of American society as well. It is this message of the worth of the human person that Thorin's unassuming, completely unpretentious, honest book gets across to us.

The first book we published on the Middle East was Nejla Izzeddin's *The Arab World* in the spring of 1953. It included an introduction by William Ernest Hocking, who, great scholar, teacher, and man of principle that he was, said something on this general subject that made a deep impression on me then and is worth repeating now:

Our Arab neighbors . . . hold the cross-roads of three continents, and their political decisions will affect the course of world history—including our own history—for years to come . . . when the Arab world speaks with decision from its own self-consciousness of mission, there is at least a chance that the external powers which today tend to shape Arab destinies through bargains, programs, condescensions and commands, will begin to realize that there is in the wealth of Arab or Iraqi oil nothing peculiarly Arabic; whereas there is everything peculiarly Arabic in, let us say, the Koranic union of law and faith. . . . The Arab cultural contribution to the world . . . will continue . . . to yield laws, constitutions, social arrangements typically Arab, as well as great literature, just in so far as that national genius is recognized and encouraged from within and from without.

The Arab World is a substantial and beautifully written book in which the author undertakes to describe the current situation and the religious, cultural, and historical traditions of her people to the Western reader. Miss Izzeddin, a Moslem of the Druse sect, is a graduate of Vassar, and did her graduate work at the University of Chicago. She is intensely loyal to her own people, and her strong feelings are evident in her chapter on Palestine; but, for all that, her book was well received and became a selection of the History Book Club.

Our next book on a subject involving the Middle East, Alfred M. Lilienthal's *What Price Israel*, published late in 1953, lit the fires of controversy. Lilienthal had become a rather notorious figure in Zionist circles with the publication in the September, 1949, issue of *Reader's Digest* of the article "Israel's Flag Is Not Mine," in which he took the position that as an American Jew he owed no political allegiance to Israel; for him, his Jewishness was a matter of religious tradition and in no sense one of nationality. Zionist circles promptly accused him of irresponsibility, anti-Semitism, even of being an outright traitor to his people.

Lilienthal's position was well known to me as a result of the *Reader's Digest* article, and one he had written for *Human Events*. I was also aware of the controversy the *Digest* article had aroused, but I felt that Lilienthal was an honorable man and that his position deserved a hearing. Before agreeing to publish his manuscript I had it read by two men whose judgment I respected. William S. Schlamm was a Jewish refugee from Austria and a distinguished journalist, and had been one of the chief editors of *Fortune*. Rabbi Elmer Berger, who was associated with the American Council for Judaism, was committed to the position that Judaism was a religious tradition and in no sense a matter of either race or nationality. As it worked out, Willi Schlamm agreed to make rather extensive editorial revisions involving matters of style, and Rabbi Berger recommended some modifications, mostly of a factual nature, all of which were incorporated in the manuscript. Both, I should add, strongly recommended its publication.

Lilienthal begins with a fairly detailed account of the history of the Zionist movement and of the circumstances of the origins of the State of Israel. He points out that Zionism had its origins in the anti-Semitism of nineteenth-century Russia, and became a world-wide movement as a result of the Dreyfus case, the migration of several million Russian Jews to the United States, and finally the trauma of German National Socialism and all that went with it.

Well aware though he is that Zionism arose out of a long history of persecution, Lilienthal is sharply critical of the methods used to make real the dream of a Jewish homeland, including the Balfour Declaration of World War I. This spoke in favor of the establishment in Palestine of a national home for the Jewish people, but contained the proviso that nothing would be done to prejudice the civil and religious rights of the existing non-Jewish communities of Palestine, or the right and political status enjoyed by Jews in any other country. Its primary motivation was not justice but political advantage, as Winston Churchill remarked in the House of Commons in July, 1937, calling it a measure taken with the object of promoting the general victory of the Allies. The British effort to support the Zionist cause was later rewarded by bitter criticism and open warfare when, following World War II, the British government, in accordance with its obligation to protect the Arab population and to maintain the peace, limited Jewish immigration into Palestine.

Lilienthal has much to say about the cynical use of the plight of the homeless Jewish refugees in Europe by the Zionists to further their political objectives, and about the tactics used by both the Zionists and the United States government to force through the United Nations the resolution that resulted in the partition of Palestine and the establishment of Israel. The politics of pressure reached its low point, perhaps, with President Truman's hasty, ill-considered, and politically motivated decision of May 14, 1948, to grant diplomatic recognition to Israel. Lilienthal's detailed, carefully documented account of this sordid episode makes it clear that Truman's sole consideration was the impact of recognition on the election the following fall. It had nothing to do with justice, with the welfare of the people involved, whether Arab or Jew, or with the national interests of the United States. It was just such considerations of the loss of the next election, Lilienthal observed, that caused James Forrestal to remark, "I think it is about time that somebody should pay some consideration to whether we might not lose the United States."

Lilienthal is also critical of the claim that Israel is not a state for its citizens alone, but for the whole Jewish people. The State of Israel exists, and it is the home of 3.5 million people, of whom some 85% are Jewish. Many have given their lives in its defense; furthermore, Israel in a sense represents the Jewish people's answer to persecution, and in particular to Hitler's "final solution." The circumstances of its origin clearly make Israel a state like no other. All this Lilienthal, I am sure, would readily admit; but in the early 1950's he believed that if Israel was to survive it would have to accept the practices and the status usually associated with a normal state. Among other things it "must solemnly withdraw all claims to the fealty of anybody but its own citizens." In addition, he said, the Jews of Israel would have to learn to live not only within but *with* their environment, which would mean living at peace with their Arab neighbors. He insisted that Israel must at least execute the various decrees of the United Nations that had created it, which include international rule over Jerusalem, the sacred home of three world religions. Nearly twenty-five years have passed since Lilienthal made these recommendations. Much blood has been spilled in the Middle East and peace seems more remote than ever, but his position still has much to be said for it.

Reading the reviews of *What Price Israel* again after more than twenty years I was pleasantly surprised at the generally balanced impression they make. Some reviewers violently rejected Lilienthal's whole argument, and in their passion distorted his viewpoint and did him an injustice; but many others presented it fairly and adequately. A long, rather violent review in the Washington *Post* began: "This anti-Israel polemic was written by a Jew whose hostility to his own people and to Judaism is quite evident. The book is a pathetic parade of abusive epithets, distorted history, and Jewish self-hate." But the Washington *Star* review observed: "The fervor and emotion with which Mr. Lilienthal writes reflect his obvious devotion to his Jewish faith and to his American nationality. . . . What he has written may be controversial but it can be read with profit by other Americans, Christian or Jewish." Erwin D. Canham, the distinguished editor of the *Christian Science Monitor*, in a long review in the *Saturday Review*, called the book important and insisted that it be taken seriously. The *National Jewish Monthly* ended a rather long review, "you will see in this book a death-blow aimed at justice and peace. There is little doubt that it will be exultingly received in every anti-Jewish, pro-Arab, reactionary quarter in the land." But Rabbi William A. Rosenblum, of Temple Israel in New York, wrote, "It is a stimulatingly written, sometimes provocative book, which every person interested in the solution of the problem should read." We could certainly not complain that the book was ignored. In spite of the reluctance of some bookstores to handle it, *What Price Israel* went through seven hardbound printings and then came out in paperback.

We published four other books on the Middle East, all in one way or another involved with the issue of Palestine. The most significant, perhaps, was Freda Utley's *Will the Middle East Go West?*, which appeared in 1957. Always the champion of the unpopular cause, Miss Utley spent some time in the Middle East in the latter part of 1956, shortly after President Eisenhower and Secretary of State Dulles had brought to a halt what came to be known as the Suez War, the British/French/Israeli attack on Egypt in retaliation for nationalization of the Suez Canal. Miss Utley, drawing a parallel with the Communist conquest of China, argued for a policy of justice and fair dealing with the Arab nations. She believed that the long record of broken promises by the Western nations in their relations with the people of the Middle East, their colonial policies, and their unqualified support of Israel could lead to a similar disaster. Fully aware of the claims of both sides in the Arab-Israeli conflict, and as always the advocate of justice, she wrote:

Unjust to the Arabs as was the partition of Palestine . . . Israel has earned her right to exist. We would be committing yet another injustice in the cycle were we to let Arab extremists acquire the means to destroy her. Nor can we demand that Israel abandon her strategy of defense by attack unless she can win security by other means. But . . . she must accept her status as one among many Middle Eastern states. The plain fact is that, without American financial and political support, Israel cannot live without the Arabs, and must learn how to live with them . . . freedom and justice for Israel depend on freedom and justice for the Arabs.

We also published in 1957 a book on the Arab refugees by the well-known Swedish photographer Per-Orlow Anderson, *They Are Human Too*. It brought us face to face with the tragedy of the Arab refugees, whom he photographed crowded into the inhospitable Gaza Strip. One unexpected consequence of the book's publication was the visit of an agent from the F.B.I., who had been sent in to make some inquiries about its author. He was obviously only carrying out orders, and as an amateur photographer soon became far more interested in Anderson's professional skill and techniques than in the purpose of his visit, whatever it may have been. This was one of the less serious calls by government agents of one kind or another that frequently followed the publication of a book that displeased some group or individual of influence.

There was also Ethel Mannin's *Road to Beersheeba*, a novel we published in 1964, whose purpose was to show the impact of the exodus of the Palestinian Arabs on the people involved. A well-known and successful English author, she came to me when her regular New York publisher found it inexpedient to bring out a book on this particular subject. Arnold Toynbee said in a letter to her: "You have succeeded in doing what is perhaps the most important thing a Westerner can do for the Arabs: you have made it impossible for the Western reader to go on supposing that the Arabs are not human beings like himself. . . . In this book you are exposing one of the biggest pieces of injustice in the present-day world."

It was too much to hope that our books on the Middle East would have any influence on the course of events. The Suez War was followed by the 1967 War. The Zionists became increasingly

intransigent, the Arabs increasingly embittered, and the plight of
the Arab refugees no better. Hearing that the Arab teacher, philosopher, and statesman Charles H. Malik was teaching at Notre
Dame University, I went to see him, to ask if he might be willing
to write something that could lead to a solution. He was a most
impressive man, serious, deeply religious, and of great experience,
but on the subject of the Arab-Israeli conflict, he was utterly pessimistic. The situation, he said, had reached such a point of hatred
and bitterness that to suggest anything would be useless and might
even make matters worse. The Jews of Israel would eventually
have to accept the fact that they live in the Middle East and must
become a part of it. Their drive, their organizational and technical
skills, their restless energy could be of great benefit to the Arab
world; and from the Arabs they could learn something of patience,
of the acceptance of things and their consequences as they are and
must be. It could be a fruitful relationship. At the time we talked,
he thought it best only to wait, pray, and work quietly.

7

THE NEW DEAL,
THE UNITED NATIONS,
LABOR UNIONS:
A RECONSIDERATION

THE location of my publishing firm, in Chicago, and the position taken by many of our books inevitably led to the rumor that, if not a subsidiary of Colonel McCormick's Chicago *Tribune*, we were at least in one way or another associated with it. Although I was on friendly terms with a number of people on the *Tribune* staff, particularly George Morgenstern, who when I first knew him was an editorial writer and later became chief of the editorial page, I met Colonel McCormick only once, and then in the company of William Henry Chamberlin, who had expressed a wish to meet the representative figure of Middle Western isolationism. The Colonel received us in his rather feudal office, high above Michigan Avenue at the top of his Gothic tower. He was a tall, erect, distinguished-looking man, who, with his white hair, blue eyes, ruddy complexion, white mustache, and in his manner and dress, conveyed the impression that he might have come from the English landed aristocracy. He was perfectly cordial, but gave us clearly to understand that our rather similar views on such matters as foreign policy and the administration in Washington were no basis for familiarity.

Although there was no connection of any kind, the *Tribune* treated us generously in its news columns, on its editorial page, and in its book-review section, and we published two books by one of its leading correspondents, Chesly Manly, who in his opinions, general attitude, and manner of expressing himself must have been as representative of McCormick's *Tribune* as it was possible to be. Manly had been for a number of years the *Tribune* correspondent at the U.S. Senate, and later at the United Nations; toward the end of his career he worked on the editorial page with Morgenstern. Manly and Morgenstern were among the last representative figures of the old Chicago *Tribune*. They were not taken in by pretense or overawed by position; they had strong opinions, and the skill and experience to express them effectively. With their rather sardonic sense of humor, and the realistic way they viewed and appraised the world, they were good company; I remember them both with esteem and affection.

For all its provincialism, the Chicago *Tribune* in those days was a strong voice and a bulwark of what we once thought were the American virtues of patriotism, self-reliance, and individual freedom. And however much one may have disagreed with it, it was always evident that it was representative not of an amorphous corporation trying to please everybody, but of a strong personality. The Chicago *Tribune* was Robert R. McCormick, for better or worse, and there was no question about where it stood. It was fashionable in certain circles to ascribe Colonel McCormick's isolationism and his antiestablishment views toward the British Empire and the eastern seaboard to an inferiority complex he had supposedly acquired as a boy in an English boarding school, when his father was American ambassador, or as a Midwestern undergraduate at Yale. This, in my opinion, was complete nonsense. Coming from a family that had played a leading part in the development of the Middle West from empty prairies to one of the most productive regions of the world, and a region, moreover, with a strong sense of identity with which he strongly identified himself, and in complete control of its leading newspaper, Colonel McCormick can have felt no compulsion to harbor inferiority complexes toward anyone.

Someone on the *Tribune* staff once told me a story that says much about the Colonel, as he was called, and about the position of the Chicago *Tribune* in the Middle West. Sometime after the war, when feelings were running high, an editorial writer on the *Tribune* spoke of the "anti-American New York *Times*." An official of the *Times* soon called the Colonel and told him that this was going too far, and that the *Times* in consequence would have to sever the relationship for the exchange of news they had had with the *Tribune* for many years. Colonel McCormick was most apologetic, assured the *Times* official that he had been out of town when the incident happened, and that the editorial writers were under strict instructions to be most circumspect in their treatment of the New York *Times*. On thinking it all over later in the day, however, the Colonel began to feel differently, and sent a telegram to the *Times* to the effect that if they wished to discontinue their relationship it would be entirely agreeable to him. This was followed by a telegram from the *Times* saying an official would be arriving the next morning in Chicago to make the necessary arrangements. By the time someone from the *Tribune* met the *Times* man at the airport, a telegram had come from New York instructing him to return at once; the old relationship would be continued as before. After a discussion at the *Times*, it had been decided that if they wanted news from the Middle West, the dominant position of the Chicago *Tribune* made it the only source.

If a further example is needed to illustrate McCormick's independence, there is this story told me by the head of the largest Chicago department store. Following a particularly virulent *Tribune* attack on Felix Frankfurter—this was after Frankfurter had appeared as a character witness for Alger Hiss—a delegation from some of the other State Street stores called on the Colonel to protest. McCormick told them, in substance, that he determined the policies of the Chicago *Tribune*, not its advertisers, and if they wished to advertise somewhere else, they were free to do so.

For all its many admirable qualities, it cannot be said that the *Tribune* was a great cultural influence. Its program for Chicago consisted of such things as a convention center on the lake front, the straightening of the Outer Drive, and a subway for the Loop. The book-review section was mediocre and of no distinction, and Claudia Cassidy, although a skillful writer with a deadly aim, did little to raise her readers' understanding of music. The editorials, on the other hand, no matter what their subject, were pointed, well written, and unequivocal, and always stimulating to read. Richard Weaver once told me that he often used editorials from the Chicago *Tribune* in his classes at the University of Chicago as examples of rhetorical excellence. As the publisher of a newspaper with a mass circulation, Colonel McCormick had to put up with such things as the *Tribune*'s "Chicagoland Music Festival," but on his editorial page he was able to demonstrate that he valued good writing and clear expression.

The first book we published by Chesly Manly had been written to appear serially in the newspaper; for some reason this idea was dropped and the manuscript was offered to us. Fred Wieck, who was our editor at the time, skillfully rearranged the manuscript and made what had been intended for publication as a series of newspaper articles into a powerful book. The title gave us some trouble, but after many tries and much discussion we settled on *The Twenty-Year Revolution: From Roosevelt to Eisenhower*, and published the book early in 1954.

It was Manly's purpose to show the fundamental change that had taken place in our country in the twenty years following the inauguration of Franklin D. Roosevelt in 1933. As an honest and experienced newspaperman, Manly considered it his task to bring the facts together. He made no attempt to analyze or explain; all he wanted to do was to tell what happened, and he did not mince words. He identified those who were in positions of influence, quoted what they said, and made it all into a coherent whole.

If one wants to know how we got where we are, how we became saddled with a staggering public debt, inflation, a gigantic bureaucracy, a world situation requiring an enormous military apparatus, and a system of taxation that makes every person a prey of the tax collector, Manly showed it all, step by step. For the quotations alone and Manly's skill in identifying the influences that determined American policy during those fateful years, *The Twenty-Year Revolution* is an invaluable source, whether one agrees with its premise or not.

In the chapter headed "Roosevelt Rebels against the Constitution," for example, Manly describes the process by which the Supreme Court, from having been the defender of the Constitution, became the means by which the arbitrary intervention of the federal government into every aspect of life was institutionalized. He pointed out that when the Supreme Court invalidated the Guffey-Vinson Coal Act, on May 18, 1936, the majority opinion held that "the relation of employer to employee is a local relation," and therefore beyond the control of the federal government. In a separate concurring opinion, Chief Justice Hughes declared that Congress has adequate authority to maintain the orderly conduct of interstate commerce but may not use it to regulate activities and relations within the states that affect interstate commerce only indirectly. Otherwise, Hughes said, in view of the multitude of indirect effects, Congress in its discretion could assume control of virtually all the activities of the people to the subversion of the fundamental principles of the Constitution. But in its decisions to uphold the Wagner Labor Relations Act, the Social Security Act, and the Agricultural Adjustment Act, which followed President Roosevelt's attempt to "pack the court," the court completely reversed itself, and opened the door to government control of virtually all the activities of the people.

One of the most revealing and devastating chapters in the book, " 'Unconditional Surrender'—to Stalin," contains an account of how, in Manly's opinion, the ending of the war with Japan was deliberately postponed several months, long enough for Russia to become at least a technical belligerent and, in consequence, to reap a lion's share of the spoils. In late May, 1945, Acting Secretary of State Joseph C. Grew gave instructions for the preparation of a document that would set forth the policies that the United States would follow in the event Japan should surrender. Dean Acheson and Archibald MacLeish, who were then both assistant secretaries, strongly objected—Manly believes at least partly on the advice of Owen Lattimore, who at the time commanded great influence in the State Department—and the project was dropped. The conditions that provided the basis of the Japanese surrender the following August, however, were almost identical to those of the Grew declaration, and Manly produced convincing evidence that the Japanese would have accepted such terms in May had they been offered, which was Grew's intention. It seems obvious, therefore, that the only purpose served by the bloody fighting from May to August, and the dropping of the atomic bombs on Nagasaki and Hiroshima, for which the United States will forever bear moral opprobrium, was to give Russia an opportunity to share in the victory. Manly quoted Lattimore, on a radio program sponsored by the University of Chicago on July 8, 1945, as having "called for a period of 'good old chaos' for Japan." The Communists may have benefited from a period of "good old chaos" in Japan, but certainly no one else.

The critical response to *The Twenty-Year Revolution* was fairly predictable. The New York *Times* ended a rather long review by R. L. Duffus, a member of its editorial board, with the recommendation that thoughtful people should avoid the impulse to drop the book into the wastebasket. "It explains in good English the way some people's minds work. Mr. Manly speaks for quite a few people who can't or won't read." The *Saturday Review*, in a very short comment, described it as "a cold blast of Midwestern air from the U.N. correspondent of the Chicago *Tribune*," and the Springfield *Republican* as "another unrealistic tirade against what appears to be inevitable social progress." But *The Twenty-Year Revolution* appeared on the New York *Times* best-seller list for four weeks, and may fairly be called a successful book.

Chesly Manly's *The U.N. Record* was written to mark the tenth anniversary of the coming into force of the United Nations Charter. For eight of those years Manly had been the Chicago *Tribune* correspondent at the U.N., had attended its sessions, had met and come to know its leading figures, and had become thoroughly familiar with its day-to-day operations and with what went on behind the scenes. He compares the rather grandiose intentions proclaimed in the Charter, in which the peoples of the United Nations expressed their determination to save succeeding generations from the scourge of war, to take effective collective measures against aggression, to practice tolerance and live together in peace, to promote respect for human rights and fundamental freedoms, with the actual accomplishments of the United Nations during the first ten years of its existence. He begins at the beginning: he compares the declaration of intention to practice respect for human rights and fundamental freedoms with what Roosevelt, Stalin, and Churchill were actually doing at the Yalta Conference when the basic lines of the Charter were agreed to. The United Nations, he concluded, was "conceived in iniquity . . . [and] born a fraud upon mankind's instinctive yearning for peace. It is a hoax of monumental proportions. . . ."

He asserts with his customary directness, "the U.N. has no moral authority, and the reason is that it has no moral integrity. . . . The member governments are composed of individuals, who are motivated not by moral principles but by what they conceive to be the best interests of their own countries if they are honorable men or by baser considerations if they are not."

After giving a number of specific examples of the complete

inability of the U.N. to maintain international peace and security, Manly devotes a chapter to Korea, which was regarded as the supreme test of the United Nations. The chapter is a masterpiece of historical writing: it is meticulously documented, tells the political history of the Korean "police action" from beginning to end, and draws the only possible conclusion. It was a war that cost the United States 136,916 casualties, including 33,417 dead, and ended with the situation exactly as it had been before it all started, with Korea divided at the thirty-eighth parallel.

It is worthwhile to recall the background of the American intervention in Korea. The decision to divide Korea between Russian and U.S. occupation forces was made at Yalta, and the thirty-eighth parallel as the dividing line, according to Dean Acheson, was suggested by Secretary of War Henry L. Stimson. In 1947 General Albert C. Wedemeyer reported that the Russians were training and equipping an army in North Korea and predicted an invasion of the South if U.S. troops should be withdrawn. This report was suppressed by General Marshall. On September 17, 1947, the Korean question was submitted to the General Assembly of the U.N., which appointed a commission to supervise nationwide elections and the formation of a national government. The Communists refused to permit the commission to enter the North, but an election was held in the South, under U.N. supervision, in May, 1948, as a result of which Syngman Rhee organized a government. On September 18, 1948, Soviet Russia informed the United States that the evacuation of its troops from North Korea would be completed by the end of the year. On December 17, 1948, the General Assembly of the U.N. adopted a resolution calling for the evacuation of all occupation forces, and on June 29, 1949, the U.N. commission reported that all American forces had been withdrawn. On January 12, 1950, in a public speech, Dean Acheson, who had succeeded General Marshall as secretary of state, declared that Korea was beyond the "defense perimeter" of the United States. On June 25, 1950, South Korea was invaded. Although the United States bore almost the entire burden of the war, it was conducted as an action of the United Nations, a fact which, as General Mark Clark was later to put it, made it "a war we were not permitted to win."

Manly makes the following observation about Truman's dismissal of MacArthur from his command:

The real tragedy was not Truman's removal of MacArthur but the failure of a supine Congress to remove Truman. If an army commander, on his own initiative, should wilfully submit to rules of combat giving the enemy an extraordinary advantage and multiplying the slaughter of his own troops he would be shot. Clearly, then, a commander-in-chief who does this should be impeached and removed from office, in the manner prescribed by the Constitution, for "high crimes and misdemeanors."

I sent a copy of the book, with a letter, to former President Truman, who, in a personal letter to me, responded as follows:

I have been reading the *U.N. Record* by Chesly Manly. It is a most interesting book for the simple reason that there is hardly a paragraph without an untrue statement in it.

I am sorry that this is the case, but of course a man who has been associated all his life with the Chicago *Tribune* would be expected to do just what Mr. Manly has done—tell the truth about nothing.

My final encounter with the Truman administration was the publication in 1956 of Jules Abels's *The Truman Scandals*. An advance copy sent to Truman brought forth the anticipated response, this time not directly from him but from his secretary:

Mr. Truman received your note of the 13th and a copy of your scandal book. A cursory examination of the publication convinced him that it is probably one of the most comprehensive collections of bold lies and calculated misrepresentations of facts to appear since the opposition party initiated its efforts to discredit the achievements of the Democratic Party.

Jules Abels was a graduate of Columbia University Law School, had been a Littauer Fellow at Harvard, a member of the editorial staff of *Newsweek*, and executive editor of the Research Institute of America. When he wrote our book he was economic adviser to the administrator of the Small Business Administration. His book is carefully documented, and for the most part is taken from the official records of the various congressional investigations conducted during the Truman and Eisenhower administrations; the rest comes from court records and other public sources. The book was not written as a campaign document or for partisan purposes, but is the work of a serious man who was outraged by the stealing, lying, influence peddling, and flagrant violations of public trust that permeated the Truman administration, and as a responsible citizen he assumed the task of gathering the facts and making them available.

Harry Truman's school of politics was the Kansas City Pendergast machine. As President, by his own attitude and that of the men around him, he set the tone of his administration. "Never," Abels remarked at the beginning of his book, "did a political party have such riches at its disposal."

There were huge governmental expenditures in a budget many times what it had been before the war. There were billions in war surplus to be disgorged. There was cheap, long-term government credit to be had. There were opportunities in new programs, such as that for housing. Most important of all, there was the tax system, the most significant element in business life in the postwar period, wonderfully intricate with countless opportunities for special rulings, immunities, and loopholes.

The stage was set for a drama that only an enormously rich country could afford, and that would be tolerated only by a country many of whose citizens have been led to believe that government is there for the benefit of those fortunate enough to be able to take advantage of its power to collect taxes.

Abels devotes one of the first chapters of his book to the "President's Pals." There was Major General Harry Vaughan, the President's military aide and an old friend from the National Guard. General Vaughan made a practice of arranging such things as special tax concessions, military contracts, or surplus-property deals in exchange for campaign contributions and favors to himself. He was the sponsor of John Maragon, who with Vaughan's help became involved, shortly after the war, in bringing large quantities of perfume and essential oils into the country on military planes without bothering to pay duty. Maragon was finally sent to prison for perjury, but he was "a lovable sort of chap," Vaughan assured the Senate subcommittee that tried to get at the bottom of it all.

The President's appointment secretary, Matthew J. Connelly, was convicted for involvement in the tax-fixing case of Irving Sachs; and his administrative assistant, Donald S. Dawson, through his position in the White House, exerted great influence on the activities of the R.F.C. He was a close friend of E. Merle Young, another Truman protégé, who was involved in arranging a number of highly questionable loans by the R.F.C. at great profit to himself, and was eventually sent to prison for perjury. The President's personal physician, General Wallace Graham, was involved in commodity speculation, as were many others with access to confidential government information. The President's close friend William M. Boyle, Jr., was forced to resign as chairman of the Democratic National Committee for influence peddling in connection with an R.F.C. loan, and the manager of Truman's 1935 senatorial campaign, Paul L. Dillon, was convicted of tax fraud. And so it went.

One activity the federal government usually conducts with some degree of efficiency is to collect taxes, but during the Truman administration even the internal revenue system was on the point of breaking down. Robert E. Hannegan, of the twenty-first ward of St. Louis, who had provided the margin of 7,000 votes Truman needed to win the Democratic nomination for the Senate in 1940, with Truman's help was made commissioner of Internal Revenue in 1943. Under Hannegan's administration and that of his hand-picked successor, Joseph D. Nunan, the system became so corrupt that Congressman Robert W. Kean, chairman of the House sub-committee that investigated the Internal Revenue Service, was led to remark in February, 1953, "If the Bureau of Internal Revenue had continued to operate as it did in the last few years, there was great danger that, through lack of confidence by the public, our whole tax-collection system might have fallen down." Nunan, it later developed, had not even bothered to report his own income while he was commissioner of Internal Revenue, and on June 28, 1954, was sentenced to five years in jail for tax evasion. When he resigned as commissioner in 1947 under the pressure of disclosures of tax fixing, favoritism, and incompetence, Truman, ever loyal to a political associate, wrote to him, "I desire to assure you of my deepest appreciation and that of the Nation whose interests you guarded with such vigilance."

Corruption at the top, needless to say, led to corruption through the entire internal revenue system; three of the worst districts, according to Abels, were Boston, New York, and San Francisco. "During the Truman administration," he wrote, "nine revenue collectors were fired in connection with tax frauds. Between January 1, 1951, and April 10, 1952, a period when Internal Revenue, under severe pressure, was moved to act to cleanse itself, a total of 177 internal revenue officials were fired—72 for 'irregularities' involving their relations with taxpayers; 18 for 'embezzlement';

and 87 for 'improper activities' not desirable in the service. More than two dozen had been jailed for shakedowns, connivance with racketeers, and for accepting fees and bribes. The loss of revenue to the United States Treasury is beyond calculation."

President Truman gave no indication that he was personally disturbed by the mounting evidence of corruption in his administration, and, instead of taking measures to clean things up, he did everything in his power to block investigations and to protect those involved. One of the worst scandals concerned the Reconstruction Finance Corporation, which had been a relatively efficient and effective government agency; under the Truman administration it was literally destroyed and finally disbanded. For his thorough, careful, and expertly conducted investigation of the R.F.C., Senator J. William Fulbright was rewarded with the epithet "an over-educated s.o.b." by the President, and his report was labeled "asinine." Truman, it appeared, was far more incensed by those who exposed corruption than by those who were responsible for it.

When the pressure for some sort of action to clean up "the mess in Washington," as Adlai Stevenson was later to call it, became irresistible, Truman characteristically chose none other than his attorney general, J. Howard McGrath, to do the job—a choice, as Abels put it, that "floored just about everybody," since McGrath, as head of the Justice Department, one of the most scandal-ridden agencies of all, had been no more energetic in rooting out corruption than had the President. McGrath appointed a New York Republican, Newbold Morris, assistant attorney general with responsibility to investigate corruption; but when it became evident that Morris took his appointment seriously and actually intended to do something, his services were quickly dispensed with. In this connection, it is interesting to recall the background of J. Howard McGrath. McGrath had succeeded Robert Hannegan as chairman of the Democratic National Committee, and following the Democratic victory in 1948 was made attorney general. He had been a U.S. senator from Rhode Island and, before that, governor, a period during which he amassed a substantial fortune, by, according to Abels, "a judicious mixture of politics and business," the business being race tracks. McGrath's department was investigated by the Chelf Committee of the Eighty-second Congress, which had this to say about him:

He exhibited a deplorable lack of knowledge of the Department he was supposed to administer. He lacked information as to its organization and personnel and specific events of importance were unknown to him. . . . Mr. McGrath showed no enthusiasm for purging his department of wrongdoers or incompetence . . . his testimony and his record as Attorney General indicate that he was content to let the status quo remain without knowing what the status quo was.

Harry Truman owed his rise in politics to the Pendergast organization of Kansas City and to the Democratic Party, and he was always intensely loyal to both. One cannot refrain from asking, however, where his loyalty to party ended and his sense of obligation to his office as President of the United States began. One of his first acts as President was to dismiss Maurice Mulligan, who as U.S. attorney for western Missouri had prosecuted the Pendergast gang, secured 259 convictions for vote fraud, and sent Tom Pendergast himself to jail for tax evasion. At the same time Truman pardoned the fifteen Pendergast people still in jail. In Mulligan's place as U.S. attorney, Truman appointed Sam Wear, who had been chairman of the Democratic State Committee of Missouri. Tom Pendergast had died in the meantime, but the office wall of his nephew and successor, James M. Pendergast, proudly displayed a photograph of the President of the United States with the inscription at the bottom, "To James M. Pendergast—friend, comrade, and adviser."

Abels gives a full account of the manner in which the 1947 investigation of wholesale vote frauds in Kansas City was frustrated and finally brought to an abrupt end when the door of the vault in which the questionable ballots had been stored was mysteriously blown open and the ballots themselves were stolen. The Democratic-controlled Chelf Committee pointed out, Abels remarked, that everyone who took part in the aborted investigation was rewarded: Tom Clark, the Attorney General, went to the Supreme Court; another official became head of the antitrust division; one who might have been subjected to embarrassing questions was given a comfortable job abroad; and Theron Lamar Caudle, Assistant Attorney General in charge of the case, was given the choice plum of assistant attorney general in charge of the tax division. But the temptations of this office proved to be too much for Caudle; he was later dismissed in disgrace in connection with a "tax fix"—it was one among many—and finally indicted and convicted.

In defense of such politics as the Truman administration practiced in almost classic fashion, it is argued that traditional machine politics, in spite of its corruption, graft, and favoritism, is less burdensome to the taxpayer than government by ideological do-gooders, who usually do not steal, but saddle society with crusades and uplift programs which, in the long run, are far more damaging. Boss Tweed, it is argued, was less destructive than Mayor Lindsay. There is no doubt a large element of truth in this argument, but Harry Truman's Fair Deal represented a conscious amalgam of the two kinds of politics: it was the politics of "compassion" in the service of a political organization operating on the principle that the primary purpose of public office is to maintain power for the organization or party. The Fair Deal was the final consummation of the merger of liberal ideology and machine politics; the effectiveness of such a combination in maintaining political power and its results are graphically demonstrated by the example of New York City.

In retrospect, after the Watergate experience, the response of the liberal press to the Abels book is most revealing. The reviewers for the New York *Times*, the New York *Herald Tribune*, the Atlanta *Journal*, the *Saturday Review*, and the Louisville *Courier-Journal* were all inclined to take a rather benign, "objective" view of corruption in the Truman administration. Such things did happen, and this was unfortunate, but they must be viewed in the context of the Truman administration as a whole. A certain amount of political larceny is unavoidable in a democracy and has always been a feature of American life; one must consider the practical needs of a political party for campaign funds; the amounts involved were petty; and so on. Walter Millis, in a review of several Truman books in the *Saturday Review*, gave Abels credit for "enormous industry" and "remarkable mastery of complicated details" but was not convinced; Millis argued that the things Abels described are an inevitable consequence of modern government, and in any case were mostly in the "peanut category." The Louisville *Courier-Journal* said that the book was "out of focus," and the New York *Times* based its rejection of the author's picture of the Truman administration on the assertion that the book was "partisan" and that there was "nothing particularly unique in these twice-told tales." The Washington *Post* did not in those days have the crusading zeal against presidential abuse of power it was later to acquire, and gave the book only a very brief notice, which said little more than that Abels "bogs down in statistical dichotomy."

None of these reviewers made any attempt to come to grips with, or even to mention, the basic issue the book raises—namely, the concept of government, and its long-run effects, of which such scandals were only the symptom. The scandals of the Truman administration were not isolated incidents; they permeated the entire structure of government and were an integral part of it. It is this fact and the reasons for it that are essential, not whether the amounts involved were large or small.

We came through all that not entirely unscathed, but we survived, and a few years later were able to survive the New Frontier and the Great Society. All of which, however, leads to the question: how much more of this sort of thing—in the age of atomic fission and intercontinental ballistic missiles, in a world grown smaller but not more friendly, with severely depleted natural resources and facing the problems of pollution, destruction of the environment, and inflation—can even a society as rich and productive as ours put up with?

In the book *Social Security: Fact and Fancy*, which we published in 1956, Dillard Stokes gives a striking and depressing account of how what began as a financially sound program with a specific, limited, and reasonable objective, has been subverted into a colossal bureaucracy, which takes an ever-growing share of the wages of more than nine-tenths of American workers, makes commitments that cannot be kept, and is well on the way to becoming a serious threat to the stability of the nation.

The first Social Security Act was passed in 1935, during the Great Depression, when more people drew relief than paid income taxes, because 10 million men were out of work. The original program was established to fulfill a specific, limited, and needed function: to provide supplemental income, beginning at age sixty-five, for those it covered. It was financed by a tax of 2% of covered wages up to $3,000 a year, of which one-half was paid by the employer; the rate was to rise to a permanent level of 6% by 1949. The only benefit provided was a monthly income of ten to eighty-five dollars per month, which began at age sixty-five. As Stokes said, under the first Social Security Act there was no way a worker could lose all the money he paid in. The act guaranteed that he or his estate would get it back with interest. The vital point is that the first Social Security Act gave a worker something definite for his money, something of fixed value, which he could not lose *while the 1935 act was in force.*

The one great flaw in the original act, in Stokes's opinion, was the escape clause, by which Congress retained the right to make amendments at its pleasure. "The plan," he goes on to say, "was put on a sound basis. The people very nearly paid for what they got and—except for the escape clause—they were sure of getting what they paid for. Social Security was in fact a means by which people were to provide for themselves; it required nobody to support anybody else."

It was not long before the bureaucrats of the new Social Security Administration began to have visions; nor did it take Congress long to discover the vote-getting possibilities in a government program that seemed to have vast sums of money at its disposal, of which every family in the country was aware. Some hint of what was to come was indicated by the line of argument taken by the government attorneys in defending the constitutionality of the first Social Security Act before the Supreme Court. Although Social Security had been presented to the public as a form of insurance, and the payments by wage earners and employers as premiums that went into a reserve fund, the government attorneys held that such payments were taxes, like any other. As for the matter of insurance, Stokes said that the insurance theory was solemnly disavowed, the savings-investment-annuity theory camouflaged, and the whole program put to the Supreme Court on the public-charity/general-welfare theory. That was the basis on which the court upheld the constitutionality of the act.

The backers of Social Security, Stokes believed, with the Supreme Court decision of 1937, had solved their original dilemma. Congress and the American public would not, in 1935, have accepted the sort of broad welfare program the administrators of the act and its original backers really wanted; and the court would not have declared the act constitutional if it had in fact been an insurance system run by the government. The real beginning of the bureaucratic colossus we now know as the Department of Health, Education, and Welfare came with the 1939 amendments of the Social Security Act, which completely changed the structure of the system. Equity ceased to be its guiding principle, said Stokes, and adequacy became the standard. Instead of paying for what they get and getting what they pay for, the people pay what the government requires and get what the government thinks they ought to have, on conditions the government imposes. The money-back guarantee disappeared, and in 1939 so did the requirement of actuarial soundness written into the law of 1935. With this it became possible for a worker to lose everything he is forced to put into Social Security.

In a moment of amazing candor, Stokes remarks, certain officials of the Social Security Administration pointed out that Congress did not know what it was doing when it wrecked the program of self-sufficiency and put the whole population on public charity in their years of retirement. But it was Congress that passed the law and Congress that increased benefits in almost every election year since, and in so doing brought the program ever closer to bankruptcy. By 1980, under the present law, Social Security taxes will come to 12.26% of the first $25,900 of salary or wages, one-half paid by the employer and one-half by the employee, but the tax is still not high enough to cover the benefits voted by Congress and by 1990 will come to 15.3% on a still-undetermined, but higher, base income. Congress has been most generous in making handsome payments to current beneficiaries out of Social Security taxes being paid by wage earners still years away from retirement, but the day of reckoning Stokes predicted in 1956 will soon be upon us. The accrued liability of the benefits voted and promised by Congress is estimated in the trillions of dollars. Where is money in such an amount to come from, and how much will it buy if and when it is paid out?

One of the objectives Dr. Arthur Altmeyer, the first administrator, had in mind when he prepared the 1939 revision of the Social Security law, was "redistribution of income." He thought that those earning more should contribute to the support of those earning less. In this respect, at least, Social Security has been eminently successful. As is the case with so many government programs, the producers support a vast horde of consumers. There are not only the hundreds of thousands who receive far more from Social Security than they have ever paid in, at the expense of those who will receive far less; there is also the army of bureaucrats who administer the program, whose salaries are paid from the payroll deductions of all those compelled by law to come into the program.

Dillard Stokes was a lawyer, a member of the bar of the District of Columbia, and admitted to practice before the Supreme Court. He had worked on special assignments for several newspapers, including the Washington *Post,* and had made it his business to become thoroughly familiar with the workings of Social Security. His book on the subject is carefully researched, competently put together, and factual in every way. Published as it was during the golden years of the Eisenhower administration, however, it attracted almost no attention. Social Security taxes exceeded current payments, though not accrued liabilities, Congress could be generous with benefits, and recipients were grateful for their government checks. Why worry about what might happen in twenty or thirty years? Among the very few reviews was one in the New York *Times* by Arthur Larson, who had been under secretary of labor. Larson was scornful about Stokes's predictions, and about the many instances he cited, all based on actual cases, of flagrant injustice. "All of his shocking examples," Larson said, "can be classified under two headings—policy limitations and transitional inequities." This same Arthur Larson appeared as the author of a bulletin issued by the government under the title "Know Your Social Security." In this bulletin we are told, "The benefits belong to you as of right. You do not have to beg or apologize. The benefits are yours—bought and paid for. They are not a handout." This is simply not true, as Larson must have known. The benefits are indeed paid for, in many cases several times over, but they do not "belong to you." They belong to the United States government, and are paid out at the discretion of Congress.

Nowhere has the combination of liberal ideology with vote-getting politics had more spectacular results than in the rise of the labor unions into a position of supreme power in the political and economic life of the country. We published four or five books on the subject, among them, in 1961, Jameson Campaigne's *Check-Off: Labor Bosses and Working Men*. After describing numerous cases of violence by labor-union officials against property and persons, including extortion, intimidation, and murder, he asked why present laws and enforcement agencies were helpless to protect the nation. His answer was that the American people cannot be protected from gangsterism, corruption, and tyranny, because too many politicians, from the lowest to the highest, owe their office to labor leaders.

Another of our books on the question was Donald R. Richberg's *Labor Union Monopoly: A Clear and Present Danger*, published in 1957. Its objective was to show the danger to individual freedom and to free institutions of uncontrolled power in the hands of labor-union leaders. An eminent lawyer, with many years of experience in the field of labor relations and labor law, Richberg described how government brought about the rise of monopoly power in the labor unions, and what it must do to bring it under control. His book and

141

Campaigne's complement each other; taken together they give a remarkably full picture of one of the most critical issues facing our country.

It is fair to ask what all this has to do with the ideology of liberalism. Joey Glimco, who Compaigne tells us had been arrested thirty-six times on charges from murder to extortion, and who won control of the Chicago Taxi Drivers Union by the use of "muscle" and quite frankly operated it for his own personal benefit, was a racketeer and a criminal, but no liberal. The "men from Detroit" sent into Kohler, Wisconsin, to man the picket lines and intimidate those who wanted to work were not liberals, nor were Jimmy Hoffa and John L. Lewis. Walter Reuther was a hero of the liberals and had many liberal credentials; but although he was a member of Americans for Democratic Action, on friendly terms with Mrs. Roosevelt and Arthur Schlesinger, Jr., and a supporter of the Kennedys, he was not a typical liberal either. As Campaigne showed, Reuther saw the labor-union movement as a means to political power, and for him the sole purpose of political power was to reshape the country in accordance with his image of a centrally planned and managed society. In his background, attitudes, and view of the world, Reuther was a product of German social democracy. He was self-righteous and a brilliant tactician; he knew what he wanted, and felt that whatever means he chose to attain his objectives were justified by his own high purpose. He knew how to use typical liberals, but he was far more ruthless than they were. It was the liberal attitude toward labor unions, rather than any active liberal participation in labor-union activity, that helped the unions gain their present position of political and economic power. As Richberg put it, the picture of a labor union as a weak, idealistic organization of downtrodden workers struggling against an oppressive concentration of property owners has assured the unions of sympathy and support from liberal intellectuals, but has nothing to do with reality; it was this attitude that has led to favorable treatment by the news media, the administration in Washington, and the courts.

When Jameson Campaigne wrote our book he was editor of the Indianapolis *Star,* where he had made a name for himself by his courage, outspokenness, and ability to put complex issues into clear and understandable language. His book was based largely on material gathered during the 1959 investigations by the McClellan

Committee of the Senate, much of which, since it was dug out by the Republican members of the committee, never got into the majority report; but he had many other sources as well. His book combined scholarship of a high order with the experienced newspaperman's ability to express himself clearly and precisely.

Donald Richberg, as the lawyer of the railway unions, was largely responsible for drafting and getting congressional approval of the Railway Labor Act of 1926, which became a milestone in the history of labor relations. He remarks that it was labor's first attempt to utilize governmental power for its own positive benefit, but although labor sought power for its own benefit, it also perforce took into consideration the interests of management and the public. In later years the unions would remember the strategy of 1926 but not its spirit. The Railway Labor Act, he declared, marks both the point at which labor's assumption of political power began, and the point to which it must return if it is to use that power legitimately.

The Clayton Act of 1914 is usually given the credit or blame, depending on the speaker, for the monopoly power of the labor unions, but Richberg felt that the Clayton Act, by itself and as originally intended by Congress, was of relatively little influence in this regard. It was through the Supreme Court's interpretation of the Clayton Act and of the Norris-La Guardia Act of 1932, and through a series of subsequent decisions, that the court extended a federal exemption to cover virtually any union activity of any substantial importance. The Clayton Act, he points out, provided only an immunity from antitrust prosecution for organizations "lawfully" carrying out their "legitimate objects." Obviously the authors of the Clayton Act and the Congressmen who voted for it had no expectation that the Supreme Court would hold that a union engaged in a sit-down strike was "lawfully" carrying out its objects, nor did they expect the court to hold that writing contracts to monopolize the sale of electrical goods in New York City was a "legitimate object" of union activity. As Justice Robert H. Jackson in a dissenting opinion expressed it, "The Court permits to employees the same arbitrary dominance over the economic sphere they control that labor so long, so bitterly and so rightly asserted should belong to no man."

In Richberg's opinion the "clear and present danger" of labor-union monopoly is the prospect of a labor government. He quotes the opposing lawyer of the American Federation of Labor in a case argued before the Supreme Court, as asserting: "The worker becomes a member of an economic society when he takes employment. . . . The union is the organization or government of this society. . . . It has in a sense the powers and responsibilities of government. . . . We can summarize the nature of union membership as a common condition of employment in an industrial society by again comparing it to citizenship in a political society. Both are compulsory upon individuals." Dr. Robert Ley of the Labor Front of National Socialist Germany could not have made the point more clearly or succinctly.

For all that, the danger may be of quite a different kind. Since Richberg's book was published, the growth of union power has continued. Teachers, firemen, postal workers, and government employees of all kinds now belong to unions and freely use the strike weapon against society to gain their objectives. Union membership is more and more generally becoming a requirement of employment. In spite of all this, however, it seems to me that it is not government by labor that may be the greatest threat to free institutions, but the kind of government that the reaction to excessive demands by the unions will bring about. The labor unions, with their featherbedding and excessive wage demands, contributed substantially to the destruction of the railroads. Thousands of young people are unemployed because of rigid, unrealistic minimum-wage laws demanded by unions. The teachers' union, with the help of the educational bureaucracy, is destroying the public schools. Many newspapers and other businesses have been forced to close because of unreasonable demands. The list could go on and on. The three great domestic problems we face are interrelated: inflation, the uncontrolled power of the labor unions, and bureaucracy. If, with our free institutions, we are unable to face and surmount these three great threats to order and individual freedom, some form of authoritarian government is inevitable, and I doubt that it will be dominated by labor.

Richberg, from the background of his enormous experience, makes a number of suggestions for meeting the problem of labor-union monopoly, but he does not think that we need to pass a "lot of laws." "It would need very little legislation," he points out, "to restore the original Clayton Act limitations. For the benefit of a Supreme Court majority which overrules the dictionary as well as itself, the word 'lawful' could be defined so that unlawful conduct would not be immunized. Careful definitions could be written in the law explaining what are 'legitimate objects' of union activity. Thus a majority instead of a minority of the Supreme Court might be induced to hold that violations of anti-trust laws and monopolistic contracts clearly in restraint of trade are not 'legitimate objects' for a labor union to pursue."

How much influence these two books had in presenting a more balanced picture of labor-union power is hard to say. The Campaigne book was largely ignored and if reviewed at all was denigrated as antilabor and one-sided. Although it is a book of 248 pages, carefully footnoted and provided with a detailed appendix, *Ethics* called it "sketchy and intemperate." The Virginia Kirkus Book Service pronounced it "hard-nosed, slow-motioned and rather one-eyed," and the *Library Journal* suggested that "a more accurate title for this book would be 'The John Birch Society Reports on Walter Reuther.'" The Richberg book, on the other hand, was widely reviewed and frequently commented on in news columns, and went into six printings. The University of Detroit *Law Journal* and the *New Republic,* not surprisingly, were outraged, and the New York *Times* pronounced that "the fear-ridden Richberg of 1957 is a dubious guide." Some twenty years later, he seems a much less dubious guide than the New York *Times.*

8

RUSSELL KIRK: CONSERVATISM BECOMES A MOVEMENT

THE critic of his time must accept the risk of being accused of negativism, but he can console himself with the knowledge that serious criticism has its source in a definite position with its own standards, values, and objectives. By the 1950's, with the work of such men as Albert J. Nock, T. S. Eliot, Richard Weaver, and Eliseo Vivas, the criticism of liberalism had grown into a substantial literature. What was lacking was a general concept that would bring the movement together and give it coherence and identity. It was the great achievement of Russell Kirk's *The Conservative Mind,* published in 1953, to provide such a unifying concept. Kirk offered convincing evidence not only that conservatism was an honorable and intellectually respectable position, but also that it was an integral part of the American tradition. It would be too much to say that the postwar conservative movement began with the publication of Russell Kirk's *The Conservative Mind,* but it was this book that gave it its name, and, more important, coherence.

When we published *The Conservative Mind,* Russell Kirk was an instructor in history at Michigan State College. He had published one book, *Randolph of Roanoke,* and numerous essays, many of them in English magazines. I met him through a mutual friend, Sidney Gair, who after his retirement as a long-time textbook trav-

146

eler for one of the large eastern publishers had become associated with our firm. Gair was a delightful man, courtly in his manner and a good conversationalist, and, confirmed conservative that he was, a great admirer of Paul Elmer More and Irving Babbitt. What it all comes down to, he used to say, is that a conservative knows that two plus two always, invariably, equal four, a fact of life a liberal, on the other hand, is not quite willing to accept.

Returning in the early part of 1952 from a trip to some of the colleges in Michigan, he told me that a young friend at Michigan State had written a manuscript he thought I would be interested in. I remember his description of Russell Kirk very clearly: ". . . the son of a locomotive engineer, but a formidable intelligence—a biological accident. He doesn't say much, about as communicative as a turtle, but when he gets behind a typewriter, the results are *most* impressive." A correspondence developed, and in reply to my expression of interest in his manuscript, Kirk told me that it was on offer to Knopf, but that if they declined it he would send it to me. "There never has been a book like it," he remarked in this letter, "so far as breadth of subject is concerned, whatever its vices may be. The subtitle is *An Account of Conservative Ideas from Burke to Santayana*." On July 31, 1952, he wrote from St. Andrews, in Scotland, that Knopf would be willing to publish his manuscript only if he would reduce it to about one-quarter of its original length, and that he was sending it to me. His manuscript, he said,

. . . is my contribution to our endeavor to conserve the spiritual and intellectual and political tradition of our civilization; and if we are to rescue the modern mind, we must do it very soon. What Matthew Arnold called "an epoch of concentration" is impending, in any case. If we are to make that approaching era a time of enlightened conservatism, rather than an era of stagnant repression, we need to move with decision. The struggle will be decided in the minds of the rising generation—and within that generation, substantially by the minority who have the gift of reason. I do not think we need much fear the decaying "liberalism" of the retiring generation; as Disraeli said, "Prevailing opinions generally are the opinions of the generation that is passing." But we need to state some certitudes for the benefit of the groping new masters of society. More than anyone else in America you have been doing just this in the books you publish.

On August 21 I acknowledged receipt of the manuscript, which I was anxious to read. I read most of it at a farm we owned in those days in the mountains of West Virginia, where we spent many happy summers with our four children. My judgment has often been faulty, but I knew that this was an important and perhaps a great book, and I was determined to publish it.

The manuscript was in beautiful shape, and could have been sent out for typesetting as it came in, except for the original title, "The Conservative Rout," which none of us thought would do. Sidney Gair suggested "The Long Retreat," which was worse, but we kept trying, until someone suggested "The Conservative Mind," which Kirk readily accepted. We gave great care also to the design of the book, which I wanted to be appropriate to the dignity of its language and the importance of what it had to say. The jacket confidently and, as it turned out, correctly predicted that the book would become a landmark in contemporary thinking. In March or April of 1953 we sent out review copies, and because the book represented a major commitment on our part, we awaited the response with some fear and trepidation. It was not long in coming, and far exceeded our most optimistic expectations.

Kirk had two great advantages in the task of presenting conservatism as a tradition relevant to our time: skill in organizing a vast body of knowledge with which he was thoroughly familiar, and a distinguished literary style. He tells us in the introductory chapter that the purpose of the book is to review conservative ideas, examining their validity for this perplexed age. It was not, he explained, a history of conservative parties, but a prolonged essay in definition.

What is the essence of British and American conservatism? What system of ideas, common to England and the United States, has sustained men of conservative instincts in their resistance against radical theories and social transformation ever since the beginning of the French Revolution? . . . Any informed conservative is reluctant to condense profound and intricate intellectual systems to a few pretentious phrases. . . . Conservatism is not a fixed and immutable body of dogma, and conservatives inherit from Burke a talent for re-expressing their convictions to fit the times. As a working premise, nevertheless, one can observe here that the essence of social conservatism is preservation of the ancient moral traditions of humanity.

Kirk then listed "six canons" of conservative thought, which I present in somewhat condensed form:

1. Belief that a divine intent rules society as well as conscience, forging an eternal chain of right and duty which links great and obscure, living

and dead. . . . Politics is the art of apprehending and applying the Justice which is above nature.

2. Affection for the proliferating variety and mystery of traditional life, as distinguished from the narrowing uniformity and equalitarianism and utilitarian aims of most radical systems.

3. Conviction that civilized society requires orders and classes. The only true equality is moral equality; all other attempts at leveling lead to despair, if enforced by positive legislation. Society longs for leadership, and if a people destroy natural distinctions among men, presently Bonaparte fills the vacuum.

4. Persuasion that property and freedom are inseparably connected, and that economic leveling is not economic progress. Separate property from private possession, and liberty is erased.

5. Faith in prescription and distrust of "sophisters and calculators." Man must put a control upon his will and his appetite, for conservatives know man to be governed more by emotion than by reason. Tradition and sound prejudice provide checks upon man's anarchic impulse.

6. Recognition that change and reform are not identical, and that innovation is a devouring conflagration more often than it is a torch of progress. Society must alter, for slow change is the means of conservation, like the human body's perpetual renewal; but Providence is the proper instrument for change, and the test of a statesman is his cognizance of the real tendency of Providential social forces.

For Russell Kirk, the teachings of Edmund Burke comprise the basic principles of conservatism. So it was quite appropriate that in the opening chapter of *The Conservative Mind,* "Burke and the Politics of Prescription," Kirk sets before us the principles of conservatism as Burke developed them. "Edmund Burke's conservative philosophy was a reply to three separate radical schools. the rationalism of the *philosophes;* the romantic sentimentalism of Rousseau and his disciples; and the nascent utilitarianism of Bentham." But it was a philosophy derived from a deep sense of piety and a profound understanding of the sources of order. "Now and again," Kirk tells us, "Burke praises two great virtues, the keys to private contentment and public peace: they are prudence and humility, the first pre-eminently an attainment of classical philosophy, the second pre-eminently a triumph of Christian discipline. Without them, man must be miserable; and man destitute of piety hardly can perceive either of these rare and blessed qualities."

Kirk sees Burke's accomplishment, taken as a whole, as the definition of a principle of order; he summarizes Burke's position in the following paragraph:

Revelation, reason, and an assurance beyond the senses tell us that the Author of our being exists, and that he is Omniscient; and man and the state are creations of God's beneficence. This Christian orthodoxy is the kernel of Burke's philosophy. God's purpose among men is revealed through the unrolling of history. How are we to know God's mind and will? Through the prejudices and traditions which millenniums of human experience with Divine means and judgments have implanted in the mind of the species. And what is our purpose in this world? Not to indulge our appetites, but to render obedience to Divine ordinance.

Russell Kirk was in his late twenties when, still a graduate student at St. Andrews University, he began the book, and in his early thirties by the time it was finished. One senses the freshness of discovery, the immense pleasure of a young man, searching for his way in a confused and confusing age, who has discovered a view of life that satisfies him, gives him direction, and seems to answer his most pressing questions. For all its maturity and sound scholarship, Kirk is able to maintain throughout the book the quality of discovery that is evident in the first chapter; he writes not only with profound knowledge of his subject, but also with the passion of a man who has discovered a great truth and wishes to communicate his discovery to others. It is perhaps this quality of the freshness of discovery that carried the day for *The Conservative Mind* and made it one of the most influential books of the postwar period.

Having laid down, in his chapter on Burke, the basic principles of conservatism, Kirk proceeded to follow the development of conservative ideas and their influence through such men as John Adams, Alexander Hamilton, Walter Scott, John Randolph of Roanoke, John Calhoun, James Fenimore Cooper, Macaulay, Tocqueville, Disraeli, and Cardinal Newman, and so down to Paul Elmer More, Irving Babbitt, George Santayana, and T. S. Eliot. To read the book again, after almost twenty-five years, was as rewarding as when I read it the first time in manuscript. A chapter that particularly impressed me at this late date of my life is "Conservatism Frustrated: America, 1865–1918," which, it seems to me, brings out with particular clarity and perception the still-unresolved contradictions, tensions, and conflicts that the rise of industrial society has created.

Kirk begins his chapter on America between the Civil War and World War I with an account of the moral confusion of the country in the decades immediately following the collapse of the Confederacy: the South prostrate, desperately trying "to make a dismembered economy stir again," too much concerned with the exigencies of life to think about anything else, and the Northern intellect, which, he said, "practically was the New England intellect," ill-equipped for the task of restoring values, for "splicing the ragged ends." New England conservatism had always been, in essence, a conservatism of negation, and its recent self-righteous flirtation with radicalism, political abstractions, and that kind of fanatic equalitarianism which Garrison represented made it even less able to meet the needs of the day than it might otherwise have been. The age of "relentless economic centralization, of dull standardization, of an insatiable devastation of natural resources," led to demands for reform, and, as the phrase went, the cure for democracy is more democracy. "If government is corrupt—why, make it wholly popular: and so the last third of the nineteenth century experiences the successful advocacy of direct democratic devices. The election of judges and of executive officials, the abolition of the last exceptions to universal manhood suffrage, the revision of constitutions, the direct primary, the popular election of United States senators, presently the popular initiative and referendum and recall—these instruments of extreme democracy are proposed, praised, and gradually enacted." It was the time of the first great strikes, which were often violent and bloody; of great extremes of wealth and poverty; of mass immigration; of "manifest destiny" and the war against Spain; of the city "bosses," and clamor that government "do something." "Jefferson's America," Kirk remarked, "is as much eclipsed as John Adams'. . . . American character, individualistic, covetous, contemptuous of restraint, always had been stubborn clay for the keepers of tradition to mould into civilization. Now it threatened to become nearly anarchic, to slip into a ditch of spiritual atomism. What can be done? Lowell speculates uneasily; Godkin scourges the age in the *Nation*; the four sons of Charles Francis Adams try to fight their way into the thick of practical affairs, but are repulsed, and Henry and Brooks Adams pry bitterly into the probabilities of social destiny."

In the rest of this chapter Kirk described the thought and influence of these four "keepers of tradition," and their attempt to fathom the currents of their time.

Kirk's presentation of the response of Brooks and, particularly, of the enigmatic Henry Adams to their age is a virtuoso demonstration of his skill in synthesizing and ordering a complex body of ideas and showing their sources and influence. After quoting

Albert J. Nock's judgment that Henry was the most accomplished of all the Adams family, Kirk observes that he "is the most irritating person in American letters—and the most provocative writer, and the best historian, and possibly the most penetrating critic of ideas. The best cure for vexation with Henry Adams is to read his detractors; for against his Olympian amusement at a dying world and his real inner modesty, their snarls and quibbles furnish a relief which displays Adams' learning and wit as no amount of adulation could."

"A case might be made that Henry Adams represents the zenith of American civilization. Unmistakably and almost belligerently American, the embodiment of four generations of exceptional rectitude and intelligence, [he was] very likely the best educated man American society has produced. . . . But the product of these grand gifts was a pessimism deep and unsparing as Schopenhauer's, intensified by Adams' long examination and complete rejection of American aspirations." His conservatism "is the view of a man who sees before him a steep and terrible declivity, from which there can be no returning: one may have leisure to recollect past nobility, now and then one may perform the duty of delaying mankind for a moment in this descent; but the end is not to be averted." By the discoveries of modern science man had released a jinni from the bottle, Adams thought, a jinni who would become his master; and the laws of thermodynamics, which teach that although the total sum of energy remains constant its usefulness is constantly dissipated, only increased his pessimism. "Once man turned from the ideal of spiritual power, the Virgin, to the ideal of physical power, the Dynamo, his doom was sure. The faith and beauty of the thirteenth century, this descendant of the Puritans declared, made that age the noblest epoch of mankind; he could imagine only one state of society worse than the rule of capitalists in the nineteenth century—the coming rule of the trade unions in the twentieth century."

What had happened in the short span of three generations to change the robust confidence of John Adams, who risked hanging for freedom and was a founder of a new nation, to the despair of his enormously gifted great-grandson? If the law of the dissipation of energy is valid, it has been valid since creation. Kirk's explanation of Henry Adams's pessimism is worth repeating, not only for what it says about Adams, but also for what it says about Kirk and his conception of conservatism:

Christian orthodoxy believes in an eternity which, as it is superhuman, is supra-terrestrial; and the real world being a world of spirit, man's fate is not dependent upon the vicissitudes of this planet, but may be translated by Divine purpose into a realm apart from our present world of space and time. In this certitude, Christians escape from the problem of degradation of energy; but Adams, however much he might revere the Virgin of Chartres as incarnation of the idea and as a symbol of eternal beauty, could not put credence in the idea of Providence. He was determined that history must be "scientific." . . . The phase of religion was far nobler, to Adams' mind, than the phase of electricity; but he felt himself borne irresistibly along by the wave of progress. One might reverence the Virgin, in the Electric phase; but one could not really worship. The blunt non-conformist piety of John Adams gave way to the doubts of John Quincy Adams, the humanitarianism of Charles Francis Adams, the despair of Henry Adams. Belief in Providence, so enduringly rooted in Burke's conservatism, was lost in the vicissitudes of New England's conservative thought.

It was, as Kirk said, a swaggering half-century, and even if conservatives had been able to command any substantial body of public opinion, they scarcely would have known what way to lead the nation. "By the time the First World War had ended, true conservatism was nearly extinct in the United States—existing only in little circles of stubborn men who refused to be caught up in the expansive lust of their epoch, or in the vague resistance to change still prevalent among the rural population, or, in a muddled and half-hearted fashion, within certain churches and colleges. Everywhere else, change was preferred to continuity."

In the last three chapters of his book, Kirk considers the situation of conservatism in the twentieth century. The last chapter, in the first edition, was called "The Recrudescence of Conservatism"; in the most recent edition, of 1972, this has become "Conservatives' Promise." He treats Irving Babbitt and Paul Elmer More, in whom "the dismayed aloofness of Henry Adams was succeeded by a dogged endeavor to achieve conservative moral reform," with particular understanding and sympathy. In Babbitt, Kirk says, "American conservatism attains maturity." With his emphasis on self-discipline, on the need of the active will to rise above the lethargy of the senses, and in his rejection of humanitarianism, Babbitt arrived at a conception of work that showed how great the gap was between him and his time: "It is in fact the quality of a man's work that should determine his place in the hierarchy that every civilized society requires." For Babbitt, according to Kirk, "the only true freedom is the freedom to work." Babbitt and More had much in common, but with More there is a different emphasis. Through all his work, Kirk believed, "runs a stern continuity: the insistence that for our salvation in this world and the other, we must look to the things of the spirit, accept the duality of human nature, remind ourselves that the present moment is of small consequence in the mysterious system of being." For More, Kirk said, "sin and redemption, justice and grace, were realities which the naturalists can ignore only at the cost of brutalizing society: and after half a century of controversy, the tide appears to be turning sharply in More's favor." Kirk concludes this discussion with the observation, "With Babbitt and More, American conservative ideas experienced a reinvigoration attesting the coquetry of History and the mystery of Providence."

Kirk, thoroughgoing realist that he is, had no illusions about the destructive forces at work in our time and country, but, believing that a divine intent rules society, he did not despair. He was well aware that conservatives had been routed, as he put it, but equally so that they had not been conquered. Although much had been lost, much was still left, and the enemies of conservatism, whether they called themselves liberals, socialists, fascists, or communists, stand discredited by history. Kirk pointed out that the federal Constitution had endured as the most sagacious conservative document in political history. "Despite the disruptive forces of mass-communication, rapid transportation, industrial standardization, a cheap press and other mass media . . . despite the radical effects of vulgarized scientific speculation and weakened private morality, despite the decay of family economy and family bonds, most men and women in the twentieth century still feel veneration for what their ancestors affirmed and built, and they express a pathetic eagerness to find stability in a time of flux." Kirk ends his book with "Cupid's curse against the hubris of the ruthless innovator":

> They that do change old love for new,
> Pray gods they change for worse.

Although I had accepted *The Conservative Mind* with as much confidence in its quality as in any book I ever published, I was not at all sanguine about its possible commercial success. I had been disappointed too many times by books I was sure had something important to say to be overly optimistic about *The Conservative*

Mind, and decided to limit the first printing to 3,000 copies. We did, however, prepare the way carefully for it, and saw that it got into the hands of people who might be helpful, and this time we were confirmed in our judgment of the book's quality.

The first indication that the response to it might be favorable was an advance notice from the somewhat unpredictable Kirkus Book Review Service, which was all we could have asked for and certainly more than I had expected: "A fine study of conservative thought in politics, religion, philosophy and literature from 1790 to 1952." This was followed by a recommendation in the *Library Journal*, and on the day before publication the *New York Times Book Review* raised our hopes and spirits immeasurably with an excellent half-page review in a prominent position by Gordon Chalmers. What really put it into the center of discussion, however, was a long, intelligent review in the July 4 issue of *Time* (dated July 6). George Washington was on the cover, and the whole book-review section was devoted to *The Conservative Mind*, which was mentioned as well in the news pages. The theme of the issue, then, seemed to be the continuity of the American conservative tradition. The review was not only favorable, it was the kind that stimulates the interest and curiosity of the reader, which is not true of every review, favorable or not. Sales increased immediately, from about one hundred copies a week to four hundred, and the first printing was sold out before the end of July. A second printing of 5,000 was delivered in August and a third before the end of the year. Russell Kirk, from having been a rather obscure instructor at what he was later to call "Behemoth U," had become a national figure.

The impact of *The Conservative Mind* when it first appeared in 1953 is hard to imagine now. After the long domination of liberalism, with its adulation of the "common man," its faith in mechanistic political solutions to all human problems, and its rejection of the tragic and heroic aspects of life, such phrases as "the unbought grace of life" and the "eternal chain of right and duty which links great and obscure, living and dead," and a view of politics as "the art of apprehending and applying the Justice which is above nature" came like rain after a long drought. August Heckscher began his review in the New York *Herald Tribune*: "To be a conservative in the United States has for so long been considered identical with being backward, and even faintly alien, that Mr. Kirk's proud justification of the term is to be welcomed." Harrison Smith, in a syndicated review that appeared in many papers, including the Washington *Post*, welcomed the book with the words, "Thoughtful Americans concerned with the rapidity with which totalitarian theories and revolutions are spreading over a large part of the world should read Russell Kirk's landmark in contemporary thinking." There was a most favorable and effective review in *Fortune*, and *Partisan Review* discussed the book at length in two separate issues. A long essay about *The Conservative Mind* by John Crowe Ransom appeared in the *Kenyon Review* and was later reprinted in a collection of his essays, and another, in part a reply to Ransome, by Brainard Cheney in the *Sewanee Review*. It was reviewed in the *Times Literary Supplement*, and both Golo Mann and Wilhelm Roepke wrote extended essays about it in German publications. The post-World War II conservative movement had attained intellectual respectability and an identity, and was on its way.

For the review in *Time* we are indebted to Whittaker Chambers. I had first met Chambers in 1952, when he was given an honorary degree by Mount Mary College in Milwaukee. Hearing that he was in Milwaukee, I called to ask if I might see him. I did this, I must say, with some hesitation, since I was reluctant to intrude on his privacy, and was therefore all the more pleased when he told me that he would be delighted to see me, and to come along at once. He was with his wife, Esther, who had made her own contribution to his achievement and firmness under fire, and who for all her gentleness and charm of manner had character and resolution of steel. The admiration I had felt for him ever since reading *Witness* quickly developed into warm friendship. I have the most pleasant memory of visits to the Chamberses at their Maryland farm, and corresponded with him to the end of his life. I had spoken to him about *The Conservative Mind* soon after having read it, and sent him a set of proofs as soon as they became available. His response was the following letter, dated June 26, 1953:

I wrote Roy Alexander, the editor of *Time,* recently, to say I thought that Russell Kirk's book was one of the most important that was likely to appear in some time, and to suggest that *Time* might well devote its entire Books section to a review of it. Since you can never count on journalists being able to count above two, I also told *Time* why I thought the Conservative Mind important, what it was and did.

Yesterday, Roy telephoned to say that *Time* agreed and that its whole forthcoming Books section will be devoted to Kirk's book. It will be the July 4 issue with G. Washington on the cover. So I am able at last to do something in a small way, for you who have done so much for us— and to do something for Kirk's book, which you and I both would agree is the big thing. Incidentally, this shows that simply by picking up a pen, things can be done if we have the will to overcome inertia.

I can make no claim that I ever did anything for Whittaker Chambers beyond offering him my friendship; I felt more than repaid by the return of his. He was one of the great men of our time, and by assuming the terrible burden of being, as he expressed it, an involuntary witness to God's grace and to the fortifying power of faith, he put all of us immeasurably in his debt.

The sense of exultation we felt when the advance copies of the *Time* review came in is still very clear in my memory. Sidney Gair was in a state bordering on ecstasy. "Just look," he said, "pictures of Paul Elmer More and Irving Babbitt in *Time* magazine, and all because *you* decided to go into the publishing business! If you had gone into oil instead, and had struck five gushers in a row, it wouldn't have given you a fraction of the satisfaction you feel now." I readily admitted that this was true, but mentally observed that the proceeds from only one oil well would have been most welcome at the moment to pay some bills, which, as always, were rather pressing—a circumstance that helped to keep my pride and sense of achievement within bounds.

Not all the reviews were favorable, of course, and neither *Harper's* nor the *Atlantic* could find space to review the book at all. Peter Gay, of Columbia University, ended his review in the *Political Science Quarterly* with the observation: "In trying to confute Lionel Trilling's position (that American conservatives have no philosophy and express themselves only in action or irritable mental gestures) Kirk has only confirmed it." Stuart Garry Brown reviewed the book in *Ethics*, a quarterly published by the University of Chicago and was not at all impressed. He reviewed Scott Buchanan's *Essays in Politics* at the same time, and called it much the better book. (He quotes with apparent approval a remark of Buchanan's to the effect that the Soviet Union is a "province of the democratic empire.") Norman Thomas, in the *United Nations World* (August, 1953), concluded a long and wordy review with the remark, "What he has given us is an eloquent bit of special pleading which is, in part, a false, and, in sum total, a dangerously inadequate, philosophy for our time."

On the other hand, Clinton Rossiter, in the *American Political Science Review*, asserted that Kirk's "scholarship is manifestly of the highest order," and concluded: "Certainly the so-called 'new conservatism' of the postwar period takes on new substance and meaning with the publication of this splendid book." L. P. Curtis reviewed *The Conservative Mind* together with Richard Pares's *King George II and the Politicians* in the *Yale Review*, and declared, "This eloquent and confident book should hearten present conservatives and open the eyes of many of them to the splendor of their moral heritage . . . in spite of shortcomings Kirk fulfills one of the higher aims of the historian: he teaches us a way of life, and one, moreover, that is tried in experience and sprung from our condition."

The acceptance of "conservatism" as the description of the growing movement of opposition to the rule of liberalism was not automatic or without strenuous opposition. Both Frank S. Meyer, who eventually became one of the acknowledged leaders of the conservative movement, and F. A. Hayek, who did as much as any other single person to give direction and a sound footing to the movement in opposition to the planned economy, wrote vigorously against conservatism as a description of their position. Hayek prefers to be known as an "Old Whig," a label requiring a prolonged explanation that probably convinces everyone who reads it except Hayek himself that he really is, at heart, a conservative.

Frank Meyer's attack on the "New Conservatism," as he called it, appeared in the July, 1955, issue of the *Freeman* and had the ominous title "Collectivism Rebaptized." He began by acknowledging that the emergence of the New Conservatism could be accurately correlated with, and was indeed precipitated by, *The Conservative Mind*. But he argued with his usual vehemence and confidence that Kirk's position, and that of the new conservatives in general, was rhetorical and without clear and distinct principle. Because Kirk "presents himself and his belief always rhetorically, never on a reasoned basis, he can succeed in establishing the impression that he has a strong and coherent outlook without ever taking a systematic and consistent position."

Meyer was particularly sharp in his criticism of Kirk's rejection of individualism. For Meyer, all value resides in the individual; all social institutions derive their value and their very being from individuals and are justified only to the extent that they serve the need of individuals. Although he did eventually call himself a conservative, Meyer always differentiated his position from the New

Conservatism, primarily on the basis of his conception of the individual and what he took Kirk's position in this respect to be.

Hayek's rejection of conservatism was first given in the form of a paper at a meeting of the Mont Pélérin Society, an international organization of economists who may be called liberal in the traditional sense, and others who share their concern for the free society. The first meeting of the society took place in Switzerland in April, 1947; ever since, its annual meetings, which are usually held in September, have provided an opportunity for the consideration on the highest level of contemporary problems and issues. Hayek is the founder of the society, and was still its president when he gave his paper "Why I Am Not a Conservative," at the 1957 meeting. Although neither *The Conservative Mind* nor Russell Kirk was specifically mentioned in the paper, it was obviously inspired by the success of Kirk's book and the influential position the ideas it set forth had attained. This is attested to by the fact that Kirk was invited to defend his position immediately afterward, which he did extemporaneously, without notes of any kind, and with great brilliance and effect. The encounter in an elegant Swiss hotel before a distinguished international audience between one of the most respected economists of his time, who had been honored by professorships at the universities of Vienna, London, and Chicago, and the young writer from Mecosta, Michigan, was a dramatic and memorable occasion. As a rather biased witness, I would not be prepared to say that the young man from Mecosta came out second best.

Hayek's rejection of conservatism, as a noun rather than a concept, may well have been unconsciously influenced by the fact that in the Austria in which he reached maturity, conservatism was identified with the House of Habsburg and clerical Catholicism. In his explanation of why he is not a conservative, however, Hayek undertook to base his argument on strictly rational grounds; but it was an argument carried through without the coherence or unremitting logic one associates with him. Conservatism, he argued, is reactionary; it may be against what all of us are against—collectivism or socialism—but by its very nature it cannot offer an alternative. Guided as they are, he said, by the belief that the truth must lie somewhere between extremes, conservatives have shifted their position every time a more extreme position appears on either wing. In consequence, the conservative lacks principle, and is essentially an opportunist. In saying that the conservative lacks principle, Hayek meant that he has no political principles that enable him to work with people whose moral values differ from his own for a political order in which both can obey their convictions. From this assertion Hayek goes on to says that "to the liberal neither moral nor religious ideals are proper objects of coercion, whereas both conservatives and socialists recognize no such limits." Finally, he tells us that one of the fundamental traits of the conservative attitude is a fear of change, a timid distrust of the new as such, but that the liberal position is based on courage and confidence, on a preparedness to let change run its course even if we cannot predict where it will lead.

Conservatism, as Kirk has repeatedly pointed out, is not an ideology or a fixed body of dogma; it can much better be described as an attitude, as a way of viewing the world that includes a willingness to come to terms with the realities of the human condition and to accept and to pass on the order of being as it has come down to us. It begins, as Kirk put it, with the premise that we must be obedient to a transcendent order. As for the assertion that conservatives lack principle, one need only point to some of the great representative conservatives, such as John Adams and the others who framed the Constitution. Hayek took conservatives to task for their fear of change, but if we have learned nothing else from the history of the last one hundred years, we should have learned that a skeptical view of change is highly desirable. As Kirk said, "innovation is a devouring conflagration more often than it is a torch of progress." As ironical as it may sound, it is quite possible that Hayek's resistance to conservatism was nothing more than resistance to change. The conservatism described by Kirk came to Hayek, with the heritage of the Austro-Hungarian monarchy behind him, as a new concept, and conservative at heart that he really is, he is not willing to accept it without a struggle.

He argued that by its very nature conservatism cannot offer an alternative to socialism. But why should it? Why should an American conservative, with the free and incredibly successful society behind him made possible by the American tradition and the U.S. Constitution, feel any compulsion to offer an alternative to socialism, a concept of government and society not only completely contrary to human nature, but also utterly discredited by experience? As for the criticism that conservatism fails to recognize that moral and religious ideas are not proper objects of coercion, has not the present age of licentiousness taught us the contrary? A society has the right to protect itself from those who would destroy the moral principles on which it rests, as well as from those who would destroy it physically.

By his tireless, unselfish, and effective devotion to the cause of the free society, Frank Meyer earned the right to nourish an aberration or two, one of which was his infatuation with individualism. In a sense so broad as to become meaningless, it is true that all social institutions derive their value from individuals, but which individuals? A society is more than the individuals who momentarily make it up; its character and quality are also determined by its history, its traditions, its symbols, its myths, and all the other things composing that "eternal chain of right and duty which links great and obscure, living and dead." The South is different from the North not so much because those now living in the South are different, as because it has had a different experience, just as German or Austrian society is different from French or English society. To say these things is to view reality as it is, and its consequences as they must be.

We published five further books by Russell Kirk, one, *Randolph of Roanoke*, a revised edition of a book first published in 1951 by the University of Chicago Press, and another, *Beyond the Dreams of Avarice*, a collection of essays, most of which, in somewhat different form, had appeared in various English and American periodicals. The other three were original works, and to some extent at least were written with encouragement and stimulation from our firm, an act of secondary creativity that is one of the proper functions of a publisher.

The reader of *Beyond the Dreams of Avarice* will soon discover that Kirk is a master of the essay form. Whether he writes on censorship, social boredom, liberalism, the island of Eigg in the Hebrides, or Wyndham Lewis, Kirk's sense of history, his skill in illuminating a contemporary subject from the perspective of the past, and his spacious style give his essays a quality all their own. A most appreciative review in the *New Yorker* ended with the comment, "As a critical tool in the hands of a writer as adept as Russell Kirk, conservatism has a sharp cutting edge indeed."

The three that were entirely original with us were *A Program for Conservatives, Academic Freedom,* and *The American Cause,* the first two published in 1955, and the last in 1957.

A Program for Conservatives was in a way a continuation of *The Conservative Mind.* In it Kirk undertook to apply to the contemporary situation the principles he had described in his earlier book. The critical response was almost as extensive as that brought forth by *The Conservative Mind,* but more varied. James Burnham, in the *Annals of the American Academy,* concluded a most favorable review: "He is not only reviving the conservative tradition, but he is rescuing it: both from sterile reactionaries who have degraded it, and from verbalists who . . . are trying to hitch a ride on the shifting Zeitgeist." Though not wholly uncritical, Raymond English, in the New York *Times,* called this book necessary and most welcome. Perhaps the most remarkable review was that in the socialist *New Leader,* by James Rorty, who ended a two-page, serious discussion of the issues Kirk raised by asserting that what he had done was to give us the most systematic, eloquent, and persuasive general statement of the conservative position that had appeared in print.

There were also voices of dissent. The review in *Partisan Review* was headed "The Conservatism of Despair," the *Progressive* predictably felt that the book represented the worst aspects of the "conservative recrudescence," and *Commonweal* called it sterile. A long review in *Harper's* was headed "Backward, Turn Backward," and accused Kirk of "utopianism," but granted that he raised the gravest questions, had real moral fervor, and was far better educated and more literate than most contemporary writers on politics and society. From all this it is evident that, having started the discussion, Kirk was well able to keep it going, and on his own terms.

Of these three books, the one that represented the most original contribution to thoughtful opinion and had the greatest influence was probably *Academic Freedom.* This was written in response to what the author felt was a widespread misuse and misunderstanding of a concept he considered vital to the well-being of the university and therefore of society as a whole. The somewhat flamboyant rhetoric of the late senator from Wisconsin, Joseph McCarthy, and even more a sense of guilt and inadequacy on the part of certain members of the academic community, had led to a state of mind bordering on hysteria. We were solemnly assured that a professor who would dare to drive a foreign car or assign a work of Thomas Jefferson to his classes was in danger of instant dismissal. When McCarthy recommended that certain books critical of American institutions in the libraries maintained in foreign countries by the U.S. government be removed, the cry of "book burning" was heard throughout the land, and the American Library Association, with great fanfare, responded with a manifesto, "The Freedom to Read." The words "academic freedom" were invoked like an incantation.

In all this welter of claim and counterclaim, Kirk felt that the real meaning of academic freedom was in danger of being lost. In his view academic freedom "belongs to that category of rights called 'natural rights,' and is expressed in custom, not in statute," which makes its proper understanding, particularly by those who claim its privilege, all the more necessary. Academic freedom does not mean "complete autonomy for teachers, or the licentious toleration of a bewildering congeries of private fancies," nor is it "freedom simply for the masters of educational institutions to enforce their opinions upon the teachers." It is a special kind of freedom, which arose from the realization that the protection it afforded was necessary if the university was to fulfill its high moral and intellectual purpose, and will survive only so long as the university remains true to such purpose.

Since, for Kirk, academic freedom derives its sanction from the purpose of the university, what does he consider that purpose to be? His book ends with the following paragraph, which deserves a place among the classic expressions of the aims of education:

To what truths, then, ought the Academy to be dedicated? To the proposition that the end of education is the elevation of the reason of the human person, for the human person's own sake. To the proposition that the higher imagination is better than the sensate triumph. To the proposition that the fear of God, and not the mastery over man and nature, is the object of learning. To the proposition that quality is worth more than quantity. To the proposition that justice takes precedence over power. To the proposition that order is more lovable than egoism. To the proposition that to believe all things, if the choice must be made, is nobler than to doubt all things. To the proposition that honor outweighs success. To the proposition that tolerance is wiser than ideology. To the proposition, Socratic and Christian, that the unexamined life is not worth living. If the Academy holds by these propositions, not all the forces of Caesar can break down its walls; but if the Academy is bent upon sneering at everything in heaven and earth, or upon reforming itself after the model of the market-place, not all the eloquence of the prophets can save it.

The critical response to *Academic Freedom* was extensive, and mostly of the kind one hopes for but does not often experience in the case of a serious work on an important subject. The book was reviewed at considerable length, and although not without some difference of opinion, most positively in the New York *Times,* by Roswell G. Ham, who called it a "brilliant and exciting study," whereas William F. Buckley, Jr., found himself joining hands with the *Nation* in completely rejecting it. Buckley's review, in the *Freeman,* was headed "Essay in Confusion," and asserted "Dr. Kirk's book on academic freedom has something in it for everybody. . . . But no one could conceivably refer to this book as a reasoned statement of a coherent position on academic freedom."

One of the most useful, conscientious, and thoughtful reviews was that by Paul Pickrel in *Commentary.* Pickrel said that although he was finally unconvinced by Kirk's historical account of academic freedom, and regarded his philosophical position as too narrow and doctrinaire, he believed it made a major contribution to the discussion of academic freedom in this country.

The last book we published by Russell Kirk, *The American Cause*, was written following the disclosure of the dismal performance of many Americans while prisoners of the Communists in North Korea. The lack of any sense of loyalty, of awareness of what their country stands for, of its traditions, history, and achievement, even of the will to survive, came as a great shock and demonstrated that something was seriously wrong with a system of education which had produced such people. To correct this situation, to whatever extent one small book can, was the purpose of *The American Cause*. That it served its purpose is suggested by the fact that it has been widely read, and, after twenty years, is still in print. Reviewing it in *Commonweal* Thomas Molnar remarked that it combined the great qualities of the philosopher's grasp of ideas and the pamphleteer's singleness of purpose.

As I mentioned earlier, Russell Kirk was an instructor of history at Michigan State College when we published *The Conservative Mind*. What is now Michigan State University is one of those vast educational conglomerates that have developed in consequence of the widely held belief that if a college education is useful and helpful to some, justice and the principles of democracy demand that it be made available to all. Courses are offered, as Kirk often remarked, in everything from medieval philosophy to elementary and advanced fly casting, and its chief function, in his opinion, is to deprive the young people who pour through its gates of whatever prejudices and moral principles they bring with them, and send them out into the world again having given them nothing in return in the way of principles or understanding to help them come to terms with the realities of life.

Not long after the publication of *The Conservative Mind* Kirk resigned his position at Michigan State, using the occasion to get off a great blast at President John Hanna as well as the whole concept of such an institution as Michigan State. When he told me of his intention to do this, I urged him to reconsider, pointing out the advantages of a relatively secure academic position, with its monthly check, as opposed to the uncertainties of living as a writer and lecturer, to say nothing of the retributions there might be from the academic establishment. To this he replied in his characteristic fashion in a letter dated October 12, 1953:

Poverty never bothered me; I can live on four hundred dollars cash per annum, if I must; time to think, and freedom of action, are much more important to me at present than any possible economic advantage. I have always had to make my own way, opposed rather than aided by the times and the men who run matters for us; and I don't mind continuing to do so.

Make his own way he did: we can truthfully say that Russell Kirk has become one of the most influential figures of our time. We listen to him because he speaks with the inner authority of a man who has thought deeply about what he says, means it, and is willing to put himself on the line for it.

He has chosen to live in Mecosta, the small town in northern Michigan where he spent many happy summers as a boy, in a region of small lakes, sand hills, and the stumps of the great pines that once covered the area. The house of his great-grandfather, where he lived as a bachelor, burned to the ground, ghosts and all, on Ash Wednesday, 1975; but the large, solid, square brick house, surmounted by a cupola rescued from a demolished public building, which was nearly finished at the time of the fire, provides ample room for his charming, down-to-earth, energetic wife and their four daughters, and for numerous visitors. Appropriately, as the home of its most prominent citizen, it dominates the village. A former woodworking shop about a quarter of a mile away has been converted into a study, and there, surrounded by the books accumulated during thirty years of disciplined study, he does his work. A student or protégé is usually in residence, and groups of students arrive during holidays for study and discussion. The rather remote, obscure village of Mecosta has become an important intellectual center, and doubtless has more positive influence in the world of ideas than the huge university Kirk abandoned in its favor.

One of the most remarkable aspects of Kirk's career has been its uninterrupted consistency. In a disorderly age he has tirelessly and eloquently made clear the necessity and sources of order. Against the false prophets who proclaim that all values are relative and derive from will and desire, he shows their immutability. And to those who believe that man is capable of all things, he teaches humility, and that the beginning of wisdom is respect for creation and the order of being.

9

MORE CONSERVATIVES

WILLIAM F. BUCKLEY, JR., RICHARD WEAVER, WILLMOORE KENDALL, JAMES JACKSON KIL-PATRICK, FELIX MORLEY, JAMES BURNHAM, FRANK S. MEYER, AMONG OTHERS

ALTHOUGH the success of Russell Kirk's *The Conservative Mind* had given the growing revolt against liberalism a name and a degree of focus, it did not yet deserve to be called a movement. No one had greater influence on this development than William F. Buckley, Jr. Through his books, articles, and public appearances, his newspaper column and his magazine *National Review,* but perhaps most of all by his manner and personality, he came to symbolize the conservative movement. It is worth remarking, however, that in *God and Man at Yale* the word *conservative* is hardly used; Buckley then described his position as "individualist." Now it would be difficult to conceive of the conservative movement without Bill Buckley. He has not only served ever since as an inspiration and a rallying point, particularly to student generations; he has given it a style and rhetoric of its own, and has done more than anyone else to reconcile potentially conflicting viewpoints into a coherent intellectual force.

It was Frank Hanighen who told me that a recent Yale graduate was working on a manuscript I should by all means have a look at, and it was at the suggestion of Frank Chodorov that I asked Buckley if we might consider his manuscript for publication. That first letter was dated April 26, 1951. On May 7 he wrote to say the manuscript was on its way. No long time was needed to make up our minds that this was a book we very much wanted to publish, as I wrote to Buckley on May 14. The only problem in working out the contract was timing: Buckley was most insistent that the book be published the following fall, which meant having page proofs no later than July, then only two months away. The reason for his urgency was compelling: the following fall, with great pomp and ceremony, Yale would be celebrating the 250th anniversary of its founding. The book was published October 15, and, as soon became apparent, the timing was perfect.

The thesis of *God and Man at Yale* is clear, unequivocal, and easily stated. Buckley argues that Yale represents itself as a great educational institution dedicated to upholding and handing on the basic values and traditions of American society, essentially Christian and individualist as opposed to collectivist, and that it derives its support on that basis. Instead, in its teaching and by its example, Yale was inculcating values that were contrary to the teachings of Christianity, and in the areas of public policy were essentially collectivist. As for academic freedom, it had become nothing more than a "handy slogan that is constantly used to bludgeon into impotence numberless citizens who waste away with frustration as they view in their children and their children's children the results of *laissez-faire* education."

Buckley supports his argument with examples of the attitudes of influential teachers and the contents of textbooks and courses and by describing the impact of a Yale education, as experienced by a recent graduate, with strong convictions of his own, who was well aware of what went on about him. He ends his book with a plea to the alumni to assert themselves, to demand as the price of their support that Yale represent the spiritual and moral values for which it claims to stand and in which the alumni themselves—or so Buckley thought—believed. Such a book was a great challenge both to Yale and to the reigning orthodoxy of liberalism. For a young man to throw such a challenge at one of the most strongly entrenched, self-satisfied, and influential groups in the country required courage and conviction. The fact that he survived is evidence not only of his strength of character, but also of the essential correctness of his position.

The response of the academic community to the book was instantaneous, and violent to the point of irrationality. The first great blast came from McGeorge Bundy, a Yale graduate who at the time was associate professor of government at Harvard. His review in the *Atlantic Monthly* can be said to have established the tone of the "official" response to the book. Bundy found it "dishonest in its use of facts, false in its theory, and a discredit to its author." A rejoinder from Buckley appeared in the December, 1951, issue of the *Atlantic,* along with a reply from Bundy, which began: "When I sat down to review Mr. Buckley's book, I was somewhat concerned lest my readers refuse to believe that so violent, unbalanced, and twisted a young man really existed." Theodore M. Greene, Professor of Philosophy at Yale, from whom one might have expected something better, began a long critique of the book in the *Yale News* with the observation: "Mr. Buckley has done Yale a great service, and he may do the cause of liberal education an even greater service, by stating the fascist alternative to liberalism so clearly that we can all see it for what it is." In the same issue of the *Yale News,* John Perry Miller, Professor of Economics, was only slightly more temperate than Greene. "The crux of Buckley's tract," his comments began, "is an authoritarian theory of university education which denies all the basic concepts of the university in a free society. Incidental to this theory, he presents a picture of religious and economic education at Yale which is warped and distorted beyond recognition and scurrilous and boorish in its reference to individuals."

In fairness to Yale and the academic profession, it must be said that not all academics became so hysterical as Professors Bundy and Greene. William K. Wimsatt, Jr., of the Yale English department, observed: "The section on religion I do not find startling. The voices of militant scepticism at Yale have always sounded to me far louder than those of evangelism. Despite the genuine religious and moral outlook of many individual members of the faculty, the prevailing secularism of the university is palpable. I agree with Mr. Buckley that a good deal of superstition currently attaches to the term 'academic freedom.' The freedom of a citizen never has been and never can be complete—unless in a society about to dissolve. And the scholar-teacher does not escape being a citizen. . . . A professor's political freedom can surely be no wider than anybody else's, and his responsibility is surely somewhat heavier than that of many others." Felix Morley, in a long review in *Barron's,* commented, ". . . his well-reasoned and well-supported argument must be taken seriously. . . . Mr. Buckley makes a case against current college instruction that cannot go unanswered." And Peter Viereck, in a not uncritical review in the New York *Times,* wrote: "As gadfly against the smug Comrade Blimps of the left, this important, symptomatic, and widely hailed book is a necessary counterbalance."

No book in the past generation has aroused more discussion and controversy, been more passionately condemned or more widely reviewed and commented on, than *God and Man at Yale.* It was an instant success, appeared on best-seller lists for weeks, and went through many printings. We had planned an extensive advertising and promotional campaign, and to help get the book noticed in New York had hired a bright and efficient lady, amusingly enough from the socialist *New Leader.* But all that was unnecessary—the vehemence of the response of the liberal establishment assured the book's success, and in William F. Buckley, Jr., we had an author whose talents for debate and for provoking his antagonists were of inestimable value.

We have come a long way since McGeorge Bundy characterized William F. Buckley, Jr., as being "violent, unbalanced, and twisted" for having pointed out a situation that subsequent events have made obvious. In spite of the storm it aroused, the immediate impact of Buckley's book, at least on Yale, was probably slight. As Bundy confidently predicted they would, Yale alumni contributed more to their university the year after publication than they ever had before. The great question the Buckley book raised, however, still remains unanswered, and asking it may well have been its greatest service. If those entrusted with interpreting and handing on what Eliseo Vivas has called the sustaining intellectual and moral structures of civilization instead disparage and subvert them, where are we to turn?

To have been the publisher of such a book was deeply satisfying. Not only was *God and Man at Yale* a great success; it made a constructive contribution to the intellectual ferment of the time, and I felt that I had played a small part in launching the career of a man who has since attained a position of great influence. But the book had one unforeseen consequence, and to explain what happened I must turn back briefly to the early days of the Henry Regnery Company.

Not long after its incorporation, while I still had my office above a drugstore in Hinsdale, I had a call from someone connected with the Great Books Foundation who asked if I would be interested in publishing the books used in the program. In those years before the "paperback revolution" it was difficult to find appropriate editions of most of the books participants in this adult-education project were expected to read, and then discuss at meetings directed by a "leader." The Foundation had itself prepared paperback editions of the eighteen works used in the first year, and had attempted to produce offset editions of some of the books used later that were particularly hard to find. But it did not have the capital, staff, or facilities to produce, store, and ship its own books; and it came to me with its problems after having first approached the University of Chicago Press, with discouraging consequences.

I myself had confidence in the idea and the people behind it, and saw an opportunity to acquire virtually overnight a solid list of books for which there would be a continuing demand—the nucleus of a "backlist," which is the basis of continuing success for any publishing house. After much discussion the Henry Regnery Company entered into an agreement in June, 1949, to publish the seventy-two books used in the first four years of the Great Books program. In 1951 we arranged to add the books used in the fifth year of the program. Although we lost money on the venture for the first two years, I was optimistic about it, and felt that it would become a substantial part of our business. The number of those participating in the program was growing, and we were developing a considerable sale of individual copies, particularly in the college bookstores. Our relations with the Foundation were also satisfactory. Its president during the early part of the association—Wilbur C. Munnecke, who had been a vice-president of the University of Chicago—was an excellent administrator and was always fair and open in his dealings with us. But his successor, though well meaning, was in my view incompetent and arrogant. And with the publication of *God and Man at Yale* we ran into serious troubles with the Foundation.

A few weeks after Buckley's book appeared, a friend of mine from another city came to my office late one afternoon directly from a meeting of the directors of the Foundation, of whom he was one. He told me that another of the directors, who was particularly influential, had been deeply angered by Buckley's book and insisted that the association between the Foundation and the Henry Regnery Company be terminated forthwith. Furthermore, he was now in a position to dispense with our services: Robert M. Hutchins had recently become head of the Ford Foundation, and support could be expected from it or from one of its subsidiaries.

Within a day or two Charles F. Strubbe, a lawyer by training who was now president of the Great Books Foundation, came to my

171

office and bluntly told me that the Foundation could indeed dispense with our services, and wished to break off the relationship. When I protested that we had a contract, he replied that any contract can be broken, that litigation would be protracted and costly, and that we would be much better off in the long run to let them buy us out and be done with it. When I pressed for reasons for this abrupt change in attitude, he remarked that our books were one-sided and that this was causing the Foundation embarrassment. He did not mention the Buckley book and of course I did not indicate that I was aware of what had gone on in the recent directors' meeting. When I pressed for a more specific description of what he meant by one-sided, he was evasive, reiterating only that our books were causing the Foundation embarrassment, that some of the directors were afraid this would hurt the program, and that our relationship would have to end.

The prospect was a serious matter for us. We had invested a substantial part of our capital and our corporate efforts in the project, and by now almost one-half of our total sales was accounted for by the paper-bound books we had published for the Foundation. On December 10, following numerous discussions with Strubbe and others connected with the Foundation, I wrote a long letter proposing an arrangement that would remove our name from the books used in the program, and eliminate the privilege of our selling sets of the books in bookstores, but still leave us with something. Under the terms of the contract, I pointed out, we had paid the Foundation more than $40,000 in royalties; in addition, the Foundation had enjoyed a substantial profit from the sale of the sets we had supplied to them, at no risk whatever to them and without the investment of a penny on their part.

Concerning any embarrassment caused to the Foundation by some of the books on our list, I remarked that although I had published a number that were undeniably controversial, I had published none that any reasonable person could consider detrimental to public morals, or that was in bad taste or dishonest. I said I felt sure our list compared favorably with that of any publisher in the United States.

All this was to no avail. The director who determined the policy of the Foundation wanted nothing to do with a publisher who would bring out such a book as *God and Man at Yale,* and with the resources of the Ford Foundation behind him he had no hesitation in breaking their contract with us. It was finally agreed that they would pay us $50,411 for our plates, which had cost us more than $65,000 (allowing nothing for proofreading or overhead), and the regular price, less an allowance for shipping and selling expenses, for our inventory of books packed in sets. We recovered our original cash investment, but were paid nothing for the value of the business we had built up, for the risk we had taken, or for the services we had performed for the Great Books Foundation.

It was a costly experience, but besides being educational, it showed me that there was a substantial market for good paperback editions of the classics, especially in college bookstores, and for a number of other titles in steady demand. As a result, we started our own series of quality paperbacks, Gateway Editions. Ironically enough, considering our reputation at that time, one of the best sellers in the series for years was the *Communist Manifesto*, which we would probably never have published at all if it had not been on the list of Great Books. In due course, Gateway Editions became a mainstay of the firm.

As for the association with Bill Buckley, it has been greatly rewarding. Our friendship has had its ups and downs, as seems often the case in the rather difficult relationship between author and publisher, but we published with great success another of his books, *McCarthy and His Enemies*, which he wrote with Brent Bozell. And we are still on good terms. Buckley was probably more sensitive to criticism in those days than he has since become, and was quick to fire off letters in reply to his critics, some of which I tried, without success, to induce him to tone down. When I sent a copy of *God and Man at Yale* to T. S. Eliot, I was disappointed that he did not think that it was suitable for publication in England by Faber & Faber, but was gratified to have him say, in his letter of reply, "Thank you . . . for sending me Mr. Buckley's book, which interested me very much. While I thought that he made one or two serious mistakes of strategy, I am glad to hear that it has attracted so much attention." Buckley, however, was incensed, and in a letter to me commented, "I am astounded and disappointed by the superficiality of T. S. Eliot's remarks about my book." I had expected him to be pleased that Eliot had read the book at all and taken the time to say something about it, but Buckley was a young man then, and his first book was, quite properly, a matter of the utmost seriousness.

We published *McCarthy and His Enemies* in 1954. It was as

perfectly timed as *God and Man at Yale*. The McCarthy episode, one of those overblown American phenomena that the communications apparatus periodically produces, had reached its climax. The liberal press would have had us believe, and would have us believe still, that the country was in the grip of a wave of terror, the universities in a state of panic, the foreign service paralyzed, books publicly burned, the press itself about to be stifled—all because of a single United States senator, acting virtually alone. College and university presidents, foreign-service officers, foundation executives, we are still solemnly told, lived in terror, all of them, haunted by the question where will he strike next? The liberal intellectual establishment gloried in the persecution to which it imagined it was being subjected, and in its own heroism, which it still recalls with the utmost self-gratification. The fact that it was far more dangerous for a professor to defend McCarthy than to attack him bothers the liberals not at all; nor, in its posture of the persecuted, does the liberal establishment consider the relative position of the antagonists—a single senator against the most powerful and influential group in the country, which, after it had recovered from the shock of his first attack and its own sense of guilt —McCarthy's accusations were by no means without foundation— proceeded to mobilize its forces and relentlessly to destroy him.

The attempt on the part of two young men to counter all this with a reasonable, carefully documented presentation of the facts and issues was probably naïve, at least insofar as reaching the intellectuals was concerned. But they made an honest try, and their book still stands as the authoritative account of the McCarthy episode.

The issue was clear and unequivocal: How does the government of the United States protect itself from subversion? The problem of treason in the world of modern technology and of Communism in the service of an enormously powerful state, is on an entirely different level from what it was, say, during the reign of Queen Victoria or President Cleveland. McCarthy's approach to the problem may have been drastic, but was far closer to the realities of the world as it is than that of the high government official Buckley and Bozell quote as having said, "A man in the employ of the government has just as much right to be a member of the Communist Party as he has to be a member of the Democratic or Republican Party." It was not, of course, so much a matter of party membership as of influence, but the attitude of this government official, as the careers of such men as Alger Hiss, Lauchlin Currie, Harry Dexter White, and Owen Lattimore demonstrate, was by no means unusual, and this, as Buckley and Bozell put it, "was the overriding problem when Senator McCarthy made his entrance on the national stage: having acknowledged the nature and immediacy of the peril, how might we get by our disintegrated ruling elite, which had no stomach for battle, and get down to the business of fighting the enemy in our midst?"

William F. Buckley, Jr., was a most satisfactory author, and the seasons of *God and Man at Yale* and *McCarthy and His Enemies* among the most memorable of my publishing career. We made several trips together to promote one book or the other, and Buckley often stayed with us—on at least one occasion with his striking and delightful wife, who in no way except perhaps skiing needs to take second place to Bill. He was a great favorite with our four children, who were quite small then. He brought them presents, played games, and told them stories. Most memorable of all for them was his performance on our piano of "Variations on the Theme *Three Blind Mice.*" It began quietly and demurely, became more and more flamboyant, and ended in a perfect torrent of pyrotechnics, at which point the children, whom we had carefully brought up on Bach and Mozart, having watched absolutely spellbound, would say in one voice, "Do it again!"

We published many books related in one way or another to conservatism, and taken together they doubtless contributed to what became the title and substance of an imposing book, *The Conservative Intellectual Movement in the United States since 1945*, written by George H. Nash. It was not with a movement in mind, however, that they were published; each book was accepted on its merits as it came along, and if, as a group, they make a remarkably coherent whole, this is more a reflection of the intellectual ferment of the time and my own estimation of what was worth publishing than any conscious intention on my part to launch a movement.

There were three books on the structure of American government: James Jackson Kilpatrick's *The Sovereign States*, Felix Morley's *Freedom and Federalism*, and James Burnham's *Congress and the American Tradition*. These three books, published within a period of less than two years, complement one another in a remarkable fashion, and taken together constitute an eloquent defense of constitutional government as it evolved, at least until 1933, in the United States.

When he wrote *The Sovereign States*, Kilpatrick was editor of the Richmond *News-Leader*. This book, which was published in 1957, may properly be considered, I think, the southern reply to *Brown* vs. *Board of Education*, the Supreme Court decision of May 17, 1954, which undertook to put an end to racial separation in the public schools. Although the school decision was the immediate stimulus to the writing of the book, its concern is with the much larger issue of the usurpation by Washington of the authority of the states.

Kilpatrick is a fine stylist, and he developed his thesis with the eloquence of the great Virginia orators he so much admires. Our government, Kilpatrick argues, was constitutionally intended to be a federation of sovereign states jointly controlling their mutual agent, the federal government. It is true that the sovereign states jointly had delegated some of their powers, but they did not become less sovereign thereafter. They remained separate, respective states. Although the Fourteenth Amendment has greatly weakened the power of the individual states, as has the income-tax amendment, the states still have the means to protect themselves if they would use it. This was the "right of interposition," as developed by James Madison in his report of 1799 to the Virginia House of Delegates during the great controversy that resulted from the Alien and Sedition Acts. Kilpatrick quotes the following sentence from Madison's report:

That, in case of deliberate, palpable, and dangerous exercise of other powers, not granted by the said compact, the States, who are parties thereto, have the right and are in duty bound, to interpose for arresting the progress of evil, and for maintaining within their respective limits, the authorities, rights, and liberties appertaining to them.

"This," Kilpatrick adds, "is the heart and soul of the 'right to interpose.' The language was to be re-affirmed, substantially verbatim, by the Hartford Convention in 1814; by the Wisconsin Legislature in 1859; and by the Virginia Assembly in 1956. When men talk of the 'Doctrine of '98,' this is the paragraph they are talking of."

Kilpatrick gives many examples of the use of interposition by individual states, which are of the greatest interest in themselves, and clearly show how much we have lost of the independence

Americans once regarded as their most treasured and characteristic possession. When the Supreme Court, in the Chisholm case brought against the state of Georgia in 1793, commanded the state to appear in court or suffer judgment in default, the sovereign state of Georgia responded in no uncertain terms. "The Georgia House of Representatives passed a bill providing that any Federal marshal who attempted to levy upon the property of Georgia in executing the court's order 'shall be . . . guilty of felony, and shall suffer death, without the benefit of clergy, by being hanged.' " There were the Kentucky and Virginia Resolutions, in the preparation of which both Jefferson and Madison had a leading part, in answer to the Alien and Sedition Acts of 1798; the Olmstead case, in which the governor of Pennsylvania ordered out the state militia to prevent a United States marshal from serving a writ against two ladies who had inherited a sum of money in a disputed prize case; and, of course, the revolt of the New England states against the Embargo Acts of 1807 and 1809. He describes all this in fascinating detail and in great style, which makes the supine acceptance by present-day Americans of any order emanating from a federal court or agency, no matter how outrageous, all the more depressing. The threat by some bureaucrat to withhold "federal" money—it comes, after all, from the taxpayers—is sufficient to bring any recalcitrant state, city, school board, or, for that matter, university promptly into line.

Although I am not at all sure that Felix Morley would care to be called a conservative—he prefers to be known as an old-fashioned liberal—his book made its own contribution to conservatism by clearly defining the nature of freedom and federalism and the distinction between a democracy and the federal system of the United States Constitution. It is the purpose of *Freedom and Federalism*, which was published in 1959, to define the principles and circumstances that had made the American form of government eminently successful—to determine why it was that the political system of this representative republic has done more for its people as a whole than any other ever devised. In addition, Morley undertakes to describe the influences that currently endanger the continuance of the American form of government as it has developed since the Philadelphia Convention. Like Kilpatrick, Morley lays great stress on the federal structure of the American system. The immediate issue that motivated him to begin his book was the threat to the independence of the Supreme Court implied in President Roosevelt's attempt to reorganize it through the "court packing bill of February 5, 1937." It was the President's Fireside Chat on the following March 9, in which he undertook to allay the mounting criticism of the bill, by, among other things, asserting that his only purpose was to make democracy succeed, which, Morley said, "for the first time brought home to me . . . the demonstrable fact that uncritical praise and practice of political democracy can readily be the highway to dictatorship, even in the United States. The collection of material for this book was begun that evening."

Morley is willing to grant that American society is democratic, but society must be distinguished from government. The democratic nature of American society, in his opinion, is based on a religious conception, that "all are brothers under the Fatherhood of God." From this, he says, derives the idea of equality that underlies American society and makes it democratic—the idea that all men are subject to the same natural laws and therefore should be treated equally by man-made laws. The American structure of government, however, is not democratic and was never intended to be. Morley puts great emphasis on the destructive influence of Rousseau, particularly his specious but superficially appealing conception of the "general will." "A single, unified popular will," Morley points out, "implies a single, unified governmental direction to make the will effective." Hitler and Stalin both doubtless considered themselves to be the embodiment of the "national will," which was the basis of the claim that their systems were democratic. That Franklin D. Roosevelt thought of himself in a somewhat similar fashion is not so farfetched as it may sound. In his State of the Union message of January 6, 1941, in which he outlined what he called the "four essential freedoms," Roosevelt proclaimed that a free nation has the right to expect full co-operation from all groups. This, Morley argues, is exactly what Rousseau meant in stating that "whosoever refuses to obey the general will must in that instance be restrained by the body politic, which actually means that he is forced to be free."

Morley is well aware of the continuing vitality of the American system and tradition of government; he is equally aware of the forces behind the growing tendency to concentrate political power in Washington, to change what he termed the "Federal Republic" into a centralized democracy. Two amendments to the Constitution, in his opinion, had "operated subtly to undermine the federal structure of the United States as originally planned. The Fourteenth Amendment in effect reversed the emphasis of the first eight Amendments, all designed to limit the powers of the central government, so as to make these limitations applicable by the central government to the States. The Sixteenth Amendment supplemented this revolutionary change by giving the central government virtually unlimited power to tax the people without regard to State needs or boundaries." It was the Sixteenth Amendment, of course, that provided the means to implement the "service state," which gradually becomes the bureaucratic state.

James Jackson Kilpatrick and Felix Morley are both journalists in the best tradition of that much maligned profession. Both are serious students of American history and government, but the particular strength of their approach to the problem of government is their intimate, firsthand knowledge of how it actually works, and their unblinking realism.

James Burnham can best be described as a political philosopher in a tradition that goes back to Plato, but when I first met him he was associated with the magazine *National Review*, and could therefore also be described as a journalist. He has thought deeply about government: how it comes into being, the basis of its legitimacy and its right to power, its purpose, its limitations, and the basis on which a particular government is to be judged. When I first talked to him about a book, I suggested that he write a study of the congressional investigating committee. In the aftermath of the McCarthy episode, and particularly in view of the liberal intellectuals' irrational response to it, I believed there was a danger that the importance and unique function of the congressional committee could be overlooked. I felt a need for a serious, solidly based book showing how the congressional investigating committee has developed and the enormously important role it has played, one that was all the more necessary as a counterweight to the constantly growing power of the executive department of government. Out of this suggestion came a much more inclusive study, not just of the place of the congressional committee in our system, but of Congress as a whole. Reading it again makes me all the more convinced that *Congress and the American Tradition* will, with time, be recognized as one of the classic books on American government.

Political philosopher that he is, Burnham quite properly begins with a discussion of the sources of government. By what right does one man rule another? There is, he says, no rational answer to the question: ". . . the problem of government is, strictly speaking, insoluble; and yet it is solved." The ancients sought the answer in myth: "In ancient times, before the illusions of science had corrupted traditional wisdom, the founders of Cities were known to be gods or demigods." Contemporary explanations of the sources of government use a less picturesque language, but they tell us little more. "Without acceptance by habit, tradition or faith of a principle which completes the justification for government," Burnham asserts, "government dissolves, or falls back wholly on force —which is itself, of course, non-rational."

The principle that Americans have traditionally accepted as the justification of government, of rule by another, is embodied in the "We, the People" of the Preamble to the Constitution. This, of course, is also a myth. The Constitution was not ordained or established by the people of the United States; it was drafted by the members of the Philadelphia Convention and ratified by the individual states. As with all myths, its acceptance makes it true, and it will remain true only so long as it lives as a part of the American tradition.

No one, I feel confident, has expressed the tradition of American government more eloquently or beautifully than James Burnham:

Surely it must have been their faith in tradition as a living and continuous force that reconciled the Fathers to a document that, as the lawyers that many of them were, they would never have accepted as a valid contract: internally contradictory, with its assertions of dual and divided sovereignty; ambiguous as well as unfinished in its definition and assignment of rights, duties and power. Pure reason could not guarantee a good government, strong, just and free. But reasonable men, drawing on the wisdom of the past shaped into institutions as well as principles, and relying on the future interplay between individuals and their inheritance of tradition, might devise an orienting directive which would itself become an essential, even critical, part of the living tradition.

So, of course, has the Constitution become, so that it seems the précis, the distillation of the entire American political tradition. Our governmental structure, whether good or not as conceived rational system, *becomes, is made,* good and even the best through time and history. The Constitution is like a man's wife who, though to tell the truth that would be revealed by an objective scale, she is not the most beautiful and talented creature in the world, nevertheless through twenty or thirty or fifty years of successful marriage *becomes,* as a living and historical being a good and indeed the best of all possible wives. . . .

. . . I accept it as right that Congress, the President and the courts shall govern me because they have been chosen by prescribed forms (however strange in themselves, and very strange they are) that have been honored by observance and prior acceptance.

Having described the place of Congress in the American system of government as it was intended by the Founders and as it developed during the nineteenth century—the "Golden Age" of parliamentary government, as he called it—Burnham goes on to consider the current position of Congress. Article I of the Constitution granted "all legislative powers" to "a Congress of the United States." In addition, Congress was to exert a strong influence over those other two attributes of government, the sword and the purse. "The size, temper and target of the sword are to be decided by Congress, just as Congress is to determine the amount, source and purpose of the monies," says Burnham. "The President wields the sword, as he opens the purse, only as attorney, steward, agent for Congress, and only through Congress for the nation and the people." The Congress, of course, still goes through the formality of passing laws, levying taxes, and appropriating money, of exercising its legislative prerogative, but more often than not the initiative for legislation comes not from Congress itself but from the executive department. In actual practice and in many ways the judiciary and the bureaucracy exert a far greater legislative power than Congress; in both legislation and fiscal control, Congress is in danger of becoming little more than a formality. As for the war-making power, once thought to be vested solely in Congress, here too the President has assumed the decisive voice. "Not only do the presidential acts, as in the case of Franklin Roosevelt's moves from 1939 to 1941, make a war inevitable, so that the Pearl Harbor occasion of its open start is, like the congressional declaration, a secondary incident; President Truman further demonstrated in Korea how one of the biggest wars of our history, in terms of casualties and cost, can now be entered and conducted without any legal authority from the legislature, simply by not calling it a 'war.' " In a process that began during the early days of the New Deal, Congress has more and more become accustomed to delegating its powers to the executive and the various agencies it had established. But, as Burnham points out, "To 'delegate' such powers as control over money, war and foreign affairs is, in reality, to renounce them, to abdicate."

It was not always so. Burnham tells us that through most of our history there has been congressional predominance within the central government. To illustrate his point, he quotes John Quincy Adams, who wrote in his diary after his first election to Congress in 1830: "My election as President of the United States was not half so gratifying to my innermost soul. No election or appointment conferred upon me ever gave me so much pleasure." Can one imagine a former President making such an observation in our day, or even giving a moment's consideration to the possibility of becoming a member of Congress? "To understand what is happening to the political structure of American society," Burnham continues. "we need to keep both facts in mind: that the legislature was, traditionally, predominant in theory and practice, and that it is no longer so." In the modern, computerized, highly bureaucratic state, in which every citizen must have his Social Security number and his every transaction is carefully monitored by the Internal Revenue Service, has Congress—with its debates, its committees, and its formalized procedures—become an anachronism, a picturesque but wholly unnecessary vestige of the eighteenth century? Burnham most emphatically believes not, and he bases his justification of Congress on a rigorous discussion of government and the threat to liberty inherent in its nature.

He distinguishes between two possible forms of government in the modern world: one based on the "general will," on "the theory that the will of the people is the ultimate sovereign," and the other on a "structure of government in which there obtains, or is thought to obtain, a 'rule of law,' certain 'rights' that are in some sense basic and inalienable, and a 'juridical defense' that protects the citizen through forms of 'due process' backed by the underlying rule of law." The first he calls the "democratic formula," which became the "democratist ideology," and the second the "constitutional principle." Between the two, he asserted, there "is no logical relation whatever."

The democratic formula necessarily ends in dictatorship, because only Caesar, whether his name be Bonaparte, Hitler, Stalin, Mussolini, or Perón, can embody the people's will. "Caesar is the symbolic solution—and the only possible solution—for the problem of realizing the general will, that is, for the central problem of democratist ideology."

Although there is no necessary connection between representative assemblies and liberty, the survival of constitutional government and liberty under the power relationship now existing between the citizen and the state depends on the survival of Congress. It is what Burnham calls the intermediary institutions that diffuse the power of the state and thereby protect the liberty of the individual citizen. Chief among these, with the reduced influence of the individual states and the subservience of local government and the judiciary to the executive and the bureaucracy, is Congress. If it ceases to be an actively functioning political institution, then political liberty in the United States will soon come to an end, Burnham asserts. If Congress continues to exercise a political function, then there will be at least a measure of political liberty. No one, he says, can deny the accuracy and cogency of many of the adverse criticisms that have been made of Congress as an institution and of many individual congressmen. But the hard relation remains: if liberty, then Congress; if no Congress, no liberty. "For Congress to survive politically," he goes on to say, "means that it shall be prepared to say *Yes* or *No,* on its own finding and responsibility, in answer to the questions of major policy; and this it cannot do unless the individual members of Congress have the courage to speak, to say *No* even against the tidal pressures from the executive, the bureaucracy, and the opinion-molders so often allied in our day with executive and bureaucracy, even against the threat that the semi-Caesarian executive will rouse his masses for reprisal at the polls—or in the streets."

During the course of his discussion of the American system of government, Burnham develops a most illuminating syndrome, as he calls it, to illustrate the contrasting characteristics of the liberal and conservative positions. This includes such attitudes toward man as belief on the part of the conservative that human nature is limited and corrupt and on the part of the liberal in its unlimited potentiality. In the area of government, Burnham finds a presumption on the part of the conservative in favor of Congress as against the executive. He believes that the liberal is inclined to view with favor the concentration and centralization of government power in the interest of social progress, whereas the conservative is suspicious of government power in any form, and therefore inclines toward states' rights and the diffusion of power.

In this connection, it is interesting to observe that the response of liberal reviewers to the Morley, Kilpatrick, and Burnham books accurately reflected the attitudes Burnham described.

C. L. Black, in the *Yale Review*, dismissed the Kilpatrick book as without serious merit, and went on to say that it "strikingly exemplifies the South's intellectual desperation in the present crisis of its caste system." Cecil Johnson, in the *Annals of the American Academy*, wrote that Kilpatrick, "if he applied himself with the same energy and enthusiasm and selected his materials as carefully . . . might produce comparable treatises in defense of slavery or in condemnation of democracy." William S. White, in the New York *Times*, was more generous. He did not agree with the book, but found it "an extraordinary essay by a gifted, if perhaps very wrong-headed man. A polemical tract, it nevertheless has grace and skill."

Two such distinguished scholars as Roscoe Pound, the former dean of Harvard Law School, and Edith Hamilton praised the Morley book in the highest terms. Cecil Miller, on the other hand, expressed the opinion in *Ethics* that Morley "is essentially apologetic with respect to the question of states' rights," and concluded, "If such tongue-in-cheek philosophizing serves a useful purpose, this reviewer fails to discern what it is." He also, I am sure, failed to read the book.

The response to the Burnham book provides an even more striking example of the refusal or inability of the liberal intellectuals to confront the serious issues these three books raise. In the *American Political Science Review*, R. H. Salisbury expressed the opinion, which he made no effort to substantiate, that "some difficult factual and theoretical contradictions are glided over simplistically." In the *Annals of the American Academy*, A. N. Holcombe criticized Burnham for not troubling himself "to consider the impact of the unplanned party system on the constitutional scheme of government"—a "strange neglect, which may explain his failure to put together a more persuasive case for his pessimistic conclusions." In the *Christian Century*, Paul Simon conceded that the book was well written and made some valid points, but concluded that it was "an effective presentation of a weak case." In the New York *Herald Tribune*, R. K. Carr found that the book was "rooted in more than one factual error," without specifying what they were, and that this was "fatal to the central thesis." It remained, however, for Lindsay Rogers, of Columbia University, to demonstrate the greatest skill in the art of evading the issue: he pontificated in the New York *Times*, "Occasionally in his book Mr. Burnham discloses that if he is not an amateur in the matters he considers, he is plowing fields that have only recently become familiar to him."

There were two other books by men who, like James Burnham, were closely associated with *National Review*: Frank S. Meyer's *In Defense of Freedom*, published in 1962, and Willmoore Kendall's *The Conservative Affirmation*, in 1963.

Willmoore Kendall was an enormously gifted and also an enormously complicated man. It must be said that he was also something of a trial for his publisher, but dealing with such people is one of the challenging and attractive aspects of the publisher's profession. Kendall was born in a small town in Oklahoma, the son of a southern Methodist minister. His father was blind, in consequence of which Kendall became accustomed from an early age to reading aloud to him and discussing what he had read. He graduated from high school at thirteen, entered Northwestern University the same year, and at the age of eighteen graduated from the University of Oklahoma. After graduate work at the University of Illinois he spent several years at Oxford as a Rhodes scholar, an experience that had a lasting influence on him. An incipient trend to the left was brought to an end, apparently, by a period he spent in Spain, shortly before the outbreak of the Spanish Civil War, as a correspondent for United Press. This made him into a lifelong, uncompromising anti-Communist. He could tolerate the Communists blowing up the plants of opposition newspapers, he is reported to have said, but deliberately killing opposition newsboys was too much.

Kendall was an original thinker, an inspiring teacher, a superb lecturer and debater when in the mood, and the master of an English style that, for all its twists and turns, is wonderfully expressive and ingratiating. He was unduly contentious, but he could also be a warm and generous friend. He was never one to accept anything at face value; he arrived at his conclusions on the basis of rigorous thought, and was without doubt one of the truly original and creative figures in the field of political science of his time. Difficult as he was as a person, we would be much poorer without his legacy.

I first met Kendall fairly early in my publishing career. He made numerous suggestions for additions to our paperback Gateway series, and gave us an accurate, scholarly translation for our edition of Rousseau's *The Social Contract*. There arrived from him one day the following letter, dated Northford, Connecticut, February 8, 1962. As was his habit at the time, he had written it in bright-green ink:

I propose to have ready to go (I'm using the sections for my lectures here at Georgetown) about two months from now an Intelligent Undergraduate's Guide to Contemporary American Conservatism, all by way of answer to the omnipresent question, What Is Conservatism Anyhow? There'll be chapters on The Old Sage of Mecosta, The Pseudo-Sage of Ithaca, the Rubbed Sage of Woodstock, the Young Sage of Stamford, the Muscleminded Sage of Kent, and the Nascent Sage of Indianapolis—and *not* all from the standpoint of the Worried Sage of Northford, but rather from that of the "movement" as he sees it to be shaping up. . . . How interested might you be in such a book, and what might you undertake to do for me in re getting it out fastish?

I answered this letter on February 12, in a manner, as his reply soon made apparent, that was much too brusque and presumptuous:

I was glad to have your letter of February 8. Your proposed book sounds most interesting, and I would like to see it. The only problem I can see is that I have already committed myself to two other books which might compete with yours, but I can tell better after I have seen it. Send along the manuscript. I look forward to reading it with pleasure.

Rather than the manuscript I expected to "read with pleasure," I received a long, violent letter, written on a typewriter, probably for greater emphasis. I will quote only enough to give its flavor:

Apparently I state myself badly in my recent letter—or, failing that, you misread it. In either case, you seem to have got the impression that I was *courting* the honor of having my book published by your company. Now: that is very far from being the case: I'd *much* rather, other things being equal, have my book published by a regular publisher on the East Coast . . . any book you publish starts with a couple of strikes against it because (see my recent letter) your lack of discrimination, at the margin, about whom you publish . . . as you indicate in your letter, your problem is to keep such books as my own from getting in each other's way—which I would *not* dream of letting mine do, on *your* list, to any of the other things you have coming up.
. . . I'd *like* to do business with you. But it seems to me that you make it impossible for one to do so, and that is to say that henceforth, failing some long overdue gestures on your part, I am not even trying to do so. Let me add, in case you might feel this letter is imprudent: My files contain many interesting things, but no unpublished manuscripts by
Yours sincerely

The letter was signed "Willmoore," in green ink, with an elegant flourish beneath—the flourish made me feel that it was not to be taken too tragically. I replied on March 5 that if he had no confidence in our competence as publishers it would be better if he went to someone else, and added that in view of this I was surprised that he had ever suggested the book to me at all. I ended my letter with the comment:

I respect your work and what you have done, and I think that I have made it clear at various times that I would like to have a book from you. For fear of causing more misunderstanding, perhaps I had better leave it at that.

It all worked out amicably, as I think was often the case with Willmoore's battles. The "regular publisher on the East Coast," not surprisingly, was not interested, and the manuscript came to us. It was not, fortunately, the "sages" manuscript announced in his first letter, but the book we published the following year as *The Conservative Affirmation*.

Superficially *The Conservative Affirmation* would appear to be a random collection of seven essays having such titles as "What Is Conservatism?," "The Two Majorities in American Politics," "McCarthyism, the Pons Asinorum of Contemporary Conservatism," "Freedom of Speech in America," "Conservatism and the 'Open Society.'" To these a preface had been added, and at the end a group of book reviews. Heterogeneous as the book might appear to be, however, it is held together and given purpose by a clearly stated and very important idea, which was basic to Kendall's conception of government and society. He sets it down thus in the essay on McCarthyism:

All political societies, all peoples, but especially I like to think our political society, this *"people of the United States,"* is founded upon what political philosophers call a consensus; that is, a hard core of shared beliefs. Those beliefs that the people share are what defines its character as a political society, what embodies its meaning as a political society, what, above all, perhaps, expresses its understanding of itself as a political society, of its role and responsibility in history, of its very destiny. . . . "We," cries the American people at the very moment of its birth . . . "hold these *truths*." That is, "we" believe that there is such a thing as Truth, believe that the particular Truths of which Truth is made up are discoverable by man's reason and thus by our reason, recognize *these* truths as those to which our reason and that of our forebears have led us, and agree with one another to *hold* these truths—that is, to cherish them as ours, to hand them down in their integrity to our descendants, to defend them against being crushed out of existence by enemies from without or corrupted out of existence by the acids of skepticism and disbelief working from within.

He goes on to say that American society could therefore pro-scribe certain doctrines and beliefs, and it must unhesitatingly proscribe those of the Communists, preferably long before they had an opportunity to become a clear and present danger. It was on the basis of this conviction that Kendall argues his case against John Stuart Mill's conception of freedom of speech and against Karl Popper's theory of the "open society"; it was on the basis of this idea, furthermore, that he defines conservatism. Conservatives, he says, are those who are defending an established order against those who seek to undermine or transform it. Conservatism "dis-tinguishes between 'change' directed at the *development and per-fection* of our heritage as *that which it is,* and 'change' calculated to transform that heritage into *that which it is not;* and far from opposing the former, stands forth as its champion." It was his deeply held conviction that the conservative's "highest political loyalty . . . is to the institutions and way of life bequeathed to us by the Philadelphia Convention."

Whereas conservatives, in Kendall's view, seek to defend an established social order, liberalism involves a principle that looks to the overthrow of that order and is therefore revolutionary.

Kendall's book was only moderately successful. We printed 6,000 copies and sold during the first year or two about 3,800. But in spite of that, we remained friends—which, all things con-sidered, I felt was no mean achievement. Kendall was an excellent and prolific letter writer; I received dozens of letters from him, some pages long, all as interesting as they were unpredictable, and all bearing the unmistakable stamp of his unique personality. The most frequent subject, not surprisingly, was some book project or other, a translation, an addition to our Gateway series, or a book of his own, which was usually to be a collection of previously published articles. When I protested that such books are always particularly difficult to sell and urged him to sit down and write a "real book," he explained his position at great length, concluding, in one letter, "I have a mind which is capable of seizing upon parts of a problem that I can sense rather than define, and feel, as of any given moment, capable merely of dealing with one by one and even that, often, only under pressure I invite, as with the Prayer Decision piece, by agreeing to lecture on it. . . ."

The last four years of his life were relatively tranquil. In 1963 he accepted a professorship at the University of Dallas, where he was appreciated, and after two unsuccessful marriages found happiness in a third. He died in 1967 at the age of fifty-eight. For all the perversity of his nature, Willmoore Kendall was a man of uncompromising intellectual integrity. Those who knew him, or who come to know him through his work, will not soon forget him.

In the previous chapter I spoke of Frank Meyer's criticism of Russell Kirk's *The Conservative Mind*. In a compact, closely argued book, *In Defense of Freedom: A Conservative Credo*, which we published in 1962, Meyer further elaborated his criticism of what he called "the New Conservatism" and undertook to set forth his own position, which he had been developing in articles in the *National Review*, the *Freeman, Modern Age*, and similar journals. He felt that Kirk and those of similar views, with their emphasis on order and tradition, were inclined to subordinate the individual to society. For him the central and primary end of political society is to vindicate the freedom of the person, and the proper end of the individual is to use his freedom for the attainment of virtue. He emphatically denied, however, that freedom itself is subordinate to moral and spiritual ends. He made freedom an absolute, unrelated to purpose: "Freedom that is not used to achieve high ends does not become something else; it does not change into another entity, 'license.' It is simply freedom that is not used to achieve high ends, freedom badly used; but it is still freedom."

Meyer's deep commitment to individual freedom was doubtless a reaction to his earlier commitment to Communism. As a young man he had been an active member of the Communist Party, and while a student at the London School of Economics he managed to get himself expelled from England for his Communist activities. Although his book presented the extreme libertarian position of conservatism, it was also his intention to reconcile the various aspects of conservatism. As it worked out, the categorical, rigidly logical manner of his presentation did have this effect because of the discussion it brought forth. In a long, carefully reasoned article in *National Review*, L. Brent Bozell took strong exception to Meyer's view of freedom: "The urge to freedom for its own sake is, in the last analysis, a rebellion against nature; it is the urge to be free from God." For Bozell, "true sanctity is achieved only when man loses his freedom—when he is freed of the temptation to displease God." In a review headed "An Ideologue of Liberty" in the *Sewanee Review*, Russell Kirk concluded: "Disdainful of duty and 'the contract of eternal society,' Mr. Meyer . . . can appeal to little but the arrogant ego." Many others joined the battle— Richard Weaver, Felix Morley, Stanley Perry, John Hallowell, and Stephen Tonsor—to Meyer's intense pleasure. Meyer enjoyed a fight as much as Willmoore Kendall, and was equally skillful in defending his position and seeking out weak points in that of his adversary. But he could also be most persuasive, as is evidenced by the fact that only two years after the battle engendered by the publication of *In Defense of Freedom* he succeeded in inducing nearly all of his critics to contribute to a collection of essays published under the title *What Is Conservatism? In Defense of Freedom* is a book of only 172 pages, but, perhaps more because of the exchange of views it stimulated than because of the position it represented, it became one of the landmark books in the development of the conservative movement.

Richard Weaver's *Ideas Have Consequence*, published by the University of Chicago Press in 1948, deserves to be considered one of the books from which the postwar conservative movement took its start. We published two books by him: *The Ethics of Rhetoric* in 1953 and *Life Without Prejudice* in 1965, after his death.

For most of his active life, Weaver was an effective and most respected teacher of English in the College of the University of Chicago. It was doubtless devotion to his subject and an affinity for the classics that explain his serious interest in rhetoric. The first of his books we published, which he once told me was his best, was the result of many years of careful study; it is a jewel of the mind, and I am sure will take its place among the classic books on the subject. He begins with a beautifully presented discussion of Plato's *Phaedrus*: "If we will bring to the reading of it even a portion of that imagination which Plato habitually exercised, we should perceive surely enough that it is consistently, and from beginning to end, about one thing, which is the nature of rhetoric." He concludes that rhetoric consists of truth plus its artful presentation, and goes on to say that at its truest it "seeks to perfect men by showing them better versions of themselves, links in that chain extending upward toward the ideal, which only the intellect can apprehend and only the soul have affection for."

It is in a chapter on Lincoln's rhetoric that Weaver's often quoted definition of conservatism appears: "The true conservative is one who sees the universe as a paradigm of essences, of which the phenomenology of the world is a sort of continuing approximation. Or, to put this another way, he sees it as a set of definitions which are struggling to get themselves defined in the real world." Characteristically, Weaver uses a quotation from Lincoln, whom he regarded as a true conservative, to illustrate his point, namely Lincoln's observation concerning the Framers of the Declaration of Independence: "They meant to set up a standard maxim for a free society, which should be familiar to all, and revered by all; constantly looked to, constantly labored for, and even though never perfectly attained, constantly approximated, and thereby constantly spreading and deepening its influence and augmenting the happiness and value of life to all people of all colors everywhere."

Life Without Prejudice is a collection of essays put together by Harvey Plotnick, a friend and former student of Weaver's, who carefully went through everything he had left and selected these as the best. In his introduction, a beautifully written tribute to an old friend, Eliseo Vivas points out that despite appearances the book is not a heterogeneous collection, because the essays are unified by a central concern—the plight of modern man. "In his urbane manner, in his courteous voice," said Vivas, "Weaver is making a devastating exposé of our plight. And he is telling us that that plight was of our own making and that it is not too late to do something about it. . . . Weaver always writes with a persuasiveness that is a result of the tensile strength and economy of his prose and thought. . . . He was a writer of distinguished prose, elegant, lucid, yet unobtrusive."

Richard Weaver was born and grew up in Weaverville, North Carolina, a small place near Asheville. During all the years he taught at the University of Chicago he went back to Weaverville every summer, always by train—he refused to fly. "You have to draw the line somewhere," he would say. His mother would have his garden ready for him to plant on his arrival; he always insisted it be plowed by a horse rather than a tractor, which became rather difficult to arrange for in his later years. He was unmarried, lived in an untidy room near the university, was rather shy and un-

191

obtrusive but very definite and decided in his opinions. He always felt himself, I think, to be somewhat of an outsider at the University of Chicago, however much he may have enjoyed his teaching and the stimulation of his students and colleagues. For all his scholarship and love of learning, Weaver was a down-to-earth sort of man who, as Albert J. Nock would put it, saw the world as it is; in the rather rarefied, overly intellectual atmosphere of the University of Chicago, which is inclined to view the world as if from a considerable distance and without commitment, Weaver felt himself, I think, to be a stranger. Shortly before he died, in 1963 at the age of fifty-three, Weaver had accepted a visiting professorship at Vanderbilt University, which he hoped might become a permanent appointment. He was much admired and respected by those who knew him; his loss, as Eliseo Vivas said, is irreparable.

We published a number of other books that contributed variously to the intellectual substance of the conservative movement, but perhaps the two that had the greatest and most lasting influence were by the German economist Wilhelm Roepke, both originally published in German by Eugen Rentsch in Zurich. Roepke, when I knew him, was teaching in the Graduate School of International Studies in Geneva. A few weeks after Hitler came to power he forfeited his professorship at the University of Marburg by his uncompromising, open opposition to National Socialism. Had he been willing to adapt himself to the times in the manner of many academics, and not only German academics, he would doubtless have had a great career in National Socialist Germany. Blond and blue-eyed, he was a brilliant lecturer and a prolific and skillful writer, and he had an outstanding war record. Instead he chose exile and managed to support his family, before receiving the appointment in Geneva, by teaching in Istanbul.

He was a principled and eloquent supporter of the free market, of whose limitations, however, he was well aware. He never lost sight of the primacy of the spiritual and ethical aspects of life, and this, perhaps, plus his moral courage, was the basis for his great influence. Characteristic of Roepke is the following: "Self-discipline, a sense of justice, honesty, fairness, chivalry, moderation, public spirit, respect for human dignity, firm ethical norms—all of these are things which people must possess before they go to market and compete with each other." But the Roepke quotation I like best of all is this: "The highest interests of the community and the indispensable things of life have no exchange value and are neglected if supply and demand are allowed to dominate the field."

The modern conservative movement cannot be properly described with such words as *boring, uniform, sterile,* nor do its leaders give the impression of having been cast from the same mold. The variety, vigorous discussion, and occasional rather violent differences of opinion that have characterized the conservative movement have added to its vitality and interest, but have probably lessened its popular influence. Popular influence, however, has not been the overriding passion of such men as I have been describing. Although they would not scorn or eschew it if it came their way, their predominant interest was in ideas, and in reaching the people for whom ideas are important; and in this they may, in the long run, have been correct. It is, in the end, ideas—not newspapers, television personalities, bureaucrats, or politicians—that rule the world. How many students Plato had in his academy I have no idea, certainly not more than a few hundred, of whom one was Aristotle. But Plato is still, after more than 2,000 years, one of the great teachers of mankind. We know the names of Herod and Pontius Pilate only because they happened to be living at the time of Christ, just as Brezhnev, according to a current bit of Russian folk wisdom, will be remembered only as a politician of the time of Solzhenitsyn.

The conservative movement is not the side of the big battalions, but it is a carrier of the traditions and values that have sustained and given substance to Western civilization, and those within it can feel that they have assumed an honorable task and are in distinguished company.

10

ROY CAMPBELL,
WYNDHAM LEWIS,
T. S. ELIOT, EZRA POUND

W HEN I began to publish, shortly after World War II, I hoped
that our firm would be swept along by such a tide of creativity as
had followed the first war. There was no such tide, as we all know,
but I did meet four of the great figures of that earlier period—
T. S. Eliot, Wyndham Lewis, Ezra Pound, and Roy Campbell—
and I published books by three of them. Roy Campbell, who was
the only one of the four I came to know well, for all his great vitality and poetic gifts, never gained the influence or reputation of the
other three. He was allied with Wyndham Lewis in several skir-
mishes with the denizens of Bloomsbury, and he knew and greatly
admired T. S. Eliot, who arranged for the publication of some of
his poetry, but he never met Ezra Pound. The association of Eliot,
Lewis, and Pound began when the two issues of *Blast* were published, in 1914 and 1915, and continued to the end of their lives.

In their creative achievement these four men were very much a
part of their time and among its chief ornaments. But in another
way they lived outside their time, since they strongly rejected the

positions of those who were popularly regarded, and who regarded themselves, as its intellectual leaders and spokesmen. They were classicists: their commitment, as Lewis put it, was to the life of reason, to what is harmonious and beautifully ordered. For the intellectual fads that captivated their contemporaries—Marxism, psychoanalysis, relativism, egalitarianism, positivism, scientism—they had no patience whatever.

I first met Roy Campbell in the spring of 1953, when he came to Chicago to give a lecture as part of a series by contemporary poets arranged by the University of Chicago. Having published his autobiographical work *Light on a Dark Horse*, I was asked to meet him at the station on his arrival from St. Louis and escort him to a reception in the former Borden mansion on Lake Shore Drive, which Ellen Borden Stevenson had made available as an art center and for the editorial office of *Poetry* magazine.

I met the train but could see no one who fitted my conception of Roy Campbell, until finally a lone, large man wearing a cloak and a broad, flat hat came staggering up the platform. I approached this formidable figure with some apprehension, and when I introduced myself at first got no response whatever. After it finally dawned on him who the rather diffident person was who had accosted him, he enveloped me in a huge embrace. He was terribly drunk. I finally got him into the station and was looking for a taxi when two men came rushing up saying, "One more drink. We will never have a chance to meet such a man again as long as we live. Just one more drink!" I protested that no more drinks were necessary, but Roy was more than willing, and off to the bar we went.

Our new friends had spent the entire time from St. Louis with Campbell in the bar car. They were both steel salesmen, they said, but had started out as professional football players. The conversation of these inebriated, aggressively masculine types soon got around to boasts about their strength. When one of the football players remarked that his legs were not what they used to be but that his arm was still "pretty good," Campbell challenged him to the trial of strength involving elbows on the table. The steel salesman went crashing to the floor, to the amusement of the other and to Campbell's intense satisfaction. When I finally managed to get Campbell to a hotel room, he passed out almost instantly. The tea given by the Chicago poets had to get along without the guest of honor.

Roy Campbell wrote two accounts of his life, *Broken Record*, published in England in 1934, and *Light on a Dark Horse*, which was published first in England in 1951 and appeared under our imprint a year later. *Light on a Dark Horse* is a very uneven book; it was obviously hurriedly written and carelessly edited. We took over the text of the English edition as it was, but reset it, added a number of Campbell's drawings and, as a frontispiece, a reproduction of the beautiful portrait by Augustus John of 1924.* In spite of its uneven quality and some obvious padding, consisting mostly of accounts of various brawls and physical exploits, the book is well worth reading and a pleasure to go back to from time to time, if for no other reason than the vitality and love of life the author imparts to it. As the book makes clear, Roy Campbell loved life in all its forms; he exulted in the gift of life, and never lost his wonder at its variety and mystery, or his gratitude to his Maker for permitting him to partake of it.

He was born in Durban, in the Cape Province of South Africa, in 1901, the son of a prominent and extremely energetic doctor and an equally energetic Scottish Highland mother. His account of his boyhood as part of a large, congenial family, and of long vacations in the bush country, is told with infectious enthusiasm, and includes descriptions of the African countryside and its people, animals, and birds that must be among the most beautiful ever written.

There is a particularly interesting account of the trip from Durban to Rhodesia, which Campbell made several times as a boy to visit relatives. The journey took four days by train and several more by ox-wagon—"a leisurely method of travel," he said, which is "surely the best in the world. It leaves the traveller free to make expeditions into the adjoining country, to follow honey-guides and take hives, or to make a hunting detour, yet never get left behind by his bed and kitchen. He treks during the cool of the morning and afternoon, outspanning during the heat of the day to let the oxen graze and drink, and to pass a pleasant siesta under some great shady fig, mahogany, or marula tree. About twenty miles a day is the average trek. The ox-wagon is the traveller's house, or his ship, with bunks and table complete."

The following description, from one of these treks, is typical of Roy Campbell:

Immediately after this scare, completely out in the open, I saw four

* This portrait hangs in the Carnegie Art Gallery in Pittsburgh.

majestic koodoo bulls on the edge of a wood of brilliant golden mimosa trees. Their beautiful shaggy silver beards, manes, and tails flashed electrically in the pure morning sunlight; and so did the dazzling white stripes that harness their red-golden bodies. They were pretending to fence and foil with their huge horns that rolled over their backs in magnificent spirals to a length of four or five feet. I have seldom seen an Arab or English horse, or a Spanish bull, that could equal them in their graceful and aristocratic carriage. They played and bounded in the sunlight as if they had just sprung from the hand of the Maker on the fifth day of Creation. When they caught sight of us, with their noble heads flung back, their horns undulating level with their backs, their great white bushy tails erected, their manes and beards streaming out, and their bodies bounding and scattering dew and pollen, they galloped off barking loudly into the labyrinths of flowers that closed behind them, firing off clouds of golden smoke in their wake.

As a young man, Campbell was a great horseman, tall, lithe, and, as the Augustus John portrait shows, strikingly handsome. When I knew him he was quite heavy, and badly crippled and ungainly from a war injury—he had served in World War II as a sergeant-major in the King's African Rifles, a fact of which he was very proud. For all his heaviness and his unconventional manner of dressing, he had a quality that set him apart, which made almost anybody who came even fleetingly within the field of his personality realize that this was no ordinary man. When I took him into a department store to get him some decent clothes for a lecture at Princeton, the clerk who had waited on him asked as we left if he might have his autograph. The clerk, of course, had no idea who Roy Campbell was, but he somehow realized that the man he had served, who might easily have been mistaken for a bum when he came in, was an extraordinary person. When Campbell left the hotel after four or five days to come to stay with us, at least a dozen employees—busboys, waiters, maids, barmen—came to see him off, with expressions of great esteem and affection. He had even struck up a friendship with the policeman on the beat.

He stayed at my house during each of his visits to Chicago, both times for several days. These visits were memorable occasions, not only for my family but also for the whole neighborhood. He told wonderful stories to the children, about his boyhood in South Africa, and about bareback riding, bullfighting, and whaling, which he would illustrate as he went along. He drew well, particularly African animals. One prized drawing was of animals fleeing from a bush fire: every possible animal is represented, each frantically running in its characteristic fashion, and each beautifully drawn. He would sing sea chanties and Scottish ballads in his peculiarly nasal but appealing voice, and although he had no understanding whatever of classical music, he was blessed with a good ear and true pitch. His own poetry took on a new dimension when he recited it, and he knew by heart a great deal of English poetry, particularly from the Elizabethan period.

Campbell had hoped, on his two visits to America, to lecture at various universities, read his poetry, and make a little money for his family, but, from a financial standpoint, both tours were unsuccessful. He was unpredictable, for one thing, as his would-be hosts at *Poetry* discovered, and did not fit the usual college English department's conception of a poet. His college visits worked out best when he could meet informally with students, and best of all with the football team. One visit, at Kenyon College, was particularly successful. Roberta Chalmers, the wife of the president and a good poet in her own right, knew Campbell's poetry, and arranged for him to meet with students in circumstances that made it possible for them to enjoy his unique qualities. A lecture at a downtown college in Chicago, on a hot, humid evening, was also most successful. The first poet on the program was Robert Lowell, who apologized for preceding such a heroic figure as Roy Campbell, and then went on to read what seemed to me to be rather dreadful poetry about incest and similar subjects. When Campbell's turn came it was as though a fresh breeze had swept into the room; he brought the audience immediately back to life with the imagery and vigor of his poetry, and ended the occasion by singing "John Brown's Body" in Swahili. Even if Campbell had made money from his American tours it would not have been of much use, because money meant nothing to him; if he had any in his pocket, he was as likely as not to give it to the first person he saw who seemed to need it more than he.

An unforgettable experience was a visit I made to the Campbells, together with my wife and older daughter, in the early fall of 1955. Roy and his striking, wonderfully loyal, strong-willed wife, Mary—she of the black hair and flashing eyes who appears in many of his poems—were living in Portugal, in an old, pretty house on a winding road above Sintra. It was painted a rosy pink, and had a lovely view of the valley below, and a rather overgrown walled garden in the back. Water for the garden flowed along the top of the wall from the mountain above, a trick, Roy remarked, the Moors had brought to the Iberian peninsula. Every morning a boy arrived with a large bottle of harsh red country wine on a little wagon, which Roy drank mixed with water—to purify the water, he explained. The Campbells went to great trouble to show us the countryside, with its villages and stone windmills, the castle in Sintra, with its enormous kitchen and chimney, and the coast, where great rollers from the Atlantic crash against the rocks—"the westmost point of Europe," as he wrote in "November Nights," "where it blows with might and main." Such trips were interspersed with frequent stops at small inns and cafés and constantly enlivened by Roy's stories.

After four or five days in Portugal we went on to Madrid, where the Campbells joined us. The immediate purpose of my stay was to arrange an interview with General Franco in the hope of inducing him to write his memoirs. I had made careful advance preparations, which included enlisting the support of the Spanish ambassador in Washington. Roy agreed to go with me. A time for the interview was finally set, and we rented the proper attire, striped trousers and all the rest. But at the last moment, the interview was canceled, and nothing came of it all. A Spanish aristocrat who was much experienced in the ways of the world told me at the time that although my idea was good, Franco would never write his memoirs. "Franco has the instincts of a Spanish peasant," he said, "and will never write a book. A book is too final."

I did meet several Spanish writers and publishers, arranged for a Spanish edition of Russell Kirk's *The Conservative Mind*, and agreed to publish an English translation of a small, imaginative book, *Picasso and the Bull,* by the gifted writer and editor Vicente Marrero-Suarez. Marrero's purpose in writing the book was to remind us that Picasso was first of all an artist who had grown out of the Spanish tradition. The circumstance of his being a Communist, which so delighted the liberals, was only incidental; had he been a monarchist, his politics would have been ignored.

It was amusing how our status in the elegant Madrid hotel rose after the Campbells arrived. Roy was a well-known and much admired figure in Spain in those days, and as his friends we were treated with a degree of deference to which we were not accustomed. The most memorable of various excursions was to Toledo, where Roy and Mary and their two children had lived during the years immediately preceding the Civil War, when Roy supported himself, or so he said, as a trader and trainer of horses. It was at this time, just when the war had started, that the Campbells joined the Catholic Church, by no means a safe thing to do in a city politically dominated by the "Reds," as Roy always called them.

It was a great experience to be shown that wonderful old city, with its layers of history, by such guides as the Campbells. As we were walking along a narrow, crooked street a man would rush out of a doorway calling "Roy." There would be a great embrace, followed by much talk and laughter. We had tea in the afternoon in the Campbells' former house, which, when we were there, had become a state-run hotel. Once the residence of a cardinal, it stands below the high wall of an ancient Carmelite cloister. One of Roy's contributions to civilization was to rescue, at great risk to himself, the priceless library of the cloister from destruction by the Communists. While we were sitting at a table in the pleasant garden, Mary Campbell, pointing to a well, remarked that Roy, coming home after a hard day and having had more to drink than was probably necessary, had fallen in. Roy laughed, and suggested that we take their picture sitting on the spot from which he had made his unexpected descent—he loved to be photographed.

Roy took us not only to El Greco's house, but also to the hill from which the composition of "The View of Toledo" was in part worked out. A nearby café had been the scene one year of the annual spring congress of poets, in which Roy had participated. The hill was covered with thyme, so he proposed that the poets conclude their recitations by rolling in the blossoms, which they did with great pleasure. Where else but in Spain, Roy asked, would people indulge themselves in such innocent pleasures as reciting their own poetry and rolling in thyme? But where else but in Spain would people burn churches and murder priests and nuns, and then ask forgiveness a few days later at confession?

In *Light on a Dark Horse* Roy spoke lovingly of the Spanish method of drinking from a wineskin. "This way of drinking," he wrote, "brings out the flavor and perfume, both of the wine and water, and once one has mastered the art without choking, drinking wine or water from a glass seems flat and insipid compared to it. The longer, thinner, and more forcible the jet, the more it aerates the bouquet of the wine or water. From two and a half feet away you can say: 'This water tastes of marble, of violets, of thyme, of iron, or of quartz; or of the shade of mulberry, white poplar trees, or cloves.' " There were many such leather wine bottles, or *botas*, in the store windows that day, and Roy could not resist buying one, which he had filled with red wine at the first opportunity. When we stopped for gas on the way back to Madrid he got out of the car and demonstrated his proficiency to several admiring bystanders, and then passed the *bota* around, for each to have a try.

This reminded him of his miracle. At the beginning of the Spanish Civil War he had made a firm vow to the Virgin not to drink a drop of wine until the Reds were defeated. Sometime later he was riding through the country and carrying such a skin of wine. Why, in view of his vow, he was carrying the wine he did not explain. In any case, the day was hot, he was thirsty, he became more and more tempted, and finally succumbed. Sitting under the shade of a tree, he opened his mouth and raised the wineskin, and what should come out but ice-cold pure water! The Virgin had saved him from breaking his vow, and he assured us that he never succumbed again. He was in Rome when the news came that Franco had entered Madrid. "I drank a whole bottle of wine in one swallow—" which he was perfectly capable of doing—"and do you know what it felt like? Like angels going down my throat in velvet slippers."

Roy Campbell was a serious poet: however much he may have enjoyed representing himself as a man of violent action, poetry was his life. After he had finished attending a good school in South Africa his father sent him to Oxford, where he met and became a close friend of William Walton and immersed himself in English poetry, particularly of the Elizabethan period. Walton, Campbell tells us in *Light on a Dark Horse*, was unable to arouse in him the least feeling for classical music, but he did give him a sense of vocation, "how a man can live for his art." Through Walton, Campbell met the people who influenced and helped him most in his literary career: the Sitwells, T. S. Eliot, Wyndham Lewis, Thomas Earp, Philip Heseltine, Cecil Grey, among others. He stayed at Oxford only one year; to exploit what he called his minor talent he felt he needed the sort of knowledge that is to be acquired only from travel, adventure, and rubbing shoulders with all sorts of people. Much of his life was spent in the active pursuit of such knowledge: as a friend of bullfighters and circus performers, and of the folk in isolated fishing villages in Wales and southern France, or as a soldier in World War II, a poet and man of letters in London, a horse trader and correspondent in Spain. Wherever it was or whatever he did, it was with all the intensity and commitment of which his strong personality was capable. Only a man of enormous energy could in addition have produced the considerable body of poetry he has left to us.

Campbell was unpretentious, warmhearted, and capable of the greatest generosity and gentleness; his love of life and his understanding and appreciation of nature derived from an innate sense of piety. On the other hand, if we are to believe his own accounts, as a young man he loved fighting and brawling, and was capable of attacking his enemies or supposed enemies with the fury of an enraged bull. The collection of poems related to his experience in the Spanish Civil War and World War II brought together under the title *Talking Bronco,* which Faber & Faber published in England in 1946, and we in a much revised edition in 1956, strikingly illustrates two sides of Roy Campbell. His mastery of poetic form, his sensitivity, and his innate humility are clearly apparent in his beautiful translation of *Una Noche Oscura* of St. John of the Cross, which begins

> Upon a gloomy night
> With all my cares to loving ardours flushed,
> (Oh venture of delight!)
> With nobody in sight
> I went abroad when all the house was hushed.

On another page we meet the enraged, irrational bull attacking his ideological enemies, in this case the "leftwing" poets who supported the other side in the Spanish Civil War, to whom Campbell gave the collective name MacSpaunday. The following from the twelve rather dreary pages of the poem which gives its name to the whole collection is an example of the less appealing side of Roy Campbell:

> While joint MacSpaunday shuns the very strife
> He barked for loudest, when mere words were rife,
> When to proclaim his proletarian loyalties
> Paid well, was safe, raked in the heavy royalties,
> And made the Mealy Mouth and Bulging Purse
> The hallmark of contemporary verse.

His strong feelings, however detrimental they may have been to his acceptance as a poet, were understandable. Although Campbell was over-age at the time of World War II, he volunteered for active service in the British army and was badly injured, whereas those who coined "the catchwords and phrases for which to be slaughtered" joined the "knife and fork brigade" in the rear. To add to Campbell's bitterness, he was called a fascist for taking what he considered to be the side of Christian Europe in the Spanish Civil War against those who would destroy it. However justified his bitterness may have been, one wishes that he had not wasted his talents on unproductive quarrels and on satirical couplets that are by now largely meaningless. W. H. Auden, one of the objects of Campbell's barbs, remarked long afterward that he regretted his political poetry from the Spanish Civil War days—the only one who benefited, he added, was he. The duty of the poet, Auden went on to say, is "to defend one's language from corruption." This Campbell also did, as his mastery of poetic forms and his beautiful lyric poetry amply testify; but he was willing, in addition, to put not only his pen but also his life and his reputation on the line for a cause he believed in.

He won his first recognition as a poet with the publication in 1924 of his long, epic poem *The Flaming Terrapin*, which caused a sensation, but by the time we published the first of three volumes of his collected poetry, in 1955, the ideological lines had hardened, in consequence of which the critics were inclined to view his writing not as poetry but as the work of a man whose politics they scorned. John Ciardi, writing in the *Nation*, for example, almost lost control of himself: "No poet writing in English has equalled Campbell's violence. None has presented a mind—to me at least—more despicable, a mind compounded of storm-trooper arrogance, *Sieg Heil* piety, and a kind of Nietzschean rant sometimes mixed with a ponderously uncomical sense of satire. The center of that mind—and its poetic style—is all sledgehammers." But then, almost in spite of himself, it would seem, Ciardi concluded, "It would be comforting to one's sense of liberalism to report that the result is merely thud-thud. What must be reported instead is that the sledgehammers are sometimes magnificent."

There was one particularly amusing incident in connection with the publication of this first volume of collected poetry. Dame Edith Sitwell, whom I had met through Campbell, told me that she would like to review the book. I immediately gave this information to Francis Brown, who was then editor of the *New York Times Book Review* and who, I must say, had treated me with great fairness over the years, as trying as some of my books must have been to him. In spite of very different views on the subject of politics, we became rather good friends, and shared an admiration for Wyndham Lewis. Brown told me that he could not ask Dame Edith to review the book because we had quoted her on the jacket, and sent it instead to Randall Jarrell, who wrote the sort of review that I suppose was expected of him: "It is a very bad-tempered Byron who writes these poems. . . . If the damned, blown willy-nilly round the windy circle of Hell, enjoyed it and were proud of being there, they would sound very much as he sounds. It's bad temper and reading Byron and Shelley that have produced his poetry; so it is only when we hate everybody, or feel we should sell our souls for a new 'Manfred' that his poems are much of a joy to us." Dame Edith was incensed, and sent off a stern letter of protest to the New York *Times* and a copy to me, written in her firm, definite hand. She concludes, after referring to Jarrell's scornful association of Campbell with Byron and Shelley, "Dr. Campbell may well dread sharing their oblivion."

Besides the three volumes of collected poetry, originally published in England by the Bodley Head, and *Talking Bronco*, in 1968 we published a one-volume collection, *Selected Poetry*, which was edited and supplied with an introduction and explanatory notes by Joseph M. Lalley. This included "Flaming Terrapin" and the first publication of Campbell's translation of Horace's *Ars Poetica*. Campbell's introduction to the Horace, which has never been published, ends with this characteristic paragraph:

At no other time was it ever more thrilling and enjoyable to be a poet, and to be *alive,* than it is today, when the life of the whole planet is triggered by a hair, when every moment is as precious as bread and wine, and when the rumble and roar of chaos is challenging us for every atom of faith, hope, and courage, in a measure which our Maker has never before done us the honour of expecting from His creatures.

Roy Campbell was a heroic figure and I think felt isolated in the modern world, which, with its noise and traffic—he hated the automobile, and predicted that he would be killed in one, as in fact he was—its great cities, its exploitation of nature, its longing for comfort and security, was hardly a place for a man like him. His preference for fishermen, bullfighters, circus performers, or horse traders over poets and intellectuals derived more from his feeling of isolation than from his desire for the sort of knowledge that is only to be had from rubbing shoulders with all sorts of people.

This is expressed, perhaps, in the following lines from one of his most beautiful poems, "To a Pet Cobra":

> There is no sea so wide, nor waste so steril
> But holds a rapture for the sons of strife:
> There shines upon the topmost peak of peril
> A throne for spirits that abound in life:
> There is no joy like theirs who fight alone,
> Whom lust or gluttony have never tied,
> Who in their purity have built a throne,
> And in their solitude a tower of pride.

Roy Campbell abounded in life and relished every moment of it, which made the news of his death in an automobile accident in Portugal in May, 1957, all the greater shock, but he had lived to the full, suffered great pain and discomfort from his war injuries, and was probably ready to go.

Our firm published four books by Wyndham Lewis, but I met him only twice, and then after he had become completely blind. By this time the old volcano had somewhat settled down; he had reached the point, or so he said, at which he was willing to let the modern world go its own self-destructive way. "People should be allowed to drop to pieces in any way they choose" is how he put it. He was not, however, prepared to give up the fight altogether: he wrote one of his last and in many ways most scathing books, *Self Condemned*, when he was unable to read a word of what he had written, composing it line by line, using a finger to mark the beginning of a line before going on to the next. He was a man not only of prodigous energy, but also of many talents. He was an important painter, and a creative influence on the art of his time. One of his books, *Time and Western Man,* will stand as a major contribution to philosophy. His novels can be read as literature of a high order and as profound social criticism, and few others have described the destructive forces loose in our time with the lucidity and penetration that are to be found in such books as *The Writer and the Absolute* and *The Art of Being Ruled.*

Lewis was not an easy man to get along with. His friend Ezra Pound once said of him, "You cannot be as intelligent, in that sort of way, without being a prey to the furies." In his relations with other people he could be unreasonable, irascible, unkind, and worse, but in his work he was utterly uncompromising. Although he may at times have been mistaken in his judgments, he never betrayed his convictions by adapting his position to the demands of his time.

Of the three works of fiction by him that we published—*Rotting Hill, Self Condemned*, and *Revenge for Love*—the last is the best known, and perhaps his greatest novel. He wrote it in the middle thirties, at the time he was painting those great portraits of T. S. Eliot, Stephen Spender, Ezra Pound, and Edith Sitwell, among others. It was first published in England in 1937; our edition, the first in the United States, appeared in 1952. If one asks why a major novel by one of the greatest writers of this century had to wait fifteen years to find an American publisher, the answer is quite simple: it ran counter to the prevailing orthodoxy of liberalism.

Revenge for Love begins shortly before the outbreak of the Spanish Civil War, in a Spanish prison, where we meet Percy Hardcaster, a stocky, red-faced, self-confident specimen of the English working class and a professional Communist, who has been caught smuggling arms. He attempts a clumsily executed escape, is shot, and loses a leg. The story then moves to London, where we meet various other characters: Jack Cruze, a tax accountant, the son of a country constable, coarse and full of animal life; Tristram Phipps, an artist, and his beautiful wife, Gillian, both Communists, consciously upper class, who "out of swank" live in a miserable basement; and Victor Stamp, an Australian, also an artist, but modeled on Roy Campbell, strong, handsome, cheerful, and penniless; and his wife, Margot. The whole cast of characters come together at a party in honor of Percy Hardcaster, who has returned from Spain a hero. It is largely through Margot Stamp's eyes that we view the proceedings. She is a simple, unassuming, completely honest Englishwoman, and is deeply in love with Victor. Gillian, aggressively Communist, in speaking to Margot, we are told, uses "the patronizing drawl with which those of the drawing room class address those of kitchen status." Margot "dreaded and disliked all these false politics of the sham underdogs (as she felt them to be), politics which made such lavish use of the poor and unfortunate, of the 'proletariat'—as they called her class —to advertise injustice to the profit of a predatory Party, of sham underdogs athirst for power: whose doctrine was a universal Sicilian Vespers, and which yet treated the real poor, when they were encountered, with such overweening contempt, and even derision. . . ."

Gillian Phipps is much taken by Percy Hardcaster; she gives him to understand that he would be welcome if he should come to her. There is some kissing, but Hardcaster's debilitated physical condition soon cools Gillian's ardor. She discovers that rather than being the romantic hero she had imagined he is nothing more than "a stupid fat little man of the working-class (treacherous and full of self pity, as the working-class always were—ready to turn around and bite the hand that feeds them!)" A rather sharp confrontation ensues in which Hardcaster, the professional Communist, explains the realities of revolution to Gillian. Gillian is furious; such an encounter with the real world was not at all what she had wanted when she invited Percy to come to see her.

She later leaves her husband and goes off with Jack Cruze, for whom women are a far more consuming interest than ideology. The coarse, obscenely sensual Jack, whose amorous adventures began at the age of fourteen in country hedgerows but who has never experienced an upper-class woman, is much taken by Gillian. It is quite apparent that Lewis has far more respect for Percy Hardcaster than for any of his "salon Reds," whatever their background or education: Hardcaster believed in something, was committed to it, and was a man.

The book ends as it began, with Percy Hardcaster in a Spanish prison. He has risked his life to go into Spain, this time to save Victor and Margot Stamp from certain arrest, those two innocents having been lured into an arms-smuggling scheme to earn a little money. It is Hardcaster's realization that Margot loves Victor that impels him, the hardened, professional revolutionary, to undertake such a dangerous and futile gamble. Margot had thought that their poverty and bad luck were the price fate exacted for their love, were "the revenge for love," but it is her love for Victor that redeems Hardcaster; and that such redemption is possible is the theme of the book. His prospects in a Spanish prison are not bright, but by his act, and through his realization of the meaning of the love of one person for another, he has redeemed himself as a man. On one level, *Revenge for Love* is a brilliant satire; but the novel has further dimensions, which make it, as Hugh Kenner said, a twentieth-century classic.

Rotting Hill and *Self Condemned* were both written in the dismal aftermath of World War II, which Lewis had predicted, dreaded, and done everything in his power to warn his countrymen to avoid. In books such as *Time and Western Man, The Writer and the Absolute,* and *The Art of Being Ruled* Lewis had fought with all the considerable resources at his command against the direction the modern world had taken. But in the two works of fiction written after World War II, when he was old, poor, and going blind, he seemed more inclined to accept it all as inevitable.

Rotting Hill (Lewis lived in London at Notting Hill Gate) is a collection of nine unconnected episodes, each illustrative of some aspect of life in socialist, postwar England. "If we exist, shabby, ill-fed, loaded with debt (taxed more than any men at any time have ever been), let us recognize that the sole explanation of this is our collective stupidity. . . . War is what is immediately responsible for the chaos which afflicts us at the present time." Two episodes involve village priests; in one, "The Bishop's Fool," Lewis's protagonist is an enthusiastic socialist who glories in the poverty and Spartan existence that are the lot of the country cleric under socialism. Lewis rather likes Rymer, as he calls him, whom he has met by chance in the reading room of the British Museum; he visits him and his attractive wife in their run-down country parsonage, but finds it difficult to make much sense of him. The story ends tragically, with Rymer losing his living and being brutally beaten by a local farmer, crude and modern, who has replaced the Squire as the man of power and influence in the countryside.

Lewis's other village priest is quite different from the cheerful, bumbling, left-wing Rymer: a young, esthetic, strong-willed man who believed that it was "an evil impulse on the part of the Government to break up the villages and to turn *all* of England into a factory." Having read of his fight to save the village school, which the educational authorities had decided to close, Lewis pays him a visit. The school is considered to be uneconomical, and, like the village of which it is a part, an anachronism in the modern world. The authorities, moreover, feel that the children would be better served if they were shipped off to what we would call a consolidated school. The villagers finally lose heart, as a result of which the young Vicar must give up the fight, or at least this round of it. But the episode gives Lewis an opportunity to describe one consequence of the "terrible colossus of Socialism," and a village priest who "belonged to the type of Englishman of which the most perfect specimens were Edmund Burke, Henry Maine, and a half dozen others. Those who experience the violent 'rebound of a powerful mind from . . . philosophical radicalism,' to use Maine's words."

The book ends with an "envoi," "The Rot Camp," the last paragraph of which makes clear that although Lewis may have given up the fight, he had lost none of his ability to satirize what is going on:

Lastly, standing by one of the gate-posts, was Britannia. She wore what Yankees call a 'liberty cap' (hired from Moss Bros). Once so robust, she was terribly shrunken: some wasting disease, doubtless malignant. The trident now employed as a crutch, she held out a mug for alms. I saw in the mug what looked like a phoney dollar bill, and dropped myself a lucky threepenny bit. I would give my last threepenny bit to poor old silly Britannia. In a cracked wheeze she sang "Land of Hope and Glory." I must confess that this last apparition, and its vulgar little song, rather depressed me.

When he delivered the manuscript of *Self Condemned,* he told his English publisher, J. Allen White, a close and loyal friend, that it was the best thing he had ever done. Whether it is or not, there can be no doubt that it is a powerful and moving book with much to say about the situation of modern man. It is also, as the story of two decent people destroyed by war, a heartbreaking book. The time is 1939, just before the outbreak of World War II. The central figure, René Harding, a professor of history in London and at the beginning of what promises to be a distinguished academic career, resigns his professorship and announces his intention to go to Canada, where he has no connections and no particular prospects. His reason for this drastic step, which stuns his family and leads to endless mis-understandings, is his conviction that he cannot teach history as the times and circumstances demand and remain an honest man.

The war begins while Harding and his wife, Hester, are in the middle of the Atlantic, on their way to Canada. Hester is pretty and sensual, but although she has no comprehension whatever of the reasons for her husband's decision, she loyally goes along. For three and one half years they lead a miserable existence in a single room in a cheap hotel in a city to which Lewis gives the name Momaco. The faculty of the nearby university regard the presence of an inter-nationally known scholar almost in their midst as a threat, and completely ignore him. Applications for employment lead to nothing, so that Harding finds it necessary to sell his books, one by one, to supplement whatever he can earn from the sale of an occasional article or review. One dreary day follows another, with the single sustaining hope the prospect of a return to England following the war.

Lewis went through a somewhat similar experience himself during the war, and in his account of the experiences of the Hardings he expresses his own strong distaste for Canada and the run-of-the-mill Canadian.

Finally the hotel burns down, late at night, with the temperature at thirty below zero. The fire leaves some twenty people dead and the hotel "an amazing iceberg. . . . It was now an enormous cave, full of mighty icicles as much as thirty feet long, and as thick as a tree, suspended from the skeleton of the roof. Below, one looked down into an icy labyrinth: here and there vistas leading the eye on to other caverns: and tunnels ending in mirrors, it seemed."

Great as the shock of the fire has been, it leads to a rather abrupt change for the better in the fortunes of the Hardings. René is offered the opportunity to write a column for the local paper on the war and foreign political developments, and it becomes quite successful; through the intervention of an Anglican priest he is invited to give a series of lectures at the university; and he begins to work on a new book.

The change in their fortunes enables the Hardings to move into an attractive apartment, to live comfortably, even to travel, and soon Harding is offered a professorship at the university, which he accepts. All this, however, is greeted by Hester with growing apprehension, not to say despair. As long as they lived in the single room in the hotel they sustained each other, and could look forward to an eventual return to London. But René's book is accepted and does well, and his success makes it apparent that they will never return. René says it would be impossible anyway: there would be nothing to return to.

Hester develops a pathological hatred for Canada, and with her hopes of return fading, ends her own life by throwing herself under a truck. The shock of her suicide and the realization of his own responsibility for it almost destroy René; he recovers superficially and is even able to resume his work, but has become a shell of a man.

Why, one is almost compelled to ask, was Lewis's character René Harding destroyed, whereas Lewis himself came out of a not dissimilar experience intact? He spent almost six years in exile in the United States and Canada, desperately trying to support his wife and himself by portrait painting, lecturing, or whatever turned up; poor, not really ostracized, but not warmly welcomed either. Then came the final blow of blindness—for an artist the greatest blow of all. But he never became a shell of a man: it was no empty shell that

wrote *Self Condemned*. Lewis possessed resources which his character Harding did not have, and perhaps, unconsciously, Lewis is
telling us that he who wishes to take a stand against the trend of the
times, defy the Gods, as he put it, had better be fully prepared, be
sure of sufficient ballast to weather the inevitable storm.

Lewis was not accepted by the New York literary establishment,
and no large American or Canadian university, when he really
needed it, was willing to offer him anything more substantial than
an occasional lecture. Nevertheless, he was able to feel himself part
of an intellectual community, of people who shared his values and
many of his convictions, as his correspondence during those difficult years with such people as Augustus John, T. S. Eliot, Naomi
Mitchison, Sir Nicholas Waterhouse, and many others, plainly
shows. Furthermore, we have every reason to believe that in spite
of his rather checkered career as a young man, his marriage was
successful. Finally, his opposition to the *Zeitgeist,* as he liked to
call it, derived from a strongly held philosophical position, which
had become a part of his personality and which he was prepared to
defend against all comers.

In *The Demon of Progress in the Arts,* which we published in
1955, Lewis considered the situation of art in the modern world
from his vantage point as painter, critic, and writer. A compact,
closely argued little book of only ninety-six pages, it was greeted
by some as a profound and important contribution, and by others
as the work of an old grouch who had seen better days and had
nothing more of significance to say. It is not so much a polemical
book as the expression of concern for the future of art by a
man for whom art was an utterly serious matter, and who wrote
about it not as an outsider, but as a practicing artist.

He believed that art, ever since the French Revolution, had been
going through a gradual process of disintegration, and was now approaching a limit beyond which there was, simply, nothing. This he
ascribed to such influences as the emergence of conflicting schools,
beginning with the romanticism and classicism of the early nineteenth century; to the fact that art had become almost totally dis-
connected from society, without any direct function in life, and was
able to exist only as the plaything of the intellect; to the perpetual
craving for something new, the feeling, which came with industrialism, that the old must be constantly superseded; and, finally, to the
influence of the dealers and critics. The consequence of all this is
extremism, which he said was symptomatic of a vacuum, and it is

extremism that has brought art close to the precipice beyond which there is nothing.

"If," Lewis remarks to illustrate his point, "in the windows of the art dealers, all that were to be seen were a few white empty canvases . . . and if, in answer to the enquiries of the newspapers' representatives, the dealer were curtly to reply that 'this is the latest kind of "movement",' all this should evoke no surprise." And it did, in fact, evoke no particular surprise when one of the major American art museums gave a prize for a picture, which the museum bought, which is exactly what Lewis described, a white, empty canvas.

He often complained that his books were ignored by the critics, that because the ideas he espoused were not fashionable he was subjected to a form of boycott. This may have been true at one point in his career, but it must be said that the four books we published were widely and carefully reviewed. The reviewers did not always agree with Lewis, but he was treated with considerable respect and accorded a degree of recognition that could make one feel the "Republic of Letters" is not entirely a creation of the imagination. There was, for example, a long, carefully written essay on Lewis by George Woodcock in the *New Yorker*, following the publication of *Self Condemned*, which considered his entire career and included the following tribute: "Lewis has probably been the most resolute intellectual of our age; he has converted an incapacity for intense emotionalism into a critical weapon against all the departures from intellectual consistency, all the manifestations of counterfeit philosophy, that, in his view, have governed contemporary art and literature." A reviewer for *Time* remarked, "A new generation is discovering Wyndham Lewis, and his publishers are reissuing his works amid applause from those who believe that he is Britain's foremost writer." In the *Saturday Review*, Ben Ray Redman said of *Self Condemned*, ". . . it is essentially a novel of ideas, and one of Mr. Lewis's greatest gifts is his ability to make ideas vital and potent in fiction. As for the range of his powers, that may be measured by the distance which separates this novel's comedy from its tragedy, its fun from its savage bitterness."

There were also, of course, voices of dissent. Irving Howe, in the *New Republic*, was particularly caustic: "That Wyndham Lewis should be revived in England and published in America is another dreary sign of the times. Lewis may figure in 20th century literary history, but the notion that he is important as a novelist or . . . as 'a prophet' must be put down to the recent turn to reaction by some rattled intellectuals." The Virginia Kirkus Service called *Revenge for Love* "a pretty lugubrious structure on which Mr. Lewis rests the same slender and bad-tempered opinions he recently voiced in the first person in *Rotting Hill.*" In contrast to a rather negative review of *Revenge for Love* by James Kelly in the New York *Times,* however, Ruthven Todd's review of *Self Condemned* in that newspaper was all any author or publisher could wish for. He began: "Wyndham Lewis has stood as one of the gigantic, but isolated, figures of modern letters," and ends: "In a world of the ready-made and mass produced, it is almost intoxicating to find a novel by a master, and one which only he could have conceived and executed."

A paragraph from *The Writer and the Absolute,* which, as concisely as anything of his I know, expresses his credo as painter and writer, forms an appropriate ending to this remembrance of Wyndham Lewis:

What holds the true apart from the false is a great force. This can be illustrated in the work of famous writers, but it is in the great masters of painting that this instinct occurs with all the publicity of the visible, within sight of all of us, and so it is there that it may be studied to the best advantage. Chardin, with a bland intensity, fastens his eye, impacts his gaze forever upon some object of daily use. Van Eyck, with the same intense animal absorption and austere tenacity, upon Arnolfini and his wife. The *true* image must be put down.

T. S. Eliot's kindness to young writers has often been mentioned. I would like to attest to his kindness to an inexperienced publisher. I saw him for the first time when, as a student, I heard the series of lectures he gave at Harvard, which must have been the winter of 1931–32. Having been brought up in the Middle West, I found his Oxford English somewhat hard to follow, and was surprised to learn that he had grown up in the Middle West also. I can now remember little of what he said—a remark that either Shelley or Keats, I don't know which, *might* have become a good poet if he had lived longer, and his telling us that "Beauty is truth, truth beauty" is not all we know on earth, or all we need to know.

In 1949, as I have related, we published a *Festschrift* for Eliot's sixty-fifth birthday. When he came to Chicago early in 1951 to deliver four lectures at the University of Chicago, it served as our introduction to each other. He invited me to lunch several times at the rather ornate hotel near the university where he had been installed.

On one of these occasions, looking around the dining room at the overfed, overdressed, middle-aged ladies who occupied most of the tables, and who later solemnly played cards, he asked if there might not be another place in Chicago we could go for lunch. I suggested the Red Star, a wonderful old German place on the North Side, no longer in existence, which proved to be a great success. As we walked in he remarked, "This smells like beer," but unfortunately it was Election Day and no beer was served. I was too overwhelmed by the presence of the great man to get as much out of these occasions as I should have, but they were pleasant, and he was most encouraging about my efforts to found a new publishing firm. I later visited him several times in his office at Faber & Faber, which was then in two or three rather dilapidated Victorian houses on Russell Square. On one of these visits, when he asked me how I was getting on, I told him that we had just become the publisher of Eddie Guest, having recently bought out the original publisher. He smiled in his quizzical, knowing way, and said, "Don't be ashamed of that. There isn't a publisher in the business who wouldn't be delighted to have Eddie Guest on his list, and, furthermore, he was an honest man, which is more than one can say of many people who write poetry these days."

Eliot approved of my decision to publish Wyndham Lewis, and offered to write a brief preface to *Self Condemned*. "To *me*," he said, "this is the best of Wyndham Lewis's novels." As for *Rotting Hill*, it was a good book—"perhaps too good to be relished by the English reviewer." I was somewhat perplexed by Lewis's very last novel, *The Red Priest*, which had been offered to us for publication. In reply to my letter about it Eliot wrote, "I am afraid that I also am disappointed by *The Red Priest*. In fact, I have not yet been able to get very far with it. The characters seem very unreal to me—at any rate, they correspond to nothing in my own experience." This persuaded me to decline the book, which probably saved me several thousand dollars.

I do not wish to give the impression that Eliot approved of everything we published. He could be sharply critical, and for such criticism I was as grateful as for his encouragement. When I sent him a copy of an inconsequential book we had published called *Chicago's Left Bank*, which included the conventional comments about Ezra Pound, I received the following, as a P.S. on the bottom of a longer letter: "I was not so happy with *Chicago's Left Bank* as I am with many of your books. I dare say that the book should do well locally, but I was incidentally annoyed by what seemed to me unnecessary attacks on Ezra Pound." To this the following is added, in longhand: "The book is trivial, inaccurate, uncritical, cheap & spiteful."

He particularly admired Russell Kirk's *The Conservative Mind* and was instrumental, as I have reported, in Faber's bringing out a British edition. He and Kirk later met, and out of this meeting there developed a warm friendship, a consequence of which is probably the best book we have on Eliot's work, Russell Kirk's *Eliot and His Age,* published by Random House in 1972. Although I received in all not more than two dozen or so letters from Eliot, and met with him only six or eight times, he left an indelible impression on me. But it is the way of great men, and a mark of their greatness, that they should make an indelible impression.

When in 1959 I received a letter from Noel Stock, with the return address Schloss Brunnenburg, Merano, asking if we would be interested in publishing a collection of essays by Ezra Pound he was putting together, I was somewhat taken aback, because I had never read a line of Ezra Pound. I knew something about the circumstances of his arrest by the American authorities in Italy, and that he had been confined in a mental hospital in Washington, but that was about all. Montgomery Belgion's *Victor's Justice,* one of the first books we had published, described in some detail the brutal way Pound had been treated when he was first arrested; a manuscript on Pound, which we had rejected, described the circumstances of his confinement in St. Elizabeth's in Washington; and at T. S. Eliot's suggestion we had published a short book about the *Cantos*, which I had read, but not the *Cantos* themselves. As a writer he had never come into my field of interest, but I was inclined to view him with favor because of the treatment he had received and the enemies he had made. So I replied to Stock that we would be interested in the manuscript he was preparing. Because I planned to be in Europe that fall, he suggested that I come to Schloss Brunnenburg and discuss the project at first hand. And after further correspondence, I also arranged to go on to Rapallo to meet Pound himself.

I mentioned the proposed trip to Eugene Davidson, a former editor of Yale University Press, who was then working in the historical archives in Munich. He offered to drive me, and so it was arranged, with his wife, Louise—an alert, attractive lady who was very good company—as the third member of the party. Schloss

Brunnenburg proved to be a medieval castle, which had been re-stored in the nineteenth century and bought for a small sum, after World War II, in a semiruined condition, by Pound's daughter Mary and her husband, Prince de Rachewiltz.

We were admitted by a little girl of about eight, who we later learned was Pound's granddaughter. She led us up a spiral stair-way, across a handsome old court, through an archway, and up another stairway to the floor where Stock and his wife were living, and where he occupied himself sorting and arranging Pound's papers. He took us up a further stairway to a large room with windows and window seats on three sides, which afforded a fine view of the valley and countryside, and there we were presented to Pound's daughter, Mary de Rachewiltz. She was in her early thir-ties, dignified, reserved, and very courteous; she had the presence and beautiful manners of a well-brought-up European. She sug-gested that I spend an hour or so with Stock, and that we all come back to the room where we were sitting for lunch. When I re-turned to Stock's apartment it was obvious from some of the things he showed me—an essay on the Jefferson-Adams correspondence, one called "Reorganize Your Dead Universities," letters to the American Academy and the Guggenheim Foundation, for example —that there would be no difficulty finding sufficient material for a provocative and interesting book; and so it was agreed.

Prince de Rachewiltz, who grew up in Rome and is an Egyptol-ogist, joined us for lunch. The meal was simple, excellently pre-pared, and properly served. It became immediately apparent that Mary de Rachewiltz was devoted to her father, and had suffered greatly because of all that had happened to him. After his arrest and confinement by the American army, the family had heard nothing whatever, for more than six months, about where he was or what had happened to him. She spoke rather bitterly of the fact that so few responsible people had gone to see him during the twelve years he had been confined in St. Elizabeth's, that he had been criticized because certain strange characters had more or less surrounded him, but that the "good" people had stayed away. She made the long trip to Washington to visit him, and had tried to get a job so that she could be of help to him, but had been unable to find anything. In her book of memoirs, *Discretions*, she remarks that when, during this visit to him in St. Elizabeth's, she asked what she could do, he replied, "All you can do is plant a little decency in Brunnenburg." Her father had been in excellent health and spirits for several months following his return to Italy, she said, but had since become somewhat depressed.

We reached Rapallo the next afternoon, after spending the night near Sermione, on Lake Garda, which must be one of the most beautiful spots in the world. Pound had reserved rooms for us in a small, attractive hotel on the Mediterranean, where he and his wife, Dorothy, joined us for dinner. He asked me to come to their apartment alone the next morning, and when we had dinner with them once again, we were joined by an old friend of his. Pound seemed quite energetic, was quick in his movements, but it was difficult for him to stand or sit for any length of time because of a problem with his neck, which had developed during his confinement in Pisa. Davidson asked about the circumstances of his arrest and imprisonment. He told us that toward the end of the war he and his family had gone back into the hills to escape the air raids, and when he heard on the radio that a price had been put on his head and that the American army had entered Rapallo, he went down to give himself up. The first soldier of the victorious American army he encountered was a large black, who had no interest whatever in Pound's situation, but instead tried to sell him, for fifteen dollars, a bicycle he had "liberated" from some hapless Italian. Pound seemed to find it difficult to recall the details of his first imprisonment, but he did mention that most of the other prisoners were blacks who had been arrested for rape, murder, and other crimes, and that the first commandant of the camp was later murdered in Genoa, apparently by an American soldier. He soon remarked that such reminiscences were a waste of time: "At least ten million people were treated far worse than I was, so why talk about it?"

The next day I went to see him in his apartment, which was bright, airy, and situated somewhat higher than the hotel. Mrs. Pound was a gracious, dignified woman, but she plainly bore the marks of all she had gone through in the years following her husband's arrest. When I told her how much I had enjoyed meeting her daughter, I sensed at once that I had said the wrong thing. Mary de Rachewiltz, I learned later, is the daughter of the violinist Olga Rudge.

We sat in Pound's study. Much of the furniture, which was simple, sturdy, and practical, had been made by him from his own design. I happened to notice on his desk a check for a thousand dollars, encased in lucite; it was made out to Ezra Pound and signed by Ernest Hemingway. When Pound observed that I had looked at it, he simply remarked, "Hem should have come to see me." He lay down much of the time, and rambled from one subject to another, always coming back to what was obviously his favorite theme, his theories of money. His study of the subject, he said, stemmed entirely from his desire to get at the causes of war. He was interested also in the history of the thought that tried to prevent World War II, and why it was unsuccessful. He recommended a book by Clark Emory called *Ideas into Action*, and spoke of a series he had started in 1924 with Hemingway, Ford Madox Ford, and William Carlos Williams, called "The Inquest Series," whose purpose was to revive normal prose after the appearance of *Ulysses*. He spoke of Ford and Alfred H. Orage as two men of the period who were "getting more important," and said that one of his regrets was his neglect of Arnold Bennett, to whom friends had called his attention about 1910; but he had been too immersed at the time studying Debussy's music to pay any attention to Bennett. He talked about William Woodward and his American history, which he thought well of, and remarked that Robert Lowell "was improving." Suddenly, in the midst of all this, he stood up, and with the greatest care and precision made the following observation, which I have recalled as accurately as possible: "One must find a way to admit one's mistakes without throwing away the glimmering of truth one has managed to acquire in making them."

He seemed tired and rather depressed at dinner that evening, and left early, but before doing so remarked that "they" had decided in advance to release him only when he was so broken that he would be able to do nothing that would bother anyone when he got out; and added that "they" had calculated correctly. The old Italian friend of the Pounds who joined us for dinner stayed after they had left, and proved to be a most interesting man. He was an old-time socialist, and had attended an international socialist meeting in Chicago in 1909. He was very likable and had a good sense of humor, and seemed to be in every way a robust and honest man. He had had something to do with Italian radio during the war, which is how his friendship with Pound had started. The Italians, he said, had tried to convince Pound that he should not make his wartime broadcasts; they knew that doing so would serve no purpose, and only make trouble for Pound later.

As is well known from portraits and photographs, Ezra Pound had been a striking-looking man. He still was when I met him, despite his twelve years in a mental hospital; furthermore, he had the manner and air of the poet, of the man to whom it is given to see and sense more than the rest of us. Whatever mistakes he may have made, Ezra Pound was one of the great creative influences of this century.

We published Noel Stock's collection of Pound essays in 1960, under the title *Impact: Essays on Ignorance and the Decline of American Civilization*. When he put the collection together, Stock was a devoted follower of Ezra Pound—he has since had second thoughts—and an admirer of his monetary and economic theories as much as of his poetry. The collection was therefore rather heavily weighted with material on economics, and there was more repetition than one would wish for. But there were flashes of great insight that makes the reading of the whole rewarding, and from beginning to end the reader is aware of the presence of a man who had a profound understanding of the basis and nature of civilization, and a passionate concern for its future. Pound may at times have played the fool, but he was not a fool, and was capable of insights which we ignore at our peril.

A frequently recurring theme of *Impact* is the role of an elite in civilization. Although Pound said emphatically that he "never cared a damn about snobbisms or for writing *ultimately* for the few," he went on to remark: "Serious art is unpopular at birth. But it ultimately forms the mass culture. . . . Mass culture insists on the fundamental virtues which are common to Edgar Wallace and Homer." In another chapter he spoke of the senseless destruction of the great English houses by taxation. "The farm hand does not eat more because the paintings by Raeburn and Constable are taken out of the Manor House and put in the dealer's cellar under a black and iniquitous inheritance tax. The obscuring of the sense of the nature of money has destroyed all these fine things uselessly. The dismantled Manor House, that could be and ought to show a model of how to live, is made a skeleton for no purpose."

In "National Culture" and "The Jefferson-Adams Letters" he developed more fully the idea of an elite, not as a privileged class leading an isolated and protected existence, but as a creative, responsible, and active group who by their standards of quality and behavior raise the level of society as a whole. He suggested that if a few hundred men who prefer good writing to bad would correspond with each other on a regular basis, maintain a periodical that correlated American thought with what is going on in other countries, insist on clear definitions of terms, and at least protest against the worst malpractices of the press and book trade and the more violent inaccuracies of the so-called books of reference, much could be accomplished in the way of raising standards. "One can not create by fiat a phalanx of great writers, or men of genius," he said. "One could however establish a certain degree of mental integrity, and an utter and blistering intolerance of certain present habits of sloppiness and bad faith."

For Pound, "nothing surpasses the evidence that CIVILIZATION WAS in America, than the series of letters exchanged between Jefferson and John Adams, during the decade of reconciliation after their disagreement." And for Pound, writing in 1938, nothing was more infuriating, or gave clearer evidence of what was wrong, than the fact that whereas Marx and Lenin were reprinted at ten cents and twenty-five cents in editions of 100,000, Adams's and Jefferson's thought was kept out of the plain man's reach. He said that what Jefferson and Adams still had that has since been lost "was the HABIT of thinking of things in general as set in an orderly universe."

To read *Impact* requires patience, as is true of almost anything Pound wrote, but he can be most rewarding. I cannot resist quoting one particularly striking sentence, which is probably a more exact summary of our situation than even Pound realized:

The drear horror of American life can be traced to two damnable roots, or perhaps it is only one root: 1. The loss of *all* distinction between public and private affairs. 2. The tendency to mess into other peoples' affairs before establishing order in one's own affairs, and in one's thoughts.

11

RELIGION
AND PHILOSOPHY

ONE of the first books published by our firm, as I have mentioned, was *Great Saints* by the Swiss Protestant pastor and professor of theology Walter Nigg. Although it was not the great success I had hoped for, it was by no means a failure, and helped to establish our new firm as a publisher of serious books. Shortly thereafter G. Ernest Wright and Floyd W. Filson, of McCormick Theological Seminary, came to us with a new series, "Studies in Biblical Theology," which we agreed to publish jointly with the Student Christian Movement Press of London. The series included works by a number of distinguished men and sold reasonably well, but I finally came to the conclusion that it was not what we were looking for. Several factors led us into the publication of Catholic books, and by the time I gave up control of the firm we had become one of the larger publishers of serious Catholic books and had a distinguished and highly respected list.

For a number of reasons, I have never felt able to make a final commitment to Catholicism, but for a long time I have been strongly attracted to the Catholic Church, because of my father's upbringing and also because of the two years I spent as a student in Europe, which made me more aware than I might otherwise have been of the great debt we owe the Roman Church as the bearer of the religious and cultural tradition of our civilization.

A religious tradition, it seems clear to me, demonstrates its truth by the depth of the faith and the level of the creative achievement it inspires.

All this reminds me of a conversation with the gifted but unpredictable German writer Luise Rinser, two of whose books we had published. She had grown up in the strong Catholic tradition of Bavaria, however lightly the demands of the Church may have rested upon her. At the time I met her she was married to the composer Carl Orff, and she invited me to have lunch with them in their new, handsome house near Diessen-am-Ammersee. After lunch we walked to the nearby village and looked into the church, which was a fine specimen of the highly decorated, light, airy baroque style which seems particularly appropriate to the Bavarian character and countryside. As we were standing in front of the beautifully made iron grill that separates the choir from the rest of the church, I remarked that such a church had a particular appeal to me, and made me feel deprived of something because I was an outsider to it.

She said in response that to those who grow up in it, the Church is like an old, old house one's family has always lived in. The floors are creaky, uneven, and on many levels; it was built over many centuries and in a completely haphazard fashion. "But we love it," she said. "It is a part of us, and we wouldn't think of living anywhere else." On the other hand, she confessed, she couldn't imagine moving into it if she had not grown up in it. Many people, needless to say, have found refuge in that old house, but however much I may at times have wished otherwise, I remain an outsider.

Another factor that helped to get us into Catholic publishing was the circumstance that two of my first associates in the firm, Philip N. Starbuck and William F. Strube, were former seminarians. The first Catholic book we published, *The Paschal Mystery*, by the French theologian Louis Bouyer, which had been strongly recommended by Starbuck, was on the Easter liturgy. The most ambitious project we undertook was the publication of three major works by Thomas Aquinas, all in new translations, which were prepared in various Jesuit Houses of Study: *On Truth*, in three large volumes, and the *Commentary on the Metaphysics* and the *Commentary on the Nichomachean Ethics* of Aristotle, each in two large volumes. Many years after these books appeared, my wife and I visited the Vatican Library to see the impressive exhibit arranged to commemorate the seven-hundredth anniversary of the death of Thomas Aquinas, which included original manuscripts, medieval manuscript copies, and printed editions going back to the fifteenth century of the works of the "Angelic Doctor." The pleasure and satisfaction it gave me to see displayed in those surroundings, entirely unexpectedly, our well-produced edition of *On Truth* was ample compensation for the financial burden the three works had placed on our struggling firm.

Our list included books by Paul Claudel, Jean Danielou, Gertrud von le Fort, Eugene Portalie, Benedict Bauer, Edith Stein, and Louis Colin, but probably our greatest contribution to contemporary religious thought was the publication of eight books by Romano Guardini, among them his major work, *The Lord*. Guardini, who as a Catholic priest was for sixteen years a professor at the University of Berlin, and after World War II at the University of Tübingen, and finally at the University of Munich, was one of the towering figures of our time. He was born in 1885 in Verona. His father for professional reasons took his family to Germany, and as a young man Guardini made the difficult decision to become a German. But he never gave up his attachment to the traditions of his birthplace, and felt himself to be, above all, a European.

In the early twenties, following the completion of his studies in systematic theology at the University of Bonn, and having qualified himself to teach in a university, Guardini received a call from the University of Berlin to assume a newly established professorship, which was described as "Philosophy of Religion and Christian *Weltanschauung*." In a speech delivered at the celebration of his seventieth birthday, at the University of Munich, he described the dilemma this offer had presented to him. His own lack of experience, and the rather vague way in which his proposed professorship was described, made it difficult for him to accept. It was the distinguished philosopher Max Scheler who was most helpful to him. "Examine, for example, the novels of Dostoyevski," Scheler told him, "and consider them from your Christian position, in order, on the one hand, to illuminate the work itself, and, on the other, your own starting point." This he did for sixteen years, he said, in the sharp air of Berlin, and in the process it became clear to him what the concept of a Christian view of the world expresses: "the constant, one can say methodical, encounter between faith and the world." From this professorship developed such books as those on Plato, Dante, Pascal, Hölderlin, Mörike, and Rilke, which were intended to be neither literary studies nor theology, but encounters.

Through his lectures at the University of Berlin, his books, and his work in the Catholic Youth Movement, Guardini had achieved considerable prominence by the 1930's, but it was in the period immediately following World War II that he became one of the most influential men in Germany. During those years of hunger and despair, of moral confusion and political uncertainty, he offered the example and counsel of a man wise in the classical philosophy of Europe and serene in the Christian faith. His university lectures, which were held in the largest available auditorium, and were always filled to the doors, as were his sermons, became the centers of university life. But his influence extended beyond students and young people of every class and faith to labor-union leaders and to men prominent in government and business. The contribution of this modest, unassuming professor-priest to the restoration of traditional values in the situation that followed twelve years of Adolf Hitler is difficult to overstate, and a witness to the power of the human personality acting on its highest level.

A book that gives some idea of Guardini's method, of the way in which he met a current issue on the basis of the Christian faith, is his study *Power and Responsibility*, which was first published in Munich in 1951, and in our edition just ten years later. He begins, quite logically, with a definition of power, which, in the sense he used it, is essentially a human phenomenon. "We may speak of power," he tells us, "in the true sense of the word only when two elements are present: real energies capable of changing the reality of things . . . and the will to establish specific goals and to launch and direct energies toward those goals." Such a natural phenomenon as lightning or a hurricane is not evidence of power but of force, as is the strength of a lion: the exercise of power requires will, and will implies freedom of choice and therefore responsibility. Having then carefully established what he means by power, Guardini begins the development of his thesis at the very beginning, with Adam and Eve in the Garden of Eden.

The Book of Genesis, Guardini reminds us, tells us not only that God created man, and in his own image, but also that he ordered man "to increase and multiply and fill the earth, and to make it yours; take command of the fishes of the sea, and all that flies through the air, and all the living things that move on the earth." Elaborating on this text, Guardini goes on to say, "Man cannot be human and, as a kind of addition to his humanity, exercise or fail to exercise power; the exercise of power is essential to his humanity. To this end the author of his existence determined him." Man's power, however, is to be exercised "with respect to the truth of things," as Guardini puts it. The sovereignty over the earth God has given him "is not meant to establish an independent world of man, but to complete the world of God as a free, human world in accordance with God's will." The essential nature of man's "first disobedience" then was his refusal to accept his role as a part of creation, his succumbing to the temptation "to be like gods." And ever since this event, which disrupted "man's relation to his creator," Guardini says, "history takes its course in a world that is marked by disorder."

Characteristic of the era following the Middle Ages, which Guardini called "the Modern World" and which, in his opinion, reached its apogee between the two world wars, is the supposition that "every increase in intellectual-technical power [is] an unquestionable gain," the fervent belief that all such increase is "progress, progress in the direction of a decisive fulfillment of the supreme meaning and value of existence." The Middle Ages, Guardini pointed out, regarded scientific knowledge as a means to confirm the will and purpose of God. The Modern World, on the other hand, regards science as a means to win greater power over nature, and to this latter attitude we owe, of course, not only modern medicine, but also the material comforts and security modern science and technology have given us. With this increase in power over nature, however, has come also a corresponding increase in the power one man, or group of men, can exercise over others; and this has come about not only because of the apparatus of control modern technology has made available to the state, but also because of the willingness of modern man to place himself at the mercy of power. "One being affects another," Guardini tells us, "as much as that other allows himself to be affected, indeed cooperates in the process. In the long run, domination requires not only the passive consent, but also the will to be dominated, a will eager to drop personal responsibility and personal effort . . . the inner barriers of self-respect and self-defense must fall before power can really violate."

Guardini was well aware that there is no turning back. As a result of the power over nature man has acquired, most conspicuously in the form of atomic fission, "to the end of time, there will be no human experience that lives without peril." Nor is a solution to be found by renouncing power: man cannot renounce power and remain human, since the exercise of power is part of his nature. Believing, however, that there is a divine plan in the unrolling of history, Guardini expressed the hope that the new era he saw superseding the Modern World, which he believed had already begun, would bring forth a new kind of man, who "will have power not only over nature, but also over his own powers. In other words, he will understand how to subordinate power to the true meaning of life and works."

We were the original publishers of eight books by Romano Guardini, in English translation, and, in addition, reissued in paperback editions five that had been originally published by other houses. By far the most successful was *The Lord*, which was the fruit of a life devoted to the study, contemplation, and interpretation of the Christian revelation. I entered into a contract for English-language rights with the original German publisher knowing nothing about the book beyond its reputation, and largely on the basis of the recommendation of Arnold Bergstraesser, who was then a professor at the University of Chicago. The overwhelming problem of putting this complex, highly sophisticated book into English solved itself almost miraculously, it seemed at the time, by the appearance in our office, entirely unannounced, of a lady who was not only willing to undertake the arduous task, but almost uniquely equipped to do it. Elinor Castendyk Briefs was the wife of the distinguished Georgetown University professor Goetz Briefs; she was well trained in theology and completely fluent in both German and English, and she had studied with Professor Guardini in Tübingen.

Ernest Strauss, the exceptionally competent man in charge of production at that time, saw to it that the manuscript was carefully edited and the book suitably produced; and an aggressive, imaginative man, Howard Clark, who was in charge of sales, made it his business to see that the book was promoted and sold as it deserved to be. It was probably Clark who suggested that we use the Rouault painting "Christ Mocked by Soldiers" for the jacket. With its vivid colors and strong presentation of the subject it was exactly what was needed, and the Museum of Modern Art in New York very generously lent us the necessary plates. Our publication of *The Lord* in 1954 was one of those all too infrequent ventures in which everything seems to go as one would wish, and it became the most successful book in our firm's history.

The author tells us in his preface that it was no scholarly documentation of history or theology. "Its chapters are the spiritual commentaries of some four years of Sunday services undertaken with the sole purpose of obeying as well as possible the Lord's command to proclaim him, his message and works." In a chapter entitled "Justice and That Which Surpasses It" the author took as his text the Parable of the Prodigal Son: that which surpasses justice is mercy. The chapter "Christian Marriage and Virginity" is not only beautiful in its presentation of a difficult subject, but also, in its observations about the deeper meaning of the relationship between man and woman, it has much to say to our licentious age. In the chapter that follows, on property and poverty, Guardini took as his text the story of the rich man who asks Jesus, "What shall I do to gain eternal life?," to which Jesus replies, "Go, sell whatever thou hast, and give to the poor, and thou shalt have treasure in heaven; and come, follow me." In this brief story, Guardini says, are revealed two Christian attitudes toward property. One, based on the commandments, is to own property, be grateful for it, manage it well, and achieve something with it, avoid dishonesty and injustice, be decent to others and help dispel need. The other, on a higher level, is what he calls the special order of things that leads those few who are able to serve God "not only in justice, but in the absolute freedom of the heart that has stripped itself of everything that is not he. . . . From this blend of vocation and freedom, of obligation and magnanimity springs the order of perfection, that state of more than ordinary Christian freedom which is the privilege of certain chosen individuals." After referring to St. Francis of Assisi as an example of what he is talking about, he adds, ". . . the realization of the order of perfection operates as a living example in human society. It proves the possibility of freedom from property, reminding those who possess it that there is freedom to be had also among possessions. He who has entirely freed himself from things helps him who retains his belongings to use them properly."

On the occasion of the eightieth birthday of Father Guardini, the University of Munich and the Catholic Academy of Bavaria arranged a great academic celebration. Following addresses by the Rector of the University, the Dean of the Faculty of Philosophy, and the Jesuit theologian Karl Rahner, Father Guardini expressed his gratitude in a brief reply, which he called "Truth and Irony." He spoke of the vehemence with which Plato fought against the destruction by the Sophists of all real values and norms, and especially

227

against their assault on truth by their raising of material success to be the highest goal of life. He then remarked, "Plato must have had an overwhelming experience of truth, of truth not merely as the determination of the correctness of things, but the inner realization of truth with all the splendour and fullness of meaning the unspoiled word expresses. . . . Truth is something absolute. It is a directing force from which the person is not only able to live a worthwhile life, but to face death with equanimity." Then, after speaking of Socrates's devotion to wisdom and to the discovery of truth and his firm refusal, in consequence of his conviction of his own inadequacy, to permit himself to be regarded by his followers as teacher or exemplar, Guardini added, "Plato experienced the directing power of truth in a way that combined the perception of the absolute validity of the idea with the experience of human inadequacy. And the irony of this perception lies in the fact that the thinking person perceives what of this perception lies beyond his capacity to bring to realization."

Guardini ended what must have been one of his last public addresses with the admonition:

I do not know whether I have made clear what I wanted to bring before you in these few words: the awareness of truth and at the same time awareness of the smallness of one's own strength in relation to it; recognition of one's own inadequacy, from which comes not scepticism, but conviction on the highest level. It would be, I think, good Platonic doctrine to say that the person who understands himself on the basis of what lies beneath him betrays his own nobility. Rather, he will live right only when he makes his life in accordance with what is above him—even if he is not able to understand it, and must at times appear strange to himself, *mala geloios*, as the young Glaucon puts it in the *Politeia*.

Other Guardini books we published included *Rilke's Duino Essays, The Church of the Lord, The World and the Person, The Virtues,* and *The Word of God: Three Essays on Faith, Hope and Charity.* All did well, but none so well as *The Lord,* which went through nine large printings.

In our pride in our wealth and apparent control of our natural surroundings it is easy to forget the debt we owe to such men as Romano Guardini; we feel we have no need of those who teach us humility, and to see ourselves as a part of creation, not as its ultimate purpose. In a conversation several years ago with the socialist mayor of Berlin, I remarked that there now seemed to be no one in Germany who spoke with authority. When he asked what I meant,

I gave Guardini's influence as an example of the kind of authority I had in mind. The mayor replied, with what struck me as a rather deprecating smile, *"Das war Modesache"* ("That was a fad"). But it was not a fad. Young people listened to Guardini in the confusion and uncertainty of the postwar period because he was able to offer them the wisdom and sense of order and direction they needed and longed for. The time may not be far off when we shall again turn to such men as Romano Guardini.

Over the years we built up not only a substantial and distinguished list of Catholic works, but of philosophical studies as well. An early book of ours was Helmut Kuhn's *Encounter with Nothingness,* on existentialism, a subject much talked of in those days and probably little understood. This was followed in 1949 by the first work of Martin Heidegger to be published in English. We called it *Existence and Being,* and it consisted of four essays—"Remembrance of the Poet," "Hoelderlin and the Essence of Poetry," "On the Essence of Truth," and "What Is Metaphysics?"—plus a long essay on Heidegger's chief philosophical work, *Being and Time,* then still untranslated, and a second one on the Heidegger essays included in the book. These had been written at Heidegger's request by his former assistant, Werner Brock, who was then teaching at Cambridge. Brock tells us that the purpose of these introductory essays, which make up more than half the book, is interpretative, on the assumption that he himself understands the text of the essays. This book, which is still in print after thirty years, has become an integral part of the literature of modern philosophy.

Gateway Editions, our paperback series, was strongly oriented toward philosophy. We began it with works of such standard authors as Plato, Aristotle, Thomas Aquinas, Hobbes, Hume, Locke, Rousseau, and Marx, all included in the Great Books list, then soon added authors we had published originally in hard-back editions, including Gabriel Marcel, Max Picard, Helmut Kuhn, James Collins, and Heidegger. We arranged for fresh translations of such standard works as Nietzsche's *Beyond Good and Evil* and *Thus Spake Zarathustra,* and Rousseau's *Social Contract,* as well as for two less available works of Nietzsche, *Philosophy in the Tragic Age of the Greeks* and *Schopenhauer as Educator.* We also published a number of books directly in the Gateway series, including Heidegger's *What Is a Thing?,* Eric Voegelin's *Science, Politics, Gnosticism,* two shorter works by Karl Jaspers, three stories by Unamuno,

St. Augustine's *Enchiridion on Faith, Hope and Love,* and Paul Ricoeur's *Fallible Man.* With the addition of several books first published by others which had been allowed to go out of print— Eliseo Vivas's *The Moral Life and the Ethical Life,* and two books of F. A. Hayek, for example—our Gateway paperbacks developed into a distinguished and useful list.

In connection with the search for additions to our list, I twice visited Karl Jaspers. When I met him he was living in Basel, on a quiet street in a rather modest house, one of a tight row, which was probably typical of the house of a German professor of a generation or two ago—walls lined with books, heavy furniture, thick curtains on the windows, and very comfortable. In contrast to his contemporary Martin Heidegger, who would spend months in complete isolation in a small hut in a remote part of the Black Forest, thinking and writing, Jaspers preferred to be in the center of things. He wrote for the newspaper on contemporary politics, made public speeches, and had strong opinions on current issues, not all of them, I thought, well founded.

The first time I went to see him was in October, 1962. We talked at first about several of his books that he thought we might wish to consider for publication, particularly his large work on Nietzsche. (In the event, this was first published by the University of Arizona Press, and later by us in paperback.) He then went on to say that he was an old man, and in his life had experienced the two great catastrophes of this century—World War I and the coming to power of Adolf Hitler—and that he now had the same feeling he did in 1914 and 1933, that events had taken over and man was powerless to change their course. I did not agree; history, I said, is made by man, not events, but we let it go at that. He then talked at some length about the Shirer book on the Third Reich, which he had just read, obviously with great care. The facts, he said, were probably nine-tenths correct, although he did mention two alleged meetings, one on the pocket battleship *Deutschland* and the other on Hindenburg's estate, which Shirer made much of but which Jaspers was sure had never taken place, and then went on to say that what Shirer wrote about philosophy and *Geistesgeschichte* (history of ideas) was incredibly primitive and wrong. "How could a man live in a country so long," he said, "and understand so little about it? He simply doesn't know us." He then spoke of the disastrous effect such a book could have on American foreign policy, an effect that involved not only Germany, but the West as a whole.

He wanted to know about Chicago, which someone had told him was not a city at all, but a large village. I told him that it was a collection of villages. He asked particularly about the newspapers, and whether they had anything serious to say about foreign policy; if it was true, as someone had told him, that the average citizen of Chicago hardly knew where Berlin was, much less had any idea of its significance. He went on to say that one of the great dangers to the West was the enormous influence of the American masses and their complete lack of understanding of how serious the world situation was. I did not entirely agree with this either, and told him that the masses largely reflect the views of those in a position to mold public opinion, and that it is the latter who constitute the danger.

As I prepared to leave, I found his wife waiting for me near the front door. She asked if I would sit down with her for a few minutes. She was quite small, with very bright eyes and a warm smile, and, as I soon learned, was altogether a pleasant lady, and much easier to talk to than her husband. She told me that she was Jewish, but that she was not so anti-German as her relatives and friends and that she had been well treated in Heidelberg all during the war, in spite of the official position toward Jews. She was not given a ration card because she was Jewish, she said, but others shared their food with them, so that they always had enough to eat. She spoke about her husband, how they did everything together, and of her distress when he lost his Heidelberg professorship because of her. When this happened, she said, they went to his father's house in Oldenburg. She spoke of her apprehension as they approached the house. Her father-in-law was a banker, and a tall, rather severe North German, which made her feel very uncertain about how she might be received as the person responsible for the loss of his son's position. She was intensely relieved, therefore, when the door opened and her father-in-law greeted her warmly and, turning to her husband, said, "My son, we don't belong in that crowd." This was another side of Germany during the Hitler period, and one that she thought, I am sure, should not be forgotten.

I visited Professor Jaspers once more, almost exactly a year later. His wife met me at the door; I thought she had aged considerably since I had chatted with her the year before, but he seemed about the same, only a little more pontifical. He complimented me on the appearance of the book of his we had published in the meantime, *World and Philosophy*. He spoke of President Kennedy in the highest terms; he obviously idolized him, as many Germans did after the

"Ich bin ein Berliner" speech—they thought he meant what he said. Jaspers was particularly impressed by Kennedy's efforts to settle the race issue, as he said, "with justice and in spite of the political consequences," and remarked that this was one ray of hope on the Western side. He went on to say, as I wrote down immediately afterward, "Political freedom is one of the great achievements of Western Europe. If the Negro issue in America can be settled in the spirit of political freedom, it will change the whole world situation, and may prevent the race war of which Hitler's murder of the Jews was only the beginning."

Jaspers intensely disliked Konrad Adenauer, partly perhaps because Adenauer was Catholic. He said that the true statesman educates his people to his ideals and aims, whereas Adenauer only used the people as pawns to keep himself in power. I did not agree with this, and asked if he did not think that the reconciliation with France was a great achievement. Jaspers admitted that it was, but refused to give Adenauer credit for it; it would have come about in any case, he said.

Jaspers had just passed his eightieth birthday when I met him the second time. He was tall and striking-looking, blond, blue-eyed, hair brushed back from a high forehead, impressive in manner, very sure of his own opinions, and a man who left his mark on the thought of his time. My friend Max Picard made an interesting remark about those two contemporary German philosophers Heidegger and Jaspers: "I don't agree with Heidegger in the slightest, but he has the head of the true philosopher, and one must respect him. As for Jaspers, he is a *Schulphilosoph.*"

William Ernest Hocking, who was most helpful to me and whom I visited several times in his house on a New Hampshire mountain— visits I remember with great pleasure—once wrote that my publication list reflected my own philosophical concerns. He was most generous to say this, but in doing so gave me more credit than I deserved. Although I enjoy reading certain works of philosophy, I must confess that I have no particular philosophical position, and no talent whatever for the sort of speculation the specialists engage in. Life has probably treated me too well for me to develop a philosophy of my own. To read such a book as Unamuno's *The Tragic Sense of Life* is for me a stimulating and enjoyable experience, but the problem he wrestled with with such intensity and passion, immortality, worries me not at all. We had no choice, so far as we can know, about the circumstances surrounding our coming into the world, and no matter how hard we may think about it can know nothing about what happens to us when we leave it. Our Maker has entrusted us with the gift of free will, and with the freedom to make choices and to decide for ourselves comes responsibility for our acts and decisions. We are given life to lead as best we can and in accordance with the gifts and circumstances allotted to us, and those who lead a good life can face death with the composure and confidence of old Bach, who, on his deathbed, asked those around him to sing his last chorale, "Before Thy Throne With This I Come," composed only a few days before, doubtless in preparation for this event. That our Maker feels kindly toward us, his creatures, the music of Bach and Mozart would be for me sufficient evidence, if there were not much more.

The fact that we published so many Catholic and philosophical books although I was neither a Catholic nor a philosopher often gave me the rather guilty feeling that I was sailing under false colors, that in a certain way I was misrepresenting myself. But the books, on the whole, were good and of high quality, and I think may have contributed something to understanding and orderly thinking, which would sufficiently justify their publication.

12

OTHER BOOKS:
GOOD AND BAD

WE published many more books than I have described in the
foregoing account, and some of them can justifiably be described
as good. But more than I like to think about were of no distinction
whatever, and although we enjoyed a number of successes, there
were many failures. We took on some of the less distinguished
works—the *White Sox Year Book*, for example—in the hope that
they might make money for the firm and help to pay for better
books. Others were the result of poor advice or poor judgment.

One of the final books published by the firm when it was still
under my direction was the first volume of Konrad Adenauer's
Memoirs. We had contracted to bring out the entire work, which
was to consist of two or, at the most, three volumes, the first covering the period before World War II and the rest the postwar period.
When the work developed into four volumes, all covering the postwar period, we found it necessary to withdraw. The one volume
we did publish, however, is of great interest and an important contribution to modern history. It begins with Allied troops reaching
the Rhine and the final capitulation in 1945, and goes on to describe Adenauer's appointment by the British as mayor of Cologne,
the catastrophic condition of postwar Germany, the beginnings of
political activity, relations with the military government, the for-

mulation of the Basic Law, and Adenauer's election as the first chancellor of the German Federal Republic.

We published it in collaboration with Weidenfeld and Nicholson of London, sharing translation and composition costs, and arranged to have the translation made in New York by Beate Ruhm von Oppen, who was a well-trained historian and scrupulously accurate—she detected several errors, in fact, in the original. One amusing incident in connection with the translation involved the letter informing Adenauer of his dismissal by the British as mayor of Cologne, for incompetence. Adenauer had been ordered to have the trees in the extensive Cologne parks, which he had had planted in the twenties during his previous administration as mayor, cut down for fuel. He refused, on the grounds that there was plenty of coal in the Ruhr, and was promptly fired. In the German edition the letter was reproduced in translation. Rather than translate it back into English we tried to find a copy of the original, at first without success, and finally wrote direct to General Barraclough, whose only claim to fame is the fact that he was the man who fired Adenauer. He obviously would have preferred to forget the whole episode, and replied that he had no copy, and no idea where one could be found. We were finally able to get it, however, from archives in London.

We published the book in May, 1966, on a day I will remember as the birthday of my first grandchild. The Adenauer memoir was well reviewed in the New York *Times*, *Time*, and almost every other publication in which books were reviewed, but the sale, though by no means insignificant, was disappointing to me. I had incorrectly assumed that the *Memoirs* of Konrad Adenauer—who was, after all, one of the great personalities and statesmen of this century, and who played a major role in its history—would be of as much interest to almost every literate person as they were to me, a mistake of a kind I have made many times.

Disappointment over the sale of the book was at least partially compensated for by the opportunity to meet Dr. Adenauer. The first time was in April, 1964, in a handsome villa high above Lake Como, at a reception for the foreign publishers of his book—French, British, Italian, Dutch, Swedish, and American. The house was built on two sides of a large, attractive garden, which had a huge beech tree in the center and afforded a fine view of the lake and surrounding hills. It was a bright, sunny day, warm enough for us to stand outside, and the atmosphere was relaxed and friendly. Adenauer instantly recognized that my name came from the Mosel, not far from where his family had originated, and this, together with the fact that I had spent two years in Bonn as a student and was quite familiar with the Cologne area, opened the door to further conversation.

It was not long before the name of General de Gaulle was mentioned. Adenauer spoke of his great admiration for De Gaulle, without whose initiative German-French reconciliation, at least on the broad basis on which it came about, would have been impossible. Adenauer's first efforts in that direction, he told us, had begun after World War I, when he was closely associated with Chancellor Wilhelm Cuno. Reconciliation with France, he thought then, was the only solution to the isolation of Germany, but there was too much bitterness on both sides, and for his efforts Adenauer was accused of being a traitor and a "separatist," accusations the Nazis revived when he was dismissed, for the first time, as mayor of Cologne.

De Gaulle's first approach to Adenauer came shortly after his return to power, through two emissaries who invited Adenauer to meet with him in Paris. Adenauer replied that it was not fitting that the representative of a defeated nation should go to the capital of France, and suggested that it ought to be done in a different way. De Gaulle sent a second message: John Foster Dulles had come to Paris, and if he had come the German chancellor could come also. To this Adenauer replied that Dulles did not come as the representative of a defeated nation, whereupon De Gaulle arranged the meeting in his private residence in Colombey-les-deux-Eglises, and it was here that this historic development began.

Adenauer invited George Weidenfeld and Lady Pamela Barry, the wife of the head of the London Sunday *Telegraph*, to sit with him at a small table, and very kindly asked me to join them. The conversation soon got around to British foreign policy, De Gaulle, and the Common Market, doubtless because it had not been long before that De Gaulle had startled the world by suddenly announcing his opposition to British entry into the Common Market. Adenauer began by remarking that he found it difficult to understand British foreign policy since World War II; it seemed to lack direction, and particularly a firm line toward Soviet Russia. When Lady Barry asked how he felt about the possibility of a Labour victory in the fall, he answered that such a prospect was of great concern to him because he was afraid that a Labour government would be even more indecisive toward Soviet Russia than the present Conservative government. To relieve whatever tenseness these remarks may have caused, Adenauer then told an amusing story. During an official visit to London, he noticed that his hotel was being picketed by a group who objected to the rearmament of Germany. It was a cold, wet, miserable day, which prompted him to invite the picketers in for tea. They solemnly stacked their placards in the hallway, he said, and joined in a pleasant conversation—nothing was said about armament—following which the refreshed protesters went back to their picketing.

On the subject of the Common Market, Britain, and De Gaulle, Adenauer said that he had never believed that Prime Minister Harold Macmillan was really serious about coming in, adding emphatically that De Gaulle did not object in principle to Britain's entering the Common Market, but to its doing so on a special basis. He took the position that Britain should accept the same responsibilities as all the nations involved. Another factor that had played a part in De Gaulle's sudden about-face was Macmillan's meeting with Kennedy in Bermuda. De Gaulle had told Adenauer that shortly before the Bermuda Conference, Macmillan had informed him that Britain could not afford to develop its atomic weapons any further. De Gaulle thereupon suggested that the British turn their knowledge and resources over to a European project. Macmillan refused to commit himself, but a few days later went to Bermuda and worked out the arrangement with Kennedy that would permit the Europeans to have the Polaris missile. De Gaulle first learned of the agreement from the newspapers, and quite rightly regarded this as an affront not only to France and to him, but also to all of Western Europe. It was in response to this and to the British demand for special status that he took the stand he did.

There was some discussion of De Gaulle's decision to take French troops away from NATO, which one of those present thought had weakened NATO. Adenauer defended the decision as the correct one at the time, because the opposition of the officer corps to the withdrawal from Algeria had made the French army a very uncertain quantity, for which reason it was better to keep it under De Gaulle than under NATO. Weidenfeld asked Adenauer if he thought that such a man as Khrushchev could, in any circumstances, be trusted. Adenauer said in substance that he would answer the question indirectly. No one who had never lived

237

under a modern dictatorship could understand the moral degradation, the deceit, the distrust of all others that this situation brings
about. It was bad enough under fascism, but was doubtless far
worse under Communism. Furthermore, Russia had been involved
in more wars than any other nation, Russia was *the* expansionist,
imperialist power, above all others, and the present leadership of
Russia considered only one circumstance in making a decision—
the effect it would have on the expansionist aims of the Russian
nation and world Communism.

Before the party broke up I again had a few minutes alone with
Adenauer. He remarked that Americans should understand that
Russia would never voluntarily let go of East Berlin and the Russian zone of Germany, now the German Democratic Republic.
These areas are not only useful in themselves to the Russians, but,
more important, are regarded as the bait with which to lure the
West Germans into the Russian orbit. He did not think that the
West Germans would fall into the trap, but he most emphatically
asserted that if this should ever happen, West Germany would become part of the Soviet realm, as would all the rest of Europe,
and clearly this would make an enormous difference to the situation of the United States.

The last time I saw Adenauer was in September, 1966, a few
months before he died. This meeting also took place in a villa near
Como, where he had gone to rest. He invited me to come to tea,
and to bring my younger daughter, who was traveling with me.
One of his daughters was with him, he was in excellent spirits, and
we had a most pleasant time. He was then ninety years old, but he
showed us the garden, talked about the different varieties of plants,
and in no way seemed like an old man. After tea he remarked,
"Since you come from the Mosel, we must have a bottle of wine."
He sent for a list of the Mosel wines that had been sent down for
the household, and selected a bottle of Eiswein, the very rare wine
that is made on those occasions when especially sweet grapes are
caught by an early freeze. We chatted about various things, and
I told him that my relatives on the Mosel, who were wine growers,
had told me that the canalization of the Mosel, for which he was
responsible, would spoil the wine. He was amused by this and said
it was merely peasant superstition. In fact, the canalization would
improve the wine, because by keeping the water level more constant it would result in more uniform moisture for the grapes.

For some reason or other he asked me if I knew that there had

been an election in our country at the time of the American Revolution to determine whether English or German should be the
national language, and that German had lost by only one vote.
I replied, not very diplomatically, that I had heard the story from
many Germans, but had never believed it. He became slightly
annoyed at this, but his daughter smoothed things over by remarking that there might well have been such an election in Lancaster,
Pennsylvania.

Konrad Adenauer was a shrewd, farsighted man. One of his
great assets was his implacable realism. He indulged in no false
heroics, made no empty promises; built up no hopes that could
not be realized. He accepted the situation of his country as it was
after twelve years of Hitler and total defeat—divided, every square
mile of it occupied by its former enemies, its economic life at a
standstill, its cities in ruins, millions homeless and on the verge of
starvation—and went on from there, slowly and patiently using
every opportunity that offered itself. At the end of his fourteen
years as chancellor, the German Federal Republic had taken its
place as a sovereign nation, had made an almost miraculous economic recovery, and had won international respect. The war leaders, great and small, had had their time on the world stage. It was
such men as Konrad Adenauer in Germany, Robert Schuman in
France, and Alcide de Gasperi in Italy who had the far less spectacular but more rewarding task of putting things back together
and making it possible for people to live again in peace.

Some books I published I am glad to forget, but there are others
I have not yet mentioned that it is pleasant to recall: for example a
collection of essays by John Dos Passos, *Occasions and Protests*,
which we published in 1964. When I first met Dos Passos I do not
now remember, but I do remember a particularly agreeable encounter with him at an international meeting of conservatives in
Rome in October, 1963. It was a delightful affair. There were some
quite brilliant papers, and several rather passionate speeches by
Italians, which even the interpreters seemed unable to follow. I
remember one sentence from one of these, "I am a Catholic of the
middle ages; I *reject* any compromise with the modern world." A
great dinner on a narrow street was followed by dancing, in which
Dos Passos took part, and there was much lively conversation.

The thoughtful, carefully worked-out paper Dos Passos delivered in the small Roman theater near Trajan's Column, where we

met, which appears in our collection of essays, expresses many of the concerns about the situation of our country and its future that occupied him in his later years. He talked about truth, how difficult it is to discover and then to convey: "Ever since man began, the pursuit of truth has been an activity beset by many occupational hazards. The institutions through which, in almost any society, the boss-type men impose their will on the workers and the producers and the builders are invariably founded on lies." After developing and illustrating what he was talking about, he went on to say, "In modern bureaucratic societies intellectuals are becoming a dominant class through their furnishing the bossmen with the slogans and delusions by which they control the general public. The twentieth century may well end by being known as the century of the intellectual. As they become giddy with power the usefulness of the intellectuals as a class to the cause of civilization becomes more and more doubtful."

Dos Passos was concerned all his adult life with the problem of what he called the "bossmen." Once when he was at our house for dinner my wife asked him if he had changed his basic position, as was often said, from left to right, from flaming liberal to arch conservative. He replied that he did not think he had changed his position at all; he had always been opposed to one group of men taking advantage of other men, bossing them around, as he put it. In his younger days it was the factory owners who were the bossmen, but later it became the men who control the labor unions; he had not changed, he said, only the identity of the bosses had changed.

In such essays as "The Use of the Past," "A Question of Elbow Room," and "The Workman and His Tools," Dos Passos uses his broad knowledge of his country and its history, his enormous skill with words, and his sharp "camera eye" to illustrate the essential nature of American society, and how it evolved. And without in any way overlooking the corrupting influences that sometimes seem in danger of overwhelming it, he never loses his faith in its essential strength. The latter is particularly emphasized in the first essay of the book, "The American Cause," which was originally written as a letter to a group of German students who asked him to explain, in three hundred words, why they should admire the United States. The following lines come from this essay:

I told them they should admire the United States not for what we were but for what we might become. . . . I told them to admire us for our unstratified society, where every man still has a chance, if he has the will and the wit, to invent his own thoughts and to make his own way. I told them to admire us for the hope we still have that there is enough goodness in man to use the omnipotence science has given him to ennoble his life on earth instead of degrading it. Self government, through dangers and distortions and failures, is the American cause. Faith in self government, when all is said and done, is faith in the triumph in man of good over evil.

Occasions and Protests presented the liberal reviewers with a serious tactical problem. Dos Passos was too big a name to ignore, but what were they do do with a man they once praised as one of theirs who without hesitation or apology could now say such outrageous things? The fact that they were true made it all the worse. His assertion that intellectuals furnish the bossmen with the slogans and delusions by which they control the general public was a particularly flagrant example. And in speaking of one of their heavyweight thinkers he had the temerity to say, "In a hundred newspapers readers seeking the balm of certainty will find in Walter Lippmann's column the roughage of daily events reduced to marketable opinions easily assimilated and stamped with the stamp of authority." The New York *Times* solved the problem by giving the book a slashing review on the front page of the Sunday book section—the only book of ours to have received that distinction. The reviewer, John Braine, a young English novelist, began with the summary judgment "a sad, drab book. Nothing is left of the Dos Passos style but his habit of omitting hyphens." Having thus suggested that the entire book is without merit, he goes on to say, "Only perhaps in 'Satire as a Way of Seeing' is the real Dos Passos evident; here, looking at the drawings of George Grosz, he is not only penetratingly acute about his subject—but has something to say about the change in the visual habits of Americans." What Braine is really saying, of course, is that the essay on George Grosz was the only one he agreed with. The review infuriated me, but Dos Passos, wiser and more experienced in such matters, did not even bother to read it.

So many of our books were involved with problems—foreign policy, education, the place of man in the world—that it is pleasant to recall three that were concerned with beauty, with the evidence of the divine spark in man that raises him above his physical surroundings and makes him human: *The Diary and Letters of Kaethe*

Kollwitz, published in 1955; *The Church Incarnate,* a book on church architecture by Rudolph Schwarz, published in 1958; and *The Quiet Eye: A Way of Looking at Pictures,* by the Chicago sculptress Sylvia Shaw Judson, published in 1954. They were very different in their subject matter, in the personalities of their authors, and in the manner of their approach, but each reflects the triumph of the human spirit over the vicissitudes of life.

Kaethe Kollwitz was born in 1867 in Königsberg, the very Prussian city of Immanuel Kant and the categorical imperative, and died in 1945 in the castle of Moritzburg, having been offered refuge by the Prince of Saxony after the destruction in an air raid of her Berlin house, where she had spent most of her life, where her children were born, and where much of her work was done. As the wife of a physician who chose to conduct a clinic in one of the poorest sections of Berlin, she had known what the grinding poverty and misery of a great modern city can mean. She lost a son in World War I, and in the second many of her friends and the material accumulation of her life. But her work, from the kneeling figures of grieving parents she made for the soldier's grave of her son to the drawing of a mother, one hand protecting her two small children and the other offered to death, displays the serenity, the self-discipline, and the sense of order only a great person, who was able to transcend whatever demands life may have placed upon her, could have achieved.

For Rudolph Schwarz the building of a church was a serious matter; he saw his task as the architect, the *Baumeister*:

To build churches out of that reality which we experience and verify every day, to take this our own reality so seriously and to recognize it to be so holy that it may be able to enter in before God. To renew the old teachings concerning sacred work by trying to recognize the body, even as it is real to us today, as creature and as revelation, and by trying to render it so; to reinstitute the body in its dignity and to do our work so well that this body may prove to be "sacred body." And beyond all this to guard ourselves against repeating the old words when for us no living content is connected with them.

On the one occasion I met Schwarz in his studio in Frankfurt, he spoke about the cathedral of nearby Mainz, that great, massive Romanesque structure of the High Middle Ages, which, like the cathedrals in Worms and Speyer, has a double apse. This, Schwarz said, expresses a typically medieval idea: the one apse houses the altar of Christ, the other the throne of the emperor, so that the whole structure represents the unity of church and state under the Fatherhood of God. I asked him why, in rebuilding the Cathedral of Cologne after the war, he had put the Shrine of the Three Kings, one of the great treasures of the Middle Ages, high above the pews in the choir. He replied, "So the art historians can't get at it." He meant, of course, that he wanted the shrine to be not a museum piece but a part of the cathedral as a place of worship.

In his brief preface, Mies van der Rohe speaks of *The Church Incarnate* as not only a great book on architecture, but also one of the truly great books that have the power to transform our thinking. It was Cynthia Harris, who later became a physician, who was responsible for our edition of *The Church Incarnate*. She knew Schwarz and admired his work, and undertook the arduous task of putting the book into English; without her moral and material support it would never have seen the light of day.

In her introduction to *The Quiet Eye: A Way of Looking at Pictures*, Sylvia Judson, who was herself an imaginative and skillful artist, tells us that one of her purposes is to help us to see works of art, in Plato's words, not as images of beauty but as realities. The pictures she chose for the book, she tells us, communicate a sense of affirmation, of wonder, of trust. *The Quiet Eye* is completely unpretentious, but no less beautiful for that, and it has given pleasure and I think solace to many people.

It is no secret that novels are especially risky, and that first novels almost invariably lose money, but the manuscript of a well-constructed novel that seems to have something to say is an almost irresistible temptation. We succumbed a number of times, and, true to form, most of the fiction we published lost money. There was a novel by Holmes Alexander, a successful Washington columnist and a most likable man, with a quick wit and the manners of a true southern gentleman. He was also a fluent writer, but his book did not sell, perhaps because he would not take the time to bring off his rather involved story of intrigue in an old Washington newspaper family. There were two novels by the German writer Luise Rinser, one of which was *Rings of Glass* (1955), a beautifully written story of a young girl brought up, during World War I, by an aunt who was herself the niece and housekeeper of the abbot of one of the great Bavarian monasteries. By way of complete contrast there was *Trumbull Park* (1959), by a gifted Chicago black,

Frank London Brown. Two of the best novels we published were moderately successful. One, *Chains of Fear* (1958), by N. Narokov, a Russian living in this country, was serialized by the *Saturday Evening Post*, and acclaimed by discerning critics as being in the great tradition of the Russian novel. *Manifest Destiny* (1963), by Russell Laman, was a novel running to more than five hundred pages and revolving about a Kansas homesteading family. It was recommended to me by Mari Sandoz, who will be remembered as the author of *Old Jules. Manifest Destiny* begins with a young man from the East taking a homestead in Kansas in the 1870's, and gives the reader the sense of complete authenticity that can be achieved only by a writer who, as Mark Twain put it, was there. It was no best seller, but we sold out the fairly large first printing. It was my hope that we might discover and develop a significant novelist, and in Frank Brown and Russell Laman had reason to think that there was such a possibility. But Frank Brown, after being appointed to the faculty of the University of Chicago, died before writing another book; and Russell Laman apparently wrote himself out with his one novel, which will stand, however, as a significant achievement.

Publishing books such as I have described in the foregoing chapters has its rewards, as I hope I have made clear, but in my case they were not, unfortunately, financial. We were constantly faced with the problem of trying to find a way to make income meet expenses, and needed some of those books every publisher longs for—cookbooks, schoolbooks, bibles, and so on—that have a continuing, steady, assured sale. One of our attempted solutions was to buy the old Chicago firm of Reilly & Lee, which had been founded as the Madison Book Company in 1902. Although it was on its last legs when we bought it, it still had a strong list of popular books. Its founder, Frank E. Reilly, had been the sales manager for the firm that first brought out Frank Baum's *The Wizard of Oz*. When it failed, he set up his own house, taking over as Baum's publisher. By 1919 the firm name had become Reilly & Lee, and it enjoyed great success for a time by publishing the unpretentious, wholesome books that appealed to the American taste before the advent of radio and TV, *Penthouse* and *Playboy*. Reilly & Lee published some of the enormously popular books of Harold Bell Wright, all those of the much beloved Edgar A. Guest, and many books for children, including all thirty-one of the Oz books, fourteen by Frank Baum, the rest written after his death by others.

We reissued a great many of these, including the complete Oz series, various other juveniles, the *Collected Verse of Edgar A. Guest*, and popular classics such as *101 Famous Poems*.

We tried to keep the tradition of Reilly & Lee alive by adding new books for children, but all of them except *The Golden Journey*, an anthology of poetry put together by Louise Bogan and William J. Smith, were unsuccessful and also uninspired. They lacked the elusive spark of imagination that Frank Baum had to a high degree, whatever one may think of the literary quality of his books. Those books of ours were neither worse nor better than the routine books for children produced in quantity every year, but I would prefer to forget our contribution to this flood of mediocrity.

An author who became a good and loyal friend is Frederick Ayer, Jr. How I became acquainted with him makes a fairly involved story. In the dining car of the Broadway Limited, on the way to New York, early in 1952, I got into conversation with the man sitting across the table from me. We talked about the usual things, mutual acquaintances, the state of the world, politics, and finally who might be the Republican candidate in the upcoming presidential election. I was strongly in favor of Senator Robert Taft, which prompted my acquaintance to ask if I would be interested in publishing the diary of General George S. Patton. I had heard rumors about the diary, that it had things to say about the conduct of the war that were not at all flattering to those who made the decisions, and replied that I would indeed be most interested. He told me that a man he knew in New York had a copy of the diary as well as Mrs. Patton's authorization to arrange for its publication. The next day, as promised, this man came to see me, the Patton diary in hand; he also showed me a letter from Mrs. Patton, which though perfectly friendly, certainly did not authorize him to arrange for its publication. When I asked how the diary had come into his possession, he told me that it had been given to him by Patton's army secretary, a technical sergeant, who had typed it each day from the General's dictation and had kept a copy. This man, for some reason, had never returned to the United States following the war. My visitor, who was of Hungarian birth and had been in naval intelligence during the war, had induced the former technical sergeant to place in his hands what really belonged to General Patton or his heirs.

He let me have his copy, which I took back with me to Chicago.

After reading it I was most anxious to become its publisher, but fully realized that permission would have to be obtained from the Patton family. I had tried to call Mrs. Patton from New York, shortly after my encounter with the mysterious Hungarian, but was told that she was out of the country. After she returned, she agreed to let me come to see her at her house in Beverly, Massachusetts. To vouch for my authenticity, so to speak, I asked my friend Colonel Truman Smith, who had known the Pattons in the army, to go with me. Mrs. Patton was most cordial and kind, invited us to stay for lunch, told us many interesting stories about her husband, and was in every way a gracious hostess. But she made it emphatically clear that she had no intention of permitting the diary to be published.

My interest, it must be said, did not derive entirely from the historical importance of the diary, great as it undoubtedly was. I thought of it primarily as a means to help Taft win the Republican nomination for the presidency, the choice having narrowed down to him or Eisenhower. Mrs. Patton, if possible, was even more strongly in favor of Taft than I was, or at any rate more strongly opposed to General Eisenhower as a presidential candidate; but she was not, as she put it, going to permit her dead husband to become involved in a political campaign. I returned to Chicago empty-handed.

After Mrs. Patton's death a year or two later, her brother, Frederick Ayer, called me to tell me that if I was still interested in the diary he could arrange for me to meet with the Patton children, who would all be in their father's house the following week. I stayed with the Ayers on this visit, which, insofar as the publication of the diary was concerned, proved to be as fruitless as the first. I did, however, come away with a manuscript by Frederick Ayer, Jr., which we eventually published under the title *Yankee G-Man,* for which I must confess we were responsible. Fred, Jr., having been rejected by the army for poor eyesight, had gone into the F.B.I., and after customary stringent training and some rather routine service in this country was assigned to a special European intelligence unit. Following the war he served in Greece as the chief intelligence officer. His book is an account of all this, and though written in the light-hearted manner Fred liked to assume, it is a serious work and has much that is important and revealing to say about the influences that guided our intelligence operations during and after the war. In the

Eisenhower administration Fred had a high policy-making position in Air Force Intelligence.

We published three more books of his, and all did well. Two were spy stories, *Where No Flags Fly* and *The Man in the Mirror,* which later appeared as a mass-market paperback; and both, because Fred knew from his own experience how such things are done in real life, had the unmistakable smell of authenticity about them. The third was an amusing account of the Ayers' amiable basset hound. Fred Ayer was a rare person; coming from a well-situated New England family, he was in a position to do what he pleased, but he was always ready to serve his country in whatever capacity was required, which he did on a number of occasions, always in his unassuming, completely competent way. He was a generous friend, and I remember him with gratitude.

One incident involving Fred Ayer sticks in my memory and may be worth repeating. Following dinner one evening at the Metropolitan Club in Washington, Fred suggested that we go to the lounge to hear what President Eisenhower would have to say on TV—it had been announced that he was to make an important statement on foreign policy. As it happened, it had to do with Berlin, and in the large, almost empty lounge we watched the President, who was in the White House, only a few blocks away, explain with map and pointer why Berlin was of vital importance to the West. I then told Fred a story I had heard from General Hobart R. Gay, when he was in command of the Vth Army in Chicago. During the war, Gay had been Patton's chief of staff, and he told me that he had been with Patton when the latter asked Eisenhower's permission to let his army take Berlin. Eisenhower refused, for several reasons, which Patton rather sharply refuted; whereupon Eisenhower, somewhat exasperated, asked, "Patton, of what use is Berlin anyhow?" To this Patton replied, "Eisenhower, history will answer that question for you."

Looking back at all those books and all that went into them, the reading and winnowing of manuscripts, the travel and correspondence, the editing and proofreading and planning, the buttering-up of reviewers—to say nothing of what the poor authors went through in writing their manuscripts, waiting for the publisher's decision, and finally for the verdict of reviewers and book buyers—one cannot help asking what it was all for and if I accomplished anything. Insofar as making money is concerned, I would have been far better off to have avoided book publishing like the plague. Insofar as discernible results are concerned, what can one say? After all those books on the public schools, *And Madly Teach, The Diminished Mind, The Public Schools in Crisis, The Right to Learn,* the test scores are lower than ever; in spite of those carefully reasoned books on economics and monetary theory by Jacques Rueff, Wilhelm Roepke, Melchoir Palyi, W. H. Hutt, the politicians go on happily spending money and deploring the inflation that is the inevitable consequence of their actions. And however convincingly all those books demonstrated the consequences of a foreign policy based on ideology and emotion instead of reason and common sense, we pursue one illusion after another, and as critical as some of our authors were of Dean Acheson, one can hardly argue that the appointment of Andrew Young represented an improvement. Whatever the immediate effect of these books, the men who wrote them did so because they had a compulsion to tell the truth as they saw it; and whatever their immediate effect, to the extent that they did impart truth, I am convinced that they were worth publishing.

Armour Institute of Technology convinced me that I would never become an engineer, M.I.T. that I would never become a mathematician, Harvard Graduate School that I would never become a scholar, my father's business that I would never become a businessman. Because of my good fortune in being the son of a successful and wise father, I did become a publisher. Although I like to think that a publisher will be judged by the quality of his books rather than by his financial success, he must operate at a profit to stay in business, and this I was never able to do, which is the reason that my old firm is now known as Contemporary Books, and publishes auto-repair manuals and sports books rather than Russell Kirk and Thomas Aquinas. For all the disappointments and failures, and there were many, those years in publishing were immensely rewarding, and I am grateful that I was given the opportunity to spend them in that fashion, grateful to my father for his encouragement and for making it possible, grateful to my family for standing by me, and above all to my wife, who never wavered in her support, and who was always ready to take in any author or would-be author who happened by. I regret only that I was not granted the tough-mindedness and the sense of realism that might have made the venture financially successful.

The true writer has a compulsion to write; he can hardly help himself. In the same way, the person once attracted by the lure of publishing has a compulsion to publish: to be confronted by a manuscript that says something a publisher thinks needs to be said presents him with an almost irresistible challenge. A striking example of such a publisher was Elkin Mathews, who in the early part of this century presided over a bookshop and published poetry at 6B Vigo Street in London. "If you had Mathews' imprint on your book of poems," Frank Morley once wrote to me, "you were in." Soon after his arrival in London in 1908, therefore, Ezra Pound went to 6B Vigo Street with a collection of his poetry and asked for Mr. Mathews. When the poet came back a few days later to inquire what his decision might be, Mathews asked, no doubt with some embarrassment—publishers hate to be put into such a position, but publishing poetry was not much more remunerative then than it is now—"Would you, now, be prepared to assist in the publication?" Pound replied that he had a shilling in his pocket, if that would help, to which Mathews responded, true publisher that he was, "Oh well, I want to publish 'em anyhow."

The publisher's role is often misunderstood. Authors find publishers grasping, obsessed by financial considerations, and unaware of the finer things of life, and most other people have no idea what they do. If the publisher makes money, he is accused of lowering standards; if he loses money, of being improvident and incompetent. The line he must walk between maintaining standards, on the one hand, and protecting his solvency, on the other, is a narrow and difficult one, but let us not forget that the quality of literature and the level of thought of any period will be decisively influenced by the standards or lack of standards of its publishers.

The publisher of Milton's *Paradise Lost,* we are told, paid its author five pounds, and is remembered, if at all, for the miserliness of his payment in comparison to the magnificence of the work he bought. But it should not be forgotten that he probably lost money on the venture, and that his participation in it, although of a quite different order from the author's, was also necessary.

INDEX

Index

Index

259